PRAISE FOR
Quarrel with the King

"A deeply felt history. . . . He has a passionate engagement with his subject."
—*Providence Journal*

"Typically supple and elegant prose. . . . Nicolson highlights the ambiguous nature of this most powerful of dynasties. . . . For fans of the Tudor and Stuart [periods], this will be a welcome treat."
—*Publishers Weekly* (starred review)

"Nicolson provides ample cultural context to keep general readers abreast of events. . . . Clear and compelling popular history."
—*Kirkus Reviews*

"Nicolson offers up a survey of the sociopolitical climate that led up to the English Civil War. . . . He details the complex rise of the Pembroke family. . . . Recommended for academic libraries."   —*Library Journal*

"Beautifully written and finely balanced. . . . A disarmingly readable contribution to the history of ideas. . . . It evokes, too, the tense worlds of the Tudor and Jacobean courts, in which violent impulses seethed behind smiling faces. . . . An elegant, thoughtful, imaginative book about the need for dreams and the ugliness of modernization. . . . His book will give abiding pleasure."   —*The Sunday Times* (London)

"A superb book, beautifully written, subtle, passionate, questioning, mind-altering, and wise."   —*Daily Mail* (London)

"Absorbing. . . . Wonderful, lyrical, and contemplative."
—*The Guardian* (London)

"A moving account of the Elizabethan golden age, retold through the varying fortunes of the Pembroke family, and a tour de force. . . . A brilliantly imaginative and beautifully written coup of scholarship."
—*The Observer* (London)

Jacky Houdret

About the Author

ADAM NICOLSON is the author of *Seamanship*, *Sea Room*, *God's Secretaries*, and, most recent, *Seize the Fire*, about Admiral Nelson and the battle of Trafalgar. He has won both the Somerset Maugham and William Heinemann awards. The son of Nigel Nicolson and the grandson of Harold Nicolson and Vita Sackville-West, he lives with his family at Sissinghurst Castle.

Quarrel with the King

QUARREL
WITH
THE KING

THE STORY *of an* ENGLISH FAMILY

on the HIGH ROAD *to* CIVIL WAR

ADAM NICOLSON

HARPER PERENNIAL

NEW YORK • LONDON • TORONTO • SYDNEY • NEW DELHI • AUCKLAND

HARPER PERENNIAL

A hardcover edition of this book was published in 2008 by HarperCollins Publishers.

HarperCollins books may be purchased for educational, business, or sales promotional use. For information please write: Special Markets Department, HarperCollins Publishers, 10 East 53rd Street, New York, NY 10022.

FIRST HARPER PERENNIAL EDITION PUBLISHED 2009.

Designed by Susan Yang

The Library of Congress has catalogued the hardcover edition as follows:

Nicolson, Adam.

Quarrel with the king: the story of an English family on the high road to civil war / Adam Nicolson—1st ed.
p.   cm.
ISBN 978-0-06-115431-7
1. Herbert, William, Sir, 1507–1570. 2. Herbert family. 3. Nobility—Great Britain—Biography. 4. Great Britain—History—Charles I, 1625–1649.

DA306.H47 N53   2008
941.06'20922—dc22   2008004262

ISBN 978-0-06-115432-4 (PBK.)
09 10 11 12 13 ID/RRD 10 9 8 7 6 5 4 3 2 1

ACKNOWLEDGMENTS

First, I want to thank Steven Hobbs, the Wiltshire County archivist, for his time and expertise, and for the patience he showed while I was researching this book. His enthusiasm for discovering key documents in the enormous and marvellously rich collections he has under his care never flagged. It has been the greatest of pleasures to work with him.

The staff of Cambridge University Library, the National Archives, the House of Lords Journal Office, the British Library, Hatfield House, and Sheffield Archives have all been equally generous and professional with the documents in their care.

In Wiltshire, Alison J. Maddock and John Chandler both steered me toward important changes of view, and Rosalind Conklin Hays, the co-editor of the Wiltshire collection in the Records of Early English Drama series, generously made available her preliminary transcriptions from the Wiltshire Quarter Sessions Rolls, in particular the libel sung by Jane Norrice of Stoke Verdon (A1/110/1631E no 151), which appears here on page 179.

The volumes published each year by the Wiltshire Record Society, including the key document for this book, *Surveys of the Manors of Philip, earl of Pembroke and Montgomery 1631–2*, edited by Eric Kerridge in 1953, have been invaluable, none more than the brilliant act of research and editorship performed by Dr. Joseph Bettey in his *Wilt-*

shire Farming in the Seventeenth Century, published by the Record Society in 2005. There is no more remarkable account of rural England on the cusp of the medieval and the modern. For membership details and past volumes, please contact the Honorary Secretary, Wiltshire Record Society, c/o Wiltshire and Swindon History Centre, Cocklebury Road, Chippenham SN15 3QN, England

At Wilton House itself, the Earl of Pembroke, Chris Rolfe, Ros Liddington, Nigel Bailey, David Colgrave, and Charlotte Spender have all gone well out of their way to help me, and I am very grateful to them all.

Katherine Duncan-Jones, Paula Henderson, Susan Koslow, the late Sir Oliver Millar, Alistair Laing, Barbara Ravelhofer, Robert Sackville-West, Alexandra Samarine, and Kim Wilkie have all in their different ways set me on better and truer paths.

I am grateful, as ever, to Caroline Dawnay, Zoe Pagnamenta, Hugh van Dusen, Vera Brice, Jane Beirn, Helen Ellis, Sammia Rafique, and above all Susan Watt for making the complex and drawn-out task of writing books like this into the pleasure it has been.

CONTENTS

The Earls of Pembroke in the Sixteenth and Seventeenth Centuries

Figures in the van Dyck painting of the family at Wilton are in CAPITALS

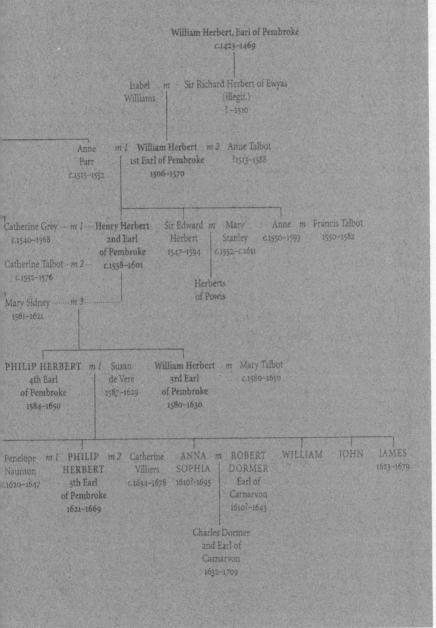

William Herbert, Earl of Pembroke
c.1423–1469

Isabel   m   Sir Richard Herbert of Ewyas
Williams   (illegit.)
                                  ? –1510

Anne   m 1   William Herbert   m 2   Anne Talbot
Parr   1st Earl of Pembroke   ?1513–1588
c.1515–1552   1506–1570

Catherine Grey — m 1 — Henry Herbert   Sir Edward   m   Mary   Anne   m   Francis Talbot
c.1540–1568   2nd Earl   Herbert   Stanley   c.1550–1593   1550–1582
                             of Pembroke   1547–1594   c.1552–c.1611
Catherine Talbot — m 2 — c.1538–1601
c.1552–1576
                                                              Herberts
                                                              of Powis
Mary Sidney ……… m 3 ………………
1561–1621

PHILIP HERBERT   m 1   Susan   William Herbert   m   Mary Talbot
4th Earl   de Vere   3rd Earl   c.1580–1650
of Pembroke   1587–1629   of Pembroke
1584–1650   1580–1630

Penelope   m 1   PHILIP   m 2   Catherine   ANNA   m   ROBERT   WILLIAM   JOHN   JAMES
Naunton   HERBERT   Villiers   SOPHIA   DORMER   1623–1679
c.1620–1647   5th Earl   c.1634–1678   1610?–1695   Earl of
                       of Pembroke   Carnarvon
                       1621–1669   1610?–1643

                                              Charles Dormer
                                              2nd Earl of
                                              Carnarvon
                                              1632–1709

The Pembroke Estates
in 16th- and 17th-
Century Wiltshire

Core Pembroke land holdings
1540s–1640s

WARMINSTER

Salisbur

W I L

Kingston Deverill

Wy

West Knoyle

Ridge • Chilmark • Teffont

Dinto

R. Nadder

Fov

Wardour • Swallowcliffe

Ebbesbourne
Wake

Alvediston

Cranborne Cha

B
C

SHAFTESBURY

Berwick
St. John

Ox Drove

DORSET

Land over 650 feet

ain

Stonehenge ⦂

Amesbury

Berwick
St. James

H I R E

Hanging
Langford

R. Avon

Wylye Little
Langford

Heale

Idmiston

Great Wishford

Roman Road

South Newton

Winterbourne
Earls

R. Bourne

Grovely Wood *Roman Road*

Old
Sarum

Roman Road

Barford
St. Martin

Ugford **WILTON** Fugglestone

Burcombe

Washerne

Bemerton

Clarendon
Park

ampton
amberlayne

Bulbridge

Netherhampton

Fisherton Anger

SALISBURY

Hare
Warren

Old Shaftesbury Drove

Ivychurch

Stratford Tony

Roman Road

R. Ebble

d Stoke
ke Farthing

Bishopstone

Odstock

N

R. Avon

W   E

nditch
hase

S

| 0 | 1 | 2 | 3 | 4 | 5 miles |

| 0 | 2 | 4 | 6 | 8 km |

QUARREL WITH THE KING

Chapter 1

THE LONG ROAD TO CIVIL WAR

1540–1650

In this book a great family, one of the richest and most glamorous of sixteenth- and seventeenth-century England, pursues a long arc of ambition, success, failure, and collapse. It is not an exclusively private story, because the family—the earls of Pembroke, their wives, children, and dependents—was deeply involved, for over a hundred years, in the central concerns of England. They saw themselves, in many ways, as an alternative to royalty. In their great house at Wilton, near Salisbury, they could entertain the king and his court as though welcoming them to a different state. They controlled tens of thousands of England's most beautiful acres, and still more in Wales, and many thousands of tenants and followers. Land, money, politics, art, and patronage were their realms. They could summon armies and, through them, impose their wills. They could gather vote-changing clusters of politicians in both houses of Parliament. As England's greatest patrons, they could sponsor poetry, plays, paintings, houses, gardens, and landscapes, all of which proclaimed their virtues, their fortitude, their antiquity, and their worth. Another England belonged to the

Pembrokes, an older and premodern country set against almost everything the modern state hoped to impose upon it.

For a century, from about 1540 onward, this family maintained a long, simmering quarrel with the king, one that flickered across the decades, part opposition, part seduction, part manipulation, and part denial. Only, finally, in the 1640s did it erupt in civil war, a dreadful and destructive conflict that released into the towns, villages, and highways of England precisely the anarchy and violence the country had dreaded for so long. The basis of the quarrel was power, a struggle between a government that needed and wanted to concentrate ever more authority in itself and its agents, and the ancient nobility of England—or at least those such as the Pembrokes, who saw themselves in that light and who thought of their role as the guardians of an ancient and balanced community of which they were the head and whose integrity the newly assertive, power-grabbing crown was disrupting and breaking.

It is a premodern story but there are many modern echoes in it: Was government a question of agreement and respect? Or authority and compulsion? What status did traditional rights have in a changing world? Did an emergency mean those rights could be ignored or overturned? Or was an emergency precisely the time when rights should be respected? This is not the usual, modern tale of freedoms struggling to assert themselves against an ancient and intolerant authority. The Pembrokes' story is the opposite of that: a long rearguard action by provincial grandees who found their ancient power, and the ancient independence of the communities they governed, under threat. In that way, this story is about the end of an old world, not the making of a new one. Almost every aspect of the Pembrokes' view of themselves was retrospective: old family, old authority, old ways of being, old values. And nearly every aspect of what they hated was new: new men, new money, new forms of authority, the new demands of the modern world.

The Pembrokes had no interest in individual freedom, only in the maintenance of their position as power brokers, with access to all the sources of money and authority they considered their due. But they were astute, and the need to survive and thrive in the modern world, combined with their energy and appetite, inevitably meant a complex engagement with that world. These "grandeez and gloriosoes" of Renaissance England were deeply embroiled in the court world from which they felt such distance. They were rebels, but they were also courtiers. For year after year, they sucked money from the crown they despised. Generation after generation carefully manoeuvred for influence and the ear of the king. Few families, in fact, managed so adroitly to surf the successive waves of royal power and favor. Each wave they caught brought another gush and surge of cash and influence. That, in fact, is their central paradox: nearly everything they had came from the king, but the more they had, the more they could afford to oppose him. The Pembrokes came to look like the ultimate cavaliers, but in the end they would be parliamentarian. At different times, they both threatened the crown and acted as its bruisingly efficient and violent agents. These were rebels not to be found plotting in a dimly lit garret but either dancing in the candlelit halls and delicious arbors of royal pleasure or actually commanding royal armies and sponsoring royal display. They were, in other words, highly ambivalent figures: flag carriers for an ancient England and time servers in some of the most corrupt courts England has ever known. The sense of distance between the Pembrokes and the crown, of the quarrel itself, was never quite absent but only rarely showed its fully naked face. It could be said that this book is a study in the ambiguity necessarily involved in the exercise and maintenance of power and status.

§   §   §

A simple act of curiosity lies behind my writing it. Many years ago, I was walking through the beautiful valley of the Nadder, in Wiltshire, in southern England, a cool and lovely clearwater stream that makes its way between the chalk downs on either side. The trout and grayling were flickering in the shallows, and bunches of meadowsweet were flowering on the banks. Just to the east of Salisbury, the river slides past the garden of Wilton House. I had been walking all day and, still in my heavy boots, I paid for my ticket, entered the house without quite knowing what to expect, and found myself in the greatest sequence of seventeenth-century rooms in England. It was a revelatory moment. I suddenly understood how wonderful a palace in the trees could be, the meaning of provincial, non-urban, exquisitely refined power.

Wilton's climax, one of the central moments of English culture, is the huge saloon known in the seventeenth century as the "great Dining-roome, or Roome of State," now called the Double Cube. It is thirty feet wide, thirty high, and sixty long—Palladian proportions, created here, almost certainly by Inigo Jones, in the 1630s. But the decoration is so rich that the harmonics of the room nearly disappear beneath it. Carved swags, gilded encrustations, and suspended pompoms hang from the walls. There is a vast fruitiness to it all; apples, peaches, and pears drip from every surface. Nothing is held back. It is grand but it is friendly grand. A giant cove, painted with putti, pan masks, and still more bowls and swags of fruit, reaches up to the ceiling. Around the marble fireplace, mannerist motifs—broken pediments, swagged consoles—jostle with the gilded statues of Bacchus and Ceres, the god and goddess of country riches. The whole complex is a shrine to fertility, a space designed for enjoyment, an arrival.

I stood there excited, bowled over by the completeness of this hidden, ancient world. But there was more: this climax of a glamour-thick room had its own climax within it. On the west wall is an enormous portrait of the family who owned and created it. Seventeen feet wide and ten deep, it is the largest painting ever made by Van Dyck, a joint portrait of the 4th Earl of Pembroke and his children. Each of the ten figures it portrays is just larger than lifesize and they dominate, as they were meant to, the gilded space in front of them. The portrait was painted in the late winter of 1634 or the spring of 1635, and it shows the Pembroke family at the sunniest and most optimistic moment of their existence. It is a wedding picture, the forerunner to and perfect model for tens of millions of paintings and photographs in the centuries to come. The oldest surviving son, fifteen-year-old Charles, Lord Herbert, in scarlet, was to marry a young heiress, the twelve-year-old Mary Villiers, who was to bring to the marriage a dowry of £25,000, roughly equivalent to two thousand years' wages of a Wiltshire shepherd.

Above them, the three dead children of the family, with garlands of roses in their hands, float on clouds as putti. The younger brothers to the left and the older sister with her husband to the right, the elegant bronzed cavalier Earl of Carnarvon, surround the Earl and Countess of Pembroke, who sit centrally, facing us, as if king and queen.

The painting is full of grace and aristocratic poise, of riches at ease with themselves, of what now would be called privilege and was then considered nobility. You can't help but stand back and gaze at its beauties as I did that afternoon. It exudes a distant and forgotten handsomeness, an abandoned world of elegance and power, neither stiff nor louche but regal and familial. But there is something not quite settled about the painting. As you look at it a little harder, that atmosphere becomes a bit uncertain. It is not blankly smug as an eighteenth-century depiction of a great family might be; nor assertive and singular as it might have been a century earlier. Inside this painting's grace are hints of anxiety and melancholy, of a world teetering on collapse, of love thwarted and happiness denied, of ambivalence as the companion of glamour.

I looked at these people, so distant and so present, in the very rooms they would have known and loved, near the great series of south windows over the valley of the Nadder, where they would undoubtedly have ridden and played. As I stood there, I wanted, above all, to hear them speak. What did they believe in? What led this family to its prominence? What did the signals in the painting mean? Why was that woman holding a pearl between her fingers? Why did that man dabble his fingers with hers? What were the implications of the strange space they were in, half public, half private, half on display, half acting out a set of hidden relationships? And what would become of them in the cataclysm of civil war that would overtake England within seven years of the painting's being finished?

The room stewards had to usher me out of the house as closing time approached, but I knew I would return, and over the last two years I have been able to plunge myself knee- and elbow-deep into the world of the Pembrokes. I soon realized that this was a world hinged to inheritance, to what the past had given it. I knew that to understand the figures in the painting, I had to go back to their grandfather, a violent and bruisingly ruthless figure in Tudor England, the 1st Earl of Pembroke, who acquired Wilton in the 1540s. More than that, though, I had to explore the world surrounding their beautiful painting: the luxurious saloon, the perfect lawns, the sliding river, the woods, fields, and villages extending from here to the horizon, all of which they owned. The Wilton landscape and the social structures embedded in it were intimately connected to their most cherished beliefs. To understand the painting, I had to understand the world in which it was made.

The story of this family, their manoeuvrings and struggles, tracks the history of Renaissance England. Tudor Wilton was a place of brutalist display. Elizabethan Wilton was the home of Sir Philip Sidney and his dazzling sister, Mary, Countess of Pembroke, who created here the dream of Arcadia, that perfect world where strife was over and turmoil done. Mary's sons William and Philip were very probably the lovers, respectively, of Shakespeare and James I, and the promoters, from the 1610s to the 1640s, of a vision of England that looked back to a more beautiful and happier time, before the corruptions, ambitions, and squalor of the Stuart court had destroyed it. Everything Shakespeare and Sidney wrote about the possibilities of a finer world found its embodiment here. Wilton became the headquarters for its own brand of Arcadian idealism, the early, aristocratic progenitor of communal and environmental ideas that set itself against the dirty, hungry power plays of city, crown, and court in Whitehall.

Few families can have had such a powerfully heritable culture. In a remarkable act of continuity, the Pembrokes transmitted their conservative, Arcadian idealism from generation to generation, fathers and mothers, sons and daughters each playing their part for more than a hundred years. Central to their idealism was the belief that the beautiful world over which they presided did not rely for its meanings on the state. They were not in the condition of servants to the king. Far from it: they represented virtues the crown and court knew little of. That was the most intriguing aspect of all: these beautiful people in their silks and their glimmering cavalier hair turned against the king in the 1640s. The great painting by Van Dyck was a picture not of conformity and settlement but of a family that had rebellion—and a longing for a better world—burning in their hearts.

THE MAKING
OF THE PEMBROKES

1527–1546

The man who would become the 1st Earl of Pembroke was as tough, powerful, and cynical, and his wife as serious and high-minded, as anyone in sixteenth-century England. Together, they embodied the two streams of Tudor life: the untrammeled brokering of power through violence, threat, and political flexibility, and the cleansing of the mind through education and integrity. William Herbert and his wife Anne were the rootstock of the Wilton Arcadia: its necessary power; its longing for goodness.

William Herbert was a Welsh hardman. He may not have been able to read and could scarcely write his own name—those signatures of his that survive, in an age of sometimes exquisite handwriting, waver and wobble from one letter to the next, unable to distinguish lower from upper case, not even pursuing a straight line across the page, but intent on a flourish here and there, the writing of a bear—a bear with pretensions—into whose paw someone has thrust a pen. According to John Aubrey, the seventeenth-century gossip, Herbert was "strong sett, but bony, reddish favoured, of a sharpe eie, sterne looke" and his portraits confirm that stark, bullish quality, depicting his feet planted four square beneath him, his eyes cold, his impatient face scarcely connected to the finery in which he has been dressed, one hand holding gloves but ready for the sword, the other clasping the staff of office as if it were a stick he might hit someone with. Everything is fixed, obdurate, immovable; the man is as substantial as the material world to which his life and passions are directed. Herbert was the acquirer of riches and the founder of a dynasty. The Elizabethan historian William Camden called him "an excellent man, who was in a manner, the Raiser of his own Fortunes," and Aubrey, "of good naturall parts, but very colorique." He was an English condottiere whose hatchet mouth and unforgiving eye founded a dynasty. Spirit barely flickered inside him. He was no Arcadian, but without him Arcadia could not have flowered.

Neither William Herbert nor his descendants wanted to see themselves as arrivistes. They wanted to look as if they had always been at the heart of significance, and throughout the sixteenth and seventeenth centuries, the Pembrokes did their best to cover up some slightly flaky origins. In the fourteenth and fifteenth centuries they had been entirely Welsh. Not until the late fifteenth century were they even called Herbert. (No one knows where the name came from.) Instead, out of the mists of Wales and time emerged Jenkyn ap Adam, who begat Gwylym ap Jenkyn, who begat Thomas ap Gwylym, who married Gladwys, the Star of Abergavenny (her dowry was a park full of deer), and together they begat William ap Thomas, who took a large body of Welsh archers to Agincourt in 1415. His son, Gwilym Ddu, "Black Will," marauded and burned his way across England in support of the Yorkist cause in the Wars of the Roses, and as his reward was made Earl of Pembroke by Edward IV. This slashingly successful warrior, the first Welshman to become an English peer, who for years ran the whole of Wales as his fiefdom, had several illegitimate children, one of whom, Richard, had as his lordship the poor, steep Vale of Ewyas in the Black Mountains, a place that is still full of small, edge-of-subsistence farms, houses pushed into the hillside, heart-stopping beauty, and unrelenting rain.

No one could ever imagine that Ewyas was the threshold of power, but it is the place from which the young William Herbert, Richard's second son, emerged to conquer his world. From a modern perspective, it is not surprising as a background to a tough, violent, imposing, and driven life—a grandfather of heroic proportions, a near-fatal lack of social standing, the stain of illegitimacy, and the fate of the second son: disinheritance even from his father's small patrimony.

That essentially meritocratic view was not how it was seen at the time. When William Herbert was finally made Earl of Pembroke in 1551, he did not boast his climb to power, nor call himself the "1st Earl." There was no honor in that. As far as he was concerned, he was the 20th Earl of Pembroke, heir in line direct to the previous nineteen, of nine different creations, who had battled their way across the Middle Ages. It was the grandest of inheritances. The pretentious George Owen, Elizabethan antiquarian and remote relation of the Herberts, whom Owen adulated, was still relishing the ancient power of the earls of Pembroke in the late sixteenth century. The earldom of Pembroke, Owen wrote, "was in auncient tyme a County Palatine," not subject to any king's power. The earl "had the commanding and leading of all the people of his country to make warres at his pleasure. He had within his Country nine castles of his owne and twelve seigniories or manors which were parcell of his Countye . . ."

In an era of increasing bureaucratization of government, and an emasculation of the old magnates of medieval England, there was a frisson to this manly independence, which a mere created earl or baron could scarcely rival. It is not surprising that any memory of the illegitimacy of William Herbert's father was quietly soothed away. Here was a man conducting his life as a power-broking baron in the mold of his ancestors.

What Owen does not mention in his catalogue of honor is that the first time this William Herbert made his mark on the world, it was as a murderer. His father had died in 1510 when William was three, and the boy went to live in the household of his relation by marriage, the Earl of Worcester. Worcester was a warrior, administrator, diplomat, and the great producer and showman of Henry VIII's court. He was responsible for the tournament ground and pasteboard palaces set up for the meeting of Henry VIII and François I at the Field of the Cloth of Gold in the summer of 1520. It was Worcester who arranged for five thousand people to be shipped across the Channel to France to organize this event. Vast quantities of timber and glass were brought to the site. Three hundred knights took part in the tournament, over which Worcester himself presided as one of the judges. William Herbert, aged thirteen, was at his side, as his page, learning the intimacy of power and glory.

Worcester died on April 25, 1526, and that year William Herbert appears as a "gentleman pensioner" at the court of Henry VIII. It was the lowest rung of court life. One could be a gentleman pensioner and still be thrown into jail for debt or be arrested on suspicion of treason, but it was the necessary first step on the road to significance. But then Herbert's career came adrift. On midsummer's eve 1527, a time for drinking and feasting, bonfires, high spirits, sex, and violence, there was an incident in Bristol, the great seaport already spreading its networks to the New World, that might have destroyed him.

The mayor of Bristol, a man known as Thomas or "Davy" Broke and later described by the hostile protestant preacher George Wishart as "a knave and gorbely [fat] knave," together with his "brethren"— perhaps "that droncken Gervys, that lubber Antony Payne, &

slovyn William Yong, and that dobyll knave William Chester," all leading Bristol merchants and all identified by Wishart as Broke's associates—were coming back into the city after some duck shooting. Unexplained, William Herbert, already with the reputation of "a mad fighting young fellow," was there with a gang of Welshmen to meet them on the bridge. They began to talk and "for want of some respect in compliment" fell into an argument and then a rage. A fight broke out, and Herbert killed one of the merchants, a man called Richard Vaughan, from an old and distinguished Bristol family.

The incident fits. Herbert's origins in South Wales were just across the Severn. The Bristol men would have known he was an illegitimate son. Herbert had by now spent most of his life in the heady atmosphere of court, wearing the badge first of his kinsman the Earl of Worcester, then of the king himself, acquiring the sheen and courteousness of that world. His own honor would have been both high and tender in his mind, and now he found himself insulted by a party of drunk, duck-hunting Bristol merchants. Of course he turned to his knife.

Herbert and the Welshmen who were with him "fled through a gate into the Marsh and escaped in a boat with the tide." After that, wanted for murder, named in a Bristol's coroner's report as the man who did it, Herbert disappeared. Nothing is known of him for the next seven or eight years. John Aubrey thought he had gone to France, to the Valois court, but as Herbert in later life was unable to speak French, that is unlikely. Maybe he went to ground in Wales, surrounded by the protective world of his Herbert connections, sheltered by the common understanding that Welsh fighters had long since been killing fat Bristol merchants. Either he, or someone else called William Herbert, killed "one honest man" in Newport in South Wales in 1533, and his servant was convicted of killing yet another Welshman the following year. Brutality lay at the center of his life.

In 1534 Herbert was still being described as a "late gentleman of the household," but soon after that he returned to court, was readmitted to the glowing circle near the king, and in 1535 was promoted to become "an esquire of the body," an honorific but one that implied a further penetration of the layers surrounding the sovereign. The story of this family over a period of more than one hundred years is hinged, at least in part, to that bodily geometry; closeness to the king, to his actual body, his breathing presence, is the one variable that governs their fortunes. Thuggery and exile among the ancestral comforts of South Wales was one thing; sharing the same physical space as the fount of all honor and the source of all lands was quite another.

On returning to court, Herbert met Anne Parr, the woman he would marry. She and Herbert may have fallen in love. Neither had any fortune to bring to the marriage. Both were orphans. Both were making their way in the world of the court. And Henry VIII's court in the 1530s was one where love affairs were frequent and courtly love admired and practiced as necessary and civilizing elements of the Italianate courtier's life. The most beautiful lines written in Tudor England are by Thomas Wyatt, in his poem bemoaning the un-Arcadian, treacherous world of calculation and disloyalty at court ("They fle from me that sometyme did me seke"), which describes just such a moment of unadorned and immediate love:

> When her lose gowne from her shoulders did fall
> And she me caught in her armes long and small
> Therewithal sweetly did me kysse
> And softly said dere hert howe like you this

Love itself might also be seen as a form of Arcadia, a private place in which the fever and anguish of being is soothed away.

William Herbert was about eight years older than Anne Parr. A drawing by Holbein, probably made when Anne was about twenty, in 1535, shows her as she was when William fell in love with her. As an image, it is a universe apart from Herbert's tense and wary assertion: calm, pure, and controlled, with a clarity and directness about her eyes and a firmness but no meanness in her mouth, she seems all spirit. It was a marriage of opposites. It is a strikingly Protestant image, nearly shadowless, a form of portraiture motivated by truth and clarity, a product of the Reformation with the removal of the dark and its substitution with the clear-eyed, clear-skinned vision of Englishwomen such as Anne Parr.

In 1531, as an orphaned sixteen-year-old after her mother died, Anne had come to court to serve as a maid-in-waiting to Henry VIII's sequence of wives. She was the daughter of a gentry family of no great wealth or standing but one that since 1483, over four generations, had served England's queens. Her mother, Dame Maud Parr, had been both confidante and lady-in-waiting to Henry's first wife, Catherine of Aragon, and now both Anne Parr and her elder sister, Katherine, were serving in the household of Catherine of Aragon's daughter, Princess Mary. Sir Thomas Parr had died in 1517, and both girls had been brought up, along with their brother, William, by the formidable Dame Maud, who was fluent in French and maybe also in Latin, a manager of lands and contracts, an educational theorist, and friend of the humanist scholars Thomas More and Roger Ascham. Dame Maud had provided her daughters with the richest possible humanist education, setting up a small school in their house in Leicestershire. Its methods had been modeled on the program Thomas More had ordained for his own family, teaching the children philosophy, mathematics, Latin, French, Italian, chess, the study of coins, art theory, medicine, and rigorous training in the Scriptures. Anne had emerged a scholar. In later life she would become patron of Fellows at St. John's College,

Cambridge. She sent two of her sons to Peterhouse. Roger Ascham, who became Elizabeth I's tutor, borrowed Anne's copy of Cicero and quoted Ovid in the letters he wrote her. The fineness and purity that glows from the face of Anne drawn by Holbein was no illusion.

Both Anne and her sister would become champions of the reformed religion that swept through England in the 1530s. It is difficult to escape the conclusion that their education in the highest and most sophisticated form of Renaissance humanism prepared the ground for a skeptical attitude toward the inherited ways of the Church. Anne Parr, in other words, looks like a Protestant in the making. She also looks like William Herbert's better half. They were probably married late in 1537, when she was twenty-two and he thirty-one.

No one could have predicted that they would be the foundation of one of the great families of England. Anne had remained no more than a maid-in-waiting, a body servant, to the evolving sequence of queens; William was still an Esquire of the King's Body. They were without any prospect of inheritance, landless, and disconnected from that great engine of power but playing their hands in the life of the court, the only place where that condition could be altered. "Upon the bare stock of their wits, they began to traffic for themselves." Over the next twenty years, the two of them played that game more successfully than anyone else in England.

William's attitude toward religion would remain equivocal for the rest of his life. He changed as circumstances required him to change. He was the heir to a great name but to nothing else. Treading carefully was an aspect of survival. He believed in the religion that the king or queen of the day required him to believe in, no more and no less. Such changes of religious allegiance were no rarity in sixteenth-century England—many justified it openly on state grounds—but his voltes-faces were among the slickest and the sweetest. In the 1590s, the old, slippery smooth courtier the Marquess of Winchester was

questioned how he stood up for thirty years together amidst
the changes and raignes of so many chancellors and great
personages. Why, quoth the Marquess, *Ortus sum ex salice,
non ex quercu*, I was made of the plyable willow, not of the
stubborn oak. And truly the old man hath taught them all,
especially William, earl of Pembroke, for they two were
ever of the King's religion, and ever zealous professors.

Meanwhile, the two young Herberts, as if in a game of grandmother's footsteps, were making their slow and careful approach to the center of power. Anne became a Gentlewoman of the Queen's Household, and William one of fifty new Gentlemen Spears, as they were called, an extravagantly equipped honor guard with gold chains and gilt poleaxes, an élite band of strong, young, capable courtiers among whom Henry felt at ease. Will Herbert soon rose again to become a Gentleman of the Privy Chamber, at a stipend of fifty pounds a year, one of a set of efficient, tough, educated officials of royal government entirely dependent on the favor and will of the king. They were no palace popinjays or playthings of the king but, for him, essential information-gathering, will-enforcing tools of government, diplomacy, and war. Herbert was approaching the crown in order to achieve his independence from it.

Needing to fund the glorious palace-building, war-waging methods of his court, the king's eyes fell on the great medieval estates of the monasteries. In the spring of 1539, the ancient abbey at Wilton, among eight hundred in England and Wales, was dissolved and its wonderful lands taken into the ownership of the crown. Much of the rest of the year at court must have been filled with speculation as to who the recipient of Wilton might be. In May 1540 the door opened: William Herbert received a twenty-one-year lease of the site of Wilton Abbey; in July he was appointed chief steward of all the abbey's lands. He was knighted, Anne became Keeper of the Queen's Jewels, and that autumn the couple's son Henry was born.

For three years, subject only to the twenty-one-year lease, Wilton remained the property of the crown, but in April 1542 Henry VIII gave it by a "mere motion"—as it is described in the enormous Exchequer document prepared for the King's Remembrancer, the official whose task it was to remember everything that had been done by the king or in his name—to "our beloved Servant William Herbert Knight and Anne his wife." The gift was for their lifetimes only. The document is vast because it lists the vastness of the gift. The house and site of the abbey "now dissolved" and all our "messuages houses edifices dove houses stables mills barns orchards gardens waters ponds parks lands soil and hereditaments whatsoever" were to go to the chosen couple. The list rolls on and on: manors, lordships, tithes, corn sheaves, grain, hay, "fisheries and the fishings of our waters," the "twenty and five quarters of salt annually extracted from the salt pits" in Dorset, the "granges mills tofts cottages meadows feedings pastures waste furze heath and marshes," and all sorts of "fees farms annuities and pensions" that the "last abbess and convent" had been entitled to. The list of places, and of every item in them, was a hymn to accumulation, the beauty of materiality, satisfying the deepest possible lust for land and property. The King's Remembrancer was transferring the ownership of an entire world, and its driving force was the "mere motion" of regal power, a fiat, a breaking of bonds that had persisted for centuries. William Herbert was now in possession of what John Aubrey would call "a countrey of lands and Mannours," a fiefdom, a power base, and a landscape.

This was good but it was not everything. After their deaths, as things stood, the great estate would revert to the crown. But in July 1543, the world of the Herberts changed. Anne's elder sister, Katherine, to whom she was exceptionally close and who shared with her a passionate attachment to the reformed religion, married the king. Katherine Parr was a beautiful widow, and the king had fallen in love with her. Both William and Anne Herbert attended the wedding, at which Henry shouted, "Yea!" when asked if he wanted to marry Katherine. Anne helped her sister prepare the black silk nightdresses the king liked his brides to wear, and William Herbert suddenly found himself the royal brother-in-law. Lands, offices, and cash began to flow toward him. As their London house, the new queen gave them the great old palace of Baynard's Castle, on the Thames. With it came the right to bind any traitor "at low tide to a pillar in the Thames near the Castle Wall, leaving him there for two floods and two ebbs." The totality of power was lapping at the Herberts' shores.

Wilton and its train of beauties became the Herberts' property forever in January 1544. Royal stewardships in Wales followed, and in 1546, William Herbert became Joint Chief Gentleman of the Bedchamber, the position with the steadiest and most regular contact with the king in his most private moments, the soft, potent heart of monarchy.

In the summer of 1543, Herbert had started to erect his new house at Wilton, "a large & high built square of hewen stone." It was in some ways a Tudor muddle, with pediments and onion domelets, classical busts in circular frames, scallop shells, and out-of-scale columns and pilasters—a collection of ideas borrowed from the Renaissance, with Corinthian capitals and exquisite entablatures all finely executed but with little understanding of the system to which they should have belonged. Herbert liked to wear a large ring on each index finger, and his new house at Wilton was rather like those rings: expensive, flashy, and big. Its lead rain heads and downpipes were decorated with a rich and barbaric mixture of green men and beautiful acanthus leaves twisted into elegant knots. All over the building, as you can still see if you creep in under the attic spaces of the later additions, there are brilliant colors and gilding and armorial beasts and legendary figures encrusting the walls. The house was an adaptation of the abbey, probably based around the abbey cloister, but it cost more than £10,000, equivalent to the cost of building a good hundred manor houses. Sixteen acres of five- and six-year-old coppice trees were felled to provide the fuel to burn the lime to make the mortar with which the stones were bound together. Those stones came either from the partly demolished abbey or from the abandoned site of the ancient city above Salisbury, Old Sarum, carted in to the palace by the River Nadder all summer long.

Parts of the Tudor house remain embedded in the seventeenth- and nineteenth-century additions, and one porch was preserved by Inigo Jones as a fine example of early Renaissance style, but the effect of Herbert's showiness can be measured by an account of it made in 1635 by a Lieutenant Hammond, who was touring the west of England. He found Wilton as it was just before the transforming Jonesian work on the house had begun. It was a building larded with richness: a gallery "richly hung and adorn'd with stately and faire pictures"; cloth of gold hangings, "over the Chimney peece the statue of King Henry 8th richly cut and gilded ouer," "the great Dyning Chamber, very richly hang'd"; in it "a most curious Chimney Peece, of Alablaster Touch-Stone and marble, cut with seuerall statues, the Kings and his lordships owne armes richly sett out." Accounts have survived of marble and jasper doorcases as well as "eight great tables" imported from France.

Buried inside this gilded case was the hidden fist—still there, remarkably, in 1635—something that Lieutenant Hammond felt "may well compare with any in the Kingdome":

> That is a most gallant Armory, which is 60 yards in length,
> the number of Armes therein will compleatly furnish, and
> fit out 1000 Foote, and Horse: besides 30 Glaues [lances],
> 30 Welsh Hookes, 60 Black Bills, 20 Holy water Springers

[?], and 60 Staues, which were weapons to guard the old
Lord's Person, with many other Offensiue, and Defensive
Armes as Coats of Maile &c.

In a special room at the end of this huge private arsenal were the
great suits of armor Herbert and his son collected: a suit of armor
made in Greenwich for Henry VIII and another for Edward VI, complete suits of Milan armor, "the Lord William his Turkish Scymiter, or
sable, and his whole armour for his Horse richly grauen and gilded."

Could the foundations of power in an English country house ever
have been quite so graphically displayed? By the time an inventory
was made of the house in 1683, there was both a "new" and an "old"
armory. The new had some pistols, blunderbusses, bullet molds, and
"bullet guns" stored in it, but the old armory spoke of an earlier world.
Piles of muskets, too many for the surveyor to count, were in there
among the "hollster pistols" and "bandiloes" (broad belts from which
a heavy weapon could be slung). Alongside them, 26 bills (hooks to
be used for slashing at hedges or men), 20 "holboards" (halberds, a
combination of axe and spear on the end of a seven-foot-long pole),
260 pikes, 92 other pikes, and most chillingly of all, "dog chains."

Outside the door, this hardman established his own Arcadia. A
garden was made with walks, fishponds, and fruit trees and a stable
built for eighty horses. The abbey's dovecote, forge, mill, and giant
grange for the grain rents from the estate were all left standing. The
entire village of Washerne, across the Nadder from the site of the
abbey, as well as the vicarage of Bulbridge, were enclosed in a new
park and demolished. What had been both common land (the open
fields) and "several" land (closes belonging to individuals) was shut
up in the park and denied to the people who had farmed it "time out
of mind." Herbert planted a copse and an avenue of trees where the
people of Washerne had previously grown their food. The avenue

would later be called Sir Philip Sidney's Walk, as it was there he would stroll, composing the *Arcadia*. Within the park, among the "diverse et pulchre perambulaciones," as a surveyor in 1562 described it, half English, half Latin, Herbert built "unum Standinge" (a platform) "in quo dominus stare potest ad super vivendum diversa loca pro placito suo" (in which the lord can stand so that he can overlook the various places for his pleasure).

Those few actions, and the few sentences used to describe them, represent the conflict of the two Arcadias. The ancient abbey is destroyed; a palace is built in its place; the poor have their ancient rights kicked away and their houses demolished; and a beautiful stretch of parkland, adorned with trees and pleasure buildings, is installed where the poor's ancestors had lived. The purpose is "pro placito suo," to calm the great man's troubled mind and to provide the Lord with an easing vision of prelapsarian bliss.

The pleasure park erased the custom of the manor. It wasn't done entirely illegally. Where lands were taken from common grazing, or even from the open field, and enclosed in a park (Herbert would have seven parks in all by the 1560s, and employed a full-time "Regarder," whose job was to travel round the parks to see that all was well), the peasants received compensation, usually in the form of lowering of rents or a relaxation of the services due to the lord. At Wilton, a seven-acre field called Lampeland was enclosed in Herbert's park. In compensation for its loss, Herbert no longer required the villagers of Washerne to pay seven shillings and eightpence every year for a marsh or meadow called Woodmersh.

That is all very well, but in a system where pressure on food and resources was tight, and where the balance of arable land with hay-growing meadow was finely tuned, removing seven acres of growing ground, not to speak of demolishing houses in a world so deeply dependent for its sense of meaning on the pattern of use of the landscape, was a form of dispossession that went far beyond the removal of an economic asset and resource. Why was it done? Not only to feed the vanity of a Tudor magnate but also to provide a place of peace and calm in a life of extreme anxiety and stress. The sufferings of the villagers of Washerne are a direct product of the tensions and struggles at the Tudor court.

The silent presence in this life is that of Anne Parr, whose portrait bust appears opposite William Herbert's on one face of the 1540s porch, said to be designed by Holbein, which still exists today in the Wilton garden. But her voice does not survive in the documents. At least at court one can be sure that she played her part in protecting her sister, the queen, in the great crisis that threatened the Parrs and the future of the English Reformation in the summer of 1546. The sickening and increasingly short-tempered Henry VIII had turned against the revolutionary forces he had unleashed through his break with Rome. In this subtly murderous atmosphere, conservatives at court, led by Bishop Gardiner, had tried to frame Katherine as a radical and a subversive. Agents and spies had rifled through the queen's apartments looking for proscribed books and pamphlets in cabinets, chests, and drawers. She kept such items, in fact, in the garderobe, and when the threat became too hot, she had them smuggled out to her uncle's house, only retrieving them after Henry had died. Anne Parr, a passionate believer in the reformed religion and well practiced at secrecy and courtiership, was central to preserving a network of Protestants right at the heart of Whitehall. For a time, in 1546 and 1547, Katherine Parr's chambers were the center of the English Reformation.

John Foxe, the great chronicler of that revolution, described the atmosphere in which Anne Parr lived. The queen was

> very much given to the reading and study of the Holy Scriptures, and that she, for the purpose, had retained divers well

learned and godly person to instruct her . . . [and] every day in the afternoon for the space of an hour one of her said chaplains in her privy chamber made some collation to her and her ladies and gentlewomen of her privy chamber, or others that were disposed to hear; in which sermons they ofttimes touched such abuses as in the church then were rife.

In February 1546, Katherine ordered some new coffers for her chamber, with new locks, metal hinges, corner bands, and handles with nails: the tools of survival. People around her were being picked off by Bishop Gardiner. In May, a young aristocratic protestant, Lord Thomas Howard, was summoned before the Privy Council and charged with "disputing indiscreetly of Scripture with other young gentlemen of the Court." Later that week it was demanded that he "confess what he said in disproof of sermons preached in Court last Lent and his other talk in the Queen's chamber and elsewhere in Court concerning Scripture." Others of her servants, the courtiers, yeomen, and physicians who attended her, were arrested and imprisoned for holding erroneous opinions and engaging in "unseemly reasoning."

In the last two weeks of July, Bishop Gardiner attempted to close the trap on the Parrs. According to John Foxe, the protestant martyrologist, Gardiner whispered in the king's ear that Katherine and her ladies were holding, discussing, and propagating views that even by the king's own laws were heretical. More than that, "he, with others of his faithful councillors, could within short time, disclose such reasons cloaked with this cloak of heresy, that his majesty could easily perceive how perilous a matter it is, to cherish a serpent within his own bosom . . ."

"They rejoice and be glad of my fall," the queen had written two years earlier in a set of private prayers.

They be assembled together against me. They strike to
kill me in the way before I may beware of them. They
gather themselves together in corners. They curse and
ban my words everyday, and all their thoughts be set to
do me harm. They watch my steps, how they may take
my soul in a trap. They do beset my way, that I should not
escape. They look and stare upon me. I am so vexed that
I am utterly weary.

The Protestant condition had martyrdom at its heart. Its self-
conceived purity was isolated in a world of sinners. A court was a
nest of enemies, and only in the sacredness of the soul's relationship
to God was there any refuge. At some level, there was a connection
here—one that will run throughout the story of this family—between
a Protestant desire for safety away from the failings of the world and
the ideal of Arcadian bliss, a place devoted to the demands of love and
purity of motive. Protestantism and Arcadianism in that way sat hand
in hand, bridging the secular and religious cultures of early modern
England. Both were driven by the demand for retreat and for a still-
ing of the clamor. Each represented an equal and opposite reaction
to the disturbance and trauma of modernity, the speeding up of the
flywheel, the sense that the world was getting old and corrupt, with
beggars on every street and every corner, where inflation and debase-
ment of the currency was rife, simplification was good, the ancient was
a refuge, rents did not produce what they had in the past, order was
under threat, bread was too expensive, old systems of authority looked
creaky and irrelevant, and there was no calm in the world.

One seventeenth-century Puritan preacher, Ralph Josselin, an
Essex clergyman, saw the grave itself as a gazebo, or a place like
the standing in the park at Wilton, as somewhere drenched in peace.

"Your Wives, your Husbandes, your Sonnes and Daughters, whose departing you so much lament," he told a funeral congregation, "are but stept aside into their retiring rooms, their cool Summer-parlours, the shady cool Grove of the Grave to take a little rest by sleep. . . ." Rest, the end of the drama, and silence: Renaissance England wanted nothing more. It is the subject that Hamlet dwelt on again and again: searching for somewhere in which the agony was over, where the flesh that he described either as too solid, too sullied, or too sallied—all three readings are relevant—would at last melt and resolve itself into a dew. Hamlet was a Protestant prince but he was also an Arcadian, at home not in the world of strife to which his ancestors had all belonged, but in the place of reflection and quiet. His soliloquy is itself an Arcadian form.

The natural end of Gardiner's plot against Katherine Parr and her circle was the arrest, interrogation, and execution of the queen and those about her. It reached its climax in the first week of August. Gardiner's men had been into the queen's apartments. Anne Parr's closet, as well as those of the other gentlewomen of the chamber, had been searched, but nothing had been found. The books were well away. Nevertheless, Gardiner felt he had enough evidence against her to persuade the king to issue a warrant for her arrest and committal to trial. Katherine guessed nothing, but by chance the warrant, at least according to John Foxe, fell out of the pocket of her enemy the Lord Chancellor, Sir Thomas Wriothesley. It was found on the paving stones by one of the queen's pages, or perhaps by her doctor, and immediately brought to her.

Her courage left her and she fell into a fit of hysterics, taking to her bed. When the king came to see her, she spoke to him without guile, asking what it might be that she had done wrong. The next day she had recovered, went to him in his chamber, told him she was "a silly poor woman"—meaning not that she was stupid but that she was innocent—and the king was her "only anchor, supreme head and governor here in earth, next unto God, to lean unto."

But there was no certainty in this court, and Gardiner continued with his plot to destroy Katherine Parr. She and the king had moved to Hampton Court, and it was there in the first week of August 1546 that the final act was played. Henry, Katherine Parr, Anne Parr, and the other gentlewomen of Katherine's court were in the Privy Gardens when suddenly, without warning, Wriothesley himself appeared among the gravel walks and box-lined beds. He had forty armed guards with him, and together they approached the royal party. Katherine watched for the king's reaction. By this stage in Henry's life, no one could be certain which way he would turn, or which set of loyalties he would respond to. The needle, quite arbitrarily, could flick either way. Would this, as it had been for other queens, be the moment of denial? Or had her confession of weakness and dependence been enough? Her life and future hung in the balance as Wriothesley approached down the gravel paths. But for Henry, there was no hesitation. The king, in an apoplectic rage, took Wriothesley roughly aside and shouted at him. "Knave! Arrant knave! Beast and fool!" Wriothesley was ordered from the palace with his men, and Gardiner's plot collapsed. The radical Protestant party, of which the Parrs were a central element, would be safe for the rest of the reign, and what the Herberts had, they would keep.

The first stage was over. William Herbert had wheedled his way into the confidences of the king. His wife, Anne Parr, had with her sister, Queen Katherine, outfaced the Roman Catholic conservatives intent on destroying her. The Herberts were in possession of Wilton but not yet secure enough to pose any threat to the crown. The stain and poverty of William's illegitimacy had been eased away. The foundations were being laid for future glory, and Wilton was to be its theater.

A COUNTREY OF LANDS AND MANNOURS

THE WORLD THE PEMBROKES ACQUIRED

England in the sixteenth century was less a single state than a gathering of separate countries, each full of intense local loyalties and habits of being. Deep communality and tight local networks lay at the heart of the country. Each landscape was a world in itself, and the fifty thousand acres or so of Wiltshire lands and manors the Herberts acquired from the crown in the 1540s were then, and remain today, among the most desirable in the kingdom. The Herberts had landed in the best that England could offer. Even though the Herbert paradox was in play—they only possessed their estate because the crown had granted it to them—this was to become their country, the place where their most rooted loyalties lay. The story of their relationship to the crown cannot be understood without the picture behind it of the world they had now acquired. Their lands and manors were the counterpoint to the cynical realties of the struggle at court. The realities of an owned estate can explain conservative rebellion. The lands themselves are the vision behind the great Van Dyck painting.

Early on a summer morning—and you should make it a Sunday, when England stays in bed for hours after the sun has risen—the chalk downland to the west of Wilton slowly reveals itself in the growing light as an open and free-flowing stretch of country, long wide ridges with ripples and hollows within them, separated by river valleys, with an air of Tuscany transported to the north, perhaps even an improved Tuscany. Seventeenth-century scientists thought the smoothness of the chalk hills meant they were part of the sea floor that had appeared after Noah's flood had at last receded. It was old, God-smoothed country and pure because of it.

This morning, you will have it to yourself. At first light, the larks are up and singing, but everything else is drenched in a golden quiet. Shadows hang in the woods, and the sun casts low bars across the backs of the hills. You will see the deer, ever on the increase in southern England, moving silently and hesitantly in the half-distance. It is a place of slightness and subtlety, wide and long-limbed, drawn with a steady pencil. Above the deeper combes, on the slopes that the Wiltshiremen call "cliffs," the grass is dotted with cowslips and early purple orchids. Gentians and meadow saxifrage can still be found on the open downland. Chalkhill Blue butterflies dance over the turf. Fritillaries and white admirals are in the woods. The whole place, as Edward Thomas once described the shape of chalkland, is full of those "long straight lines in which a curve is always latent . . ."

This feeling of length—slow changes, a sense of distance—is at the heart of the Wiltshire chalk. It is not a plain, because everywhere the ground surface shifts and modulates, but it is nowhere sharp. It is full of continuity and connectedness, a sense that if you set off in any direction you would have two or three days' journey before anything interrupted you. This, in other words, is a place that feels like its own middle, the deepest and richest of arrivals.

John Aubrey, the great seventeenth-century gossip and antiquarian, whose family rented a farm in one of these valleys, called his treasured country "a lovely *campania*," a perfect Champagne country. There is no marginality; instead, settlement, rootedness, stability, removal from strife and trouble. "The turfe is of a short sweet grasse," Aubrey wrote of the place he loved, "good for the sheep, and delightfull to the eye, for its smoothnesse like a bowling green." The most delicious things here were the rabbits, "the best, sweetest, and fattest of any in England; a short, thick coney, and exceeding fatt. The grasse is very short, and burnt up in the hot weather. 'Tis a saying, that conics doe love rost-meat." The rabbits' tastiness was a sign of the country's beneficence.

These wonderful lands—the chalk downs and the lush watered valleys of the rivers that run between them—spread over eighty square miles, were the core of the Herbert estate. Every element of the perfect life is here. High on the chalk ridge just to the west of Wilton is the great royal hunting ground of Grovely Wood, set up as a forest by the Saxon kings, so old that it formed no part of the system of parishes that were created around it before the Norman conquest. It is one of the twenty-five hunting forests mentioned in the Domesday Book, the precious reserves in which the king alone had the right to kill game. Grovely—its name perhaps a memory of the patches of rough woodland growing here when the Saxons first arrived—is still thick with bluebells and wood anemones in the early summer.

From the top of the downs, long droves descend into the valleys of the rivers that cut through the chalk tableland. Honeysuckle and wild clematis drape themselves across the hedges. The sun breaks into the droves past the thorns that are thick with mayflower. Cow parsley is just sprouting in the verges, the wheat and barley still a dense green in the fields beside you. It doesn't matter which river valley you choose: the Ebble, or the Nadder, or the Wylye. Each of them will still greet you like a vision of perfection, the perfect interfolding of the human and the natural that is at the heart of the Arcadian idea. The chalk streams (all three of them still have the Celtic names they had in pre-Roman Britain) emerge in bubbling springs all along the valley sides. The water that has percolated down through the chalk hits a layer of clay and comes to the surface. Along that springline, below the arable fields but above the floodable valley bottoms, are the villages. Their emergences are beautiful, soft, weed-rimmed places where the water erupts in shallow mushrooms and riffles. It is as if the water is simmering in the pools before making its easy way down to the main rivers that slope off to the east.

So mudless is this spring water that the rivers remain entirely clear as they move over their pale beds. The banks are spotted with kingcups, and there are islands of white-flowered watercrowsfoot in midstream. The hairy leaves of water mint grow on the gravel banks, coots and moorhens scoot between them, and if you wade out barefoot into the shockingly cold water of the river, the small, wild brown trout flicker away in front of you, running from your Gulliver-in-Lilliput intrusion. Among the trout are the pale bodies of the graylings, called *Thymalus thymalus* because their flesh smells of the wild thyme that grows on the downland turf, and which in the seventeenth century were known here as "umbers," shadow-fish, their silvery grayness scarcely to be distinguished from the most beautiful river water in England.

This was ancient country, drenched in continuities. In common with the rest of southern England, it looked in the sixteenth and seventeenth centuries much as it had for at least a thousand and maybe two or three thousand years. There would have been differences in details: woods had grown up where fields had been before; fields had been cleared where trees had once clothed the landscape. There were more people and more houses. But the villages, as ever, were made of the materials the land could provide. Wheat straw—thatched the roofs, cut not with a scythe but more carefully and more slowly with a sickle—a smaller, neater tool but justifiable in economic terms because it would guarantee a good length in the roofing material: longer straw made dryer roofs. In the walls, the oak frames were infilled with hazel panels, made with exactly the same technique as the hurdles used to enclose the sheep in the folds, the young pliant wands woven between the uprights or "sails" (the wattle), smeared with mud and straw (the daub), and then painted with limewash. Occasionally, for the walls, a mixture of chalk, or "clunch," blocks would be used, quarried from the hill and then mixed with brick from the valley clays. All of this one can still see in the houses of these valleys. Nothing would have come from more than a mile or two away. This was an immutable pattern, the intimate folding of men, their farming, and their habits of life on to the opportunities and constraints the landscape offered them.

The high chalkland would have been nothing without the river valleys. Settlement needs water, and the dew ponds on the downs—in fact, enormous clay-lined dishes to catch the rain—provided water good enough for sheep but desiccating to human taste. Each sip seems to leave a residue of chalk in your mouth. The spring-fed valley water is different, as bubblingly restorative as any in England, marvellous to lie in on a hot summer afternoon, your back on the pebbles, the water dancing around your head and shoulders. The Arcadian world of the Pembrokes' Wiltshire valleys relied for its existence on the constant and mutually supportive relationship of these two environments, the high chalkland and the damp wet valleys, each providing what the other lacked.

The same system of land management, and the virtually immobile social structure it created, had persisted across the centuries. It was, apart for some alterations at the margins, a profoundly conservative and unchanging world. Farming patterns and social relationships had lasted here essentially unchanged from before the ninth century. This extraordinary continuity, even as the world was revolutionized around them, became the dominant fact of the Pembroke estates. This was the old world. Its ancient methods looked like a version of Arcadia. And it was a world the Pembrokes were intent on protecting.

Its roots stretched back into the Dark Ages, perhaps to the moment when the Viking armies were threatening the well-being of much of the Midlands, East Anglia and Wessex, perhaps before then, when violence was still endemic among the Saxon chieftains and their war bands. The documents are thin on the ground, but it seems certain that the system of the manor emerged from a world of violence and the need for protection within it. A warlord offered land and defense, a villein—a man of the village—supplied in return labor and loyalty.

This was certainly how the landowning class of the sixteenth and seventeenth centuries understood the history of what they owned. John Norden, the preeminent surveyor of the early seventheenth century, a professional and a devout Christian, conservative in his ideals, first published his *Surveiors Dialogue* in 1607. It was a popular book that went through three large editions, and was the leading text on the meaning of land, its duties and rewards, in early modern England. With it, Norden was voicing the accepted nostrums of the society he was addressing.

After the departure of the Romans, Norden told his audience of gentlemen, the country was left as

> a very Desert and Wildernesse, full of woods, fels, moores, bogs, heathes, and all kind of forlorne places: and how-soeuer wee finde the state of this Island now, Records do witness vnto us, that it was for the most part a vniuersall wildernesse, until people finding it a place desolate and forlorne began to set footing here, and by degrees grew into multitudes; though for a time brutish and rude.

In that wild time, when life was lawless, there was mutual benefit
to be had in community. The arrangement was originally voluntary
on both sides.

> In the beginning of euery Mannor, there was a mutuall
> respect of assistance, betweene the Lord who gave parcels
> of land . . . and the tennants of euery nature, for ayding,
> strengthening and defending each other:

But time passed and what had begun as a voluntary arrangement
stiffened into the "custom of the manor." Both service to the Lord and
the rights of the tenants had become obligatory "and either, in right of
the custome due to the other, constraineth each other to do that which
in the beginning was of either part voluntary."

Central to the system was the idea of balance and mutuality in
community. In Norden's pages you can hear the discussions of the
English ruling class before the Civil War, the vision of what they
still saw as the organic integrity of the manors they owned and controlled. Norden derived the word *manor* itself from the French verb
mainer—to keep a place in hand, or in check. Control was the essence
of good management, but in harness with control and discipline was
the idea that the landlord's own life, that of his family, his "posterity,"
the lands they held, the lives of those who lived on their lands, were all
part of a single, organic whole.

It is, in this ideal and moralized world, a picture of a profoundly
hierarchical community, deriving its security and well-being from
the natural relationship of parts. "And is not euery Mannor a little
common wealth," Norden asked, tapping big political issues in the use
of that phrase, "whereof the Tenants are the members, the Land the
body, and the Lord the head?" That organic analogy worked in detail.
Above all, the land's bodily nature needed to be attended to:

If it be not fed with nutriture, and comforted and adorned
with the most expedient commodities, it will pine away,
and become forlorne, as the mind that hath no rest or recreation, waxeth lumpish and heauy. So that ground that
wanteth due disposing & right manurance, waxeth out of
kinde: euen the best meddowes will become ragged, and
full of unprofitable weedes, if it be not cut and eaten.

This idea of organic health, and of balance as the source of that
health, runs unbroken from the farming of the fields to the management of the country. It is an undivided conceptual ecology that can
take in the workings of the physical body, the court at Whitehall, the
family, the village, the land itself, the growing of crops, the trans-
mission of well-being to the future, the inheritance of understanding
from the past, and above all the interlocking roles of nobility, gentry,
and commonalty. It is the ideology of an establishment concerned
with keeping itself in the position of wealth and power. There is not a
hint of democracy, let alone radicalism, but it is a frame of mind that
also sets itself against any form of authoritarianism. The workings of
the medieval and post-medieval community depend at their heart on
a balance of interests, contributions, and rewards. It is what, in the
sixteenth and seventeenth centuries, was called, quite consciously, a
"common wealth": well-being derived from a life lived and considered in common. The custom of the manor was not to do with the
regulations of the state, or with individual freedom. It was a deeply
conservative premodern and pre-market system that recognized no
overriding rights of the individual or of national interest. It believed,
to an extent the modern world can scarcely grasp, in the rights of the
community as a living organism.

Again and again in *The Surveior's Dialogue*, Norden emphasized the
point. Good decisions in the management of land were "the meanes to

enable the Honourable to shelter the virtuous distressed." Increasing revenues from a manor allowed the tenants to be treated well. This was a form of obligation, just as, in a family, duty was owed both ways:

> As children are bound to their parents by the bonds of obe-
> dience, so are the parents bound to their children by the
> bond of education; and as servants are bound to their mas-
> ters in the bond of true service, so are the Masters bound to
> their servants in the bond of reward. In like manner, ten-
> ants being bound unto their Lords in the bond of duety, so
> are Lords bound vnto their Tennants in the bond of loue.

That last word recurs. Tenancy is not a matter of rent, or at least not only of rent; it is, Norden says quite explicitly, a love structure. The relationships within a manor, he tells the landlords, must be "in a mutual manner, you to be helpful vnto them, and they louing unto you. And by this meanes, should your strengths increase far more by their loue then by your lucre, & their comfort grow as much by your fauour as doth their groanes vnder your greediness." There was, Norden warned his gentlemen readers, "no comforte in a discontented people" and discontent in them came from avarice and indifference in their landlord. His own well-being, as the head of the body, was utterly dependent on their well-being as its limbs. Extortionate rents and the application of raw market principles would destroy the lord as much as the people.

These questions, and their implications of bodily and moral bal-ance, would, on a far larger scale, become the central concern of seventeenth-century England. Did the king owe the same duty of care to the kingdom as the earl owed to the inhabitants of these ridges and valleys? Was his authority as bound up with love as Norden's para-graphs imply? Did he in fact derive that authority from the people he ruled? Was rule a form of duty? These questions, lurking in the ambiguities of lordship, would lead to civil war, and in that civil war these Arcadian ideas were ranged on the side of Parliament and the ancient constitution and against a king and his ministers, who were seen to have broken the ancient bonds of love and duty. Conservatism was at the heart of Arcadia as it was of the English revolution.

This old, inherited mutuality in social relationships was mirrored by a carefully interfolded relationship to the land itself. The whole system of the chalkland manors depended on people adapting the way they farmed to what the land could tolerate and what the land could offer. On that basis, the manors were divided into three layers: at the top the wide grazing of the open downland; in the valley floor, the lush damp meadows and marshes; and between the two, on the valley sides, the arable fields and woods. Throughout the Middle Ages and in the centuries that followed, sheep were grazed by day on the downs, and in the evening were led downhill along the droves to the arable fields to manure them; in effect, they were used to transfer the nutrients from the chalk on to the arable land. They also served the purpose of fixing the seed corn into the tilth.

The lush valley meadows were the third part of the system. In the early spring, the grass started to grow there before there was any available on the down. There, too, in the summer, the big hay crops could be grown that would feed the animals in the winter, particularly the oxen of the manor's plough team. Good valley grazing allowed the village to keep a larger flock, which meant that more arable ground could be cultivated, which meant that more grain could be grown. Although wool and meat were produced from the flocks, their essential product was grain, the stuff of life, the food on which people depended for survival. All was connected: chalk turf and valley hay, down and meadow, the digestive system of the sheep, and the well-being of men, women, and children.

Ownership of this means of production was not shared. Each farmer owned his own beasts, his own seed corn, his own house, his own garden, barns, and backyard. He also owned his own strips in the huge open, arable fields. But this assemblage of private property was managed in common. Sheep were owned by individual farmers but were grazed in communal flocks, tended by white-caped shepherds whose wages were paid in proportion by all those whose sheep they looked after. Flocks of several hundred sheep were usual on chalkland manors, and in many ways they dictated the shared nature of the farming. It was only practical to graze them together and to fold them together on the same arable field. Villages, as elsewhere in the Midlands and in the chalk country, usually had three open fields (sometimes two, occasionally four or more), of which one lay fallow every year. It was usually laid down in the custom of the manor that the folding of the sheep on to the fields should begin one year at one end, the next at the other. Only that way would the fertility delivered by the sheep be spread evenly across the strips from year to year. Each farmer had to provide winter hay for the sheep, and contribute his few pence toward the employment of a cowherd, hogward, hayward, and even a mole catcher for the manor. Those who failed to meet their obligations to the community would be denied "the fold"—that life-giving manure from the sheep—without which their land would not grow the grains on which they relied for their existence. It was a brutal sanction, but as the manor records show, not one the villagers were slow to impose.

The shepherd in sixteenth- and seventeenth-century Wiltshire, far from being the careless lover of the Arcadian imagination, was one of the best paid and most responsible men in the village. In his hands was the critical job of safeguarding the communal flock that was the basis of the entire village's survival. By the fifteenth century, he was earning ten or twelve shillings a year (for which one could rent thirty acres or more of arable ground) plus an allowance of grain, a lamb in the spring, a fleece at the summer shearing, a whole cheese, the milk of those ewes whose lambs had died, and the milk of all ewes on Sundays. He was allowed to keep some of his sheep in the lord's pasture and was absolved from all communal duties. The shepherd was not the poorest of the poor, but even something of a village grandee.

A fascinating document in the Wiltshire records called simply "Concerning the Shepherd" describes the reality of life for a Wiltshire downland shepherd in September 1629. It consists of the requests laid down by the people of Heale, a small community in the valley of the Avon a few miles north of Wilton, his collective employer. They required of him

> That in person he diligently Attende and keepe his flocke.
> That he absent not himself from them, but upon urgent and necessary cause, and then put the same to some sufficiente body, and not to Children either boyes or girles.

There is a hint there of independence and even truculence in their employee. He also had to keep the sheep out of the corn. Any damage done by the sheep to the growing crops will be docked from his wages "according as two other tenants not interested in the said damage shall value the same." If a sheep died, he had to bring the carcass to the owner's house, to prove he had not merely sold the sheep and was cheating his employers. He had to look after the communal hay rick on which the flock would depend in the winter. He was to prevent "wool-pickers"—and this is a measure of the poverty and tightness in these valleys—from coming to pick the tiny scraps of wool that caught on the hurdles around the fold at night. He must "mend the scabby," carefully cut and destroy the blackthorn furze that always threatens to take over downland grazing, must drive "alien" sheep or pigs into the communal pound and not keep any except the community flock, a temptation to free enterprise he was to resist. If any of the community pay him in "naughty corne, the shepherd upon complainte to be righted by the lord of the mannor on the party soe offendinge."

This was scarcely the Arcadian picture of ease and contentment. Its regulatory tightness was a symptom of real pressure on the resource. At the same time, the existence of the regulations, the communal management of a shared resource, and the expectation that they would be obeyed, that the shepherd should stay with his flock and not deputize except in emergency, that he should look after both animals and grazing—one can see in the presumptions behind those requests a version of the cooperative and even the authentic world of which the sophisticated would always dream. The regulations are evidence of communality working for real.

The system operated hard up against its limits. Animal diseases could devastate flocks, with no understanding among the villagers of where the disease might have come from or what to do about it. In the seventeenth century, the habit developed of feeding tobacco to ill sheep in half-magical attempts to cure them of the many disgusting diseases sheep are prone to. Up to a third of each year's crop had to be held back for the following year's seed corn. Fertility was always at a premium, and any opportunity to receive the dung, or "soil" as it was called, which should have gone to one's neighbor, was always welcome. If someone was found to have done wrong or strayed outside the limits laid down by custom, punishment would be swift. In these ways, the manor could be seen either as a system of cooperative balance or, like a coral reef, a world of such intense internal competitiveness that its struggles and rivalries had been frozen into a set of symbiotic duties and obligations, the rivals in a clinch, by which life alone was sustainable.

Those obligations were all-pervading. Women and children were set to weeding the arable crops in the early summer. Husbands and fathers lived under a fearsome burden of communal work, or work done for the good of the lord of the manor. At the height of the Middle Ages, every year the villager had to thresh a bushel each (seventy or eighty pounds in weight) of wheat, rye, barley, beans, peas, and two bushels of oats; mow two swathes of a meadow; and reap, bind, and carry half an acre of it. Agreement after agreement specified the amount of dung each man had to carry from his own yard to the arable fields, the number of hurdles he had to make for the fold (a practiced man could make two and a half hurdles a day), and the regular amounts of money he had to contribute to the lord of the manor in return for his right to farm the land: nutsilver at the time of nuts, a rental penny at Easter, lardersilver at one or twopence a head, the substantial tax of tallage at six shillings, eightpence each, the threepence per head for the compulsory and customary drinking sessions called "scotales," and the cock and three hens at Martinmas, in November.

This system of obligation and dominance, even as early as the twelfth century, had started to evolve. The work duties of the villeins had often been changed into money payments, threepence or sixpence for "all autumn work." These villages were not designed to be self-sufficient but to produce, in the grain, a crop that could be sold for cash. Cash played a part in a complex picture of partly "customary" labor—the obligations entered into in the far distant past—and wage-based labor. Some men were paid particular rates for particular jobs; others were taken on for a year or half a year; some simply had rent-free holdings in return for work.

The Black Death in 1348 and 1349, which killed between a third and a half of the population of England, changed the balance of this world. Entire villages died. In some, lone men were found still alive among houses full of the dead. The relationship between lord and villein shifted. Too much land and a shortage of labor meant vacant holdings, decayed tenements, and collapsing rental values. The bargain on which the ancient communities had worked—land in return for duties—was no longer worth making. After 1350, those with labor to offer found themselves in a suppliers' market, and the age of compulsory labor on the lord's land was largely, although not entirely, over. From then onward, people occupied their houses and lands by what became known as "copyhold"—literally a written copy of what they had agreed with the lord, or in fact with his steward, as written down in the manor records. Until the end of the seventeenth century, this was the dominant form of tenure on the Wilton estate.

The copyhold manor sounds such a dry and legalistic term, but is in fact the label for an intriguing social experiment, lasting two hundred years or so, in the villages of rural England. It occupies a middle ground, which we would hardly recognize today, between the tight and oppressive lordly control of the early Middle Ages, which came to an end with the Black Death, and the almost equally oppressive regime of the eighteenth and nineteenth centuries, against which Cobbett and others would rail, where the sheer financial dominance of the landlords had erased any rights of the ordinary people. The sense of mutuality in community relationships, which was the dominant note in the copyhold manor, was never stronger than from about 1450 to about 1650. It is at least an interesting coincidence that the second half of that period was almost precisely the time when the fashion for the pastoral, for the Arcadian vision, was most central to English culture. Was pastoralism—like the modern environmental movement—the expression of a world realizing that something real and valuable, which previously had been taken for granted, was now under threat and disappearing from under its nose? If imagination is the cousin of memory, then are the dream worlds of Renaissance England in fact the reassembled fragments of a remembered existence that people's fathers and grandfathers might have considered normal?

The copyhold system was, of course, both good and bad. The tenancy was usually given for three lives, sometimes to a man, his wife, and a son; a man, his sister, and her husband; a man and two sons; or a widow and her son and daughter. It gave security to the farmers and allowed them to invest in improvements that a short lease could not allow. Land and buildings were only rarely let to single individuals; the lease for three lives, if to a man, his wife, his sons, meant that the terms of the lease would extend to whichever of these was the last to die. No one, in other words, would be ejected from their house and farm on the death of a husband or a father. Leases for three lives meant that the maintenance of the social fabric was built into the economic structure of the place.

But the system's conservatism was also a brake. The entire system was presided over by the memory of how things had always been done. Wisdom was essentially proverbial: what was known was good; what was strange was bad. Anything inherited was to be held on to; anything innovatory to be looked at with suspicion. The real story of this ancient form of life was not freedom but imposition, the restrictions on the individual that the workings of the community required. No modern surveillance society could match the reality of a chalk-land village in which work patterns, sexual habits, the ability to sell and trade, and forms of inheritance and friendship were all closely supervised, not by the distant lord of the manor but by the other villagers themselves. The all-seeing eyes of neighbors deeply familiar with "the custom of the manor," that inherited habit, monitored every inch and second.

Whether and where you could collect sticks for firewood, the thickness of the hedge around your garden, the suitability of your chimney for fires, the state of your roof, the dirtiness of the path up to your door, the ringlessness of your pigs' noses, the size of your back room, the clothes your wore, the way you spoke in public, the amount you could drink, your behavior in church: on every conceivable issue, the village could police the habits and trangressions of its inhabitants, and having "presented" the offenders, could sentence and punish them. Village stocks and ducking stools were both the symbols and instruments of control. Right up until the seventeenth century, villagers guilty of theft or adultery were beaten in English villages "until their backs were bloody." Wilton had its own "cage, pillory and stocks." The tumbrel and "cucckingstool" ("a chair in which scolds were sat down to be dunked [*demergebantur*] in the river") were kept in the little "parrock" (an enclosure fenced in with hurdles) belonging to a townsman called Richard Hatchett.

The village was never more vigilant than on the question of land— its boundaries, uses, and access. Common land was not common to anyone: it was common to the few villagers who had rights over it. Others were excluded. The great open fields were not open in any democratic sense: their individual strips, even if reallocated each year among the villagers, were individually named and individually owned, marked, and policed. You could be had up for trespassing on them just as much as on any enclosed land. Acres of parchment were devoted to precise and enforceable rights to and exclusions from wood, marsh, and moor.

Why so tight? Because most of rural England, from the Middle Ages onward, spent most of the time under stress. There was a desperate shortage of fertility: farming systems could only just sustain the human populations that depended on them. If for every grain sown the average return was between three and four grains, one of which had to be kept as seed for the next year, the land was an asset to be cosseted. Nothing could be allowed to disrupt the habits that, so far at least, had allowed the village to feed its people. Poverty bred fear, fear bred conservatism, and conservatism shut out strangers.

This, in many ways, was the reality of the lands the Herberts had acquired, a reliance on rules inherited from "a time beyond which the memory of man runneth not to the contrary," not because those rules stemmed from a golden age but because the risk that changing them would dissolve the system on which survival depended. Communal memory was the arbiter of life. The "custom of the manor" from "time out of mind" was both a moral duty and a set of practical requirements. There was to be no private dealing of which the court and village did not know the details. The manor court, which in its different forms could deal with petty crimes and with all property transactions and transfers, was to be the place in which grievances were to be aired and arrangements made, because only in the openness of those courts, which all copyholders could attend, was communal well-being—common wealth—to be found.

The closed-circuit supervision of one's neighbors' prying eyes ensured that people would not cut down their timber trees, sublet their land for longer than a year, or sell any part of it except in open court. They had to maintain their buildings. If they did not, they would be warned three times, at six-month intervals. On the third time, a stake would be driven into the ground by the front door (said to be the origin of an asset being "at stake"). If nothing had been done by the fourth time, the property would be forfeit. Then the "customary tenant"—the expression means "the holder of the land by the custom of the manor"—would be driven out of his "tenement," the "held thing." Although there were freeholders in these villages, they were only free of the labor and money dues that the copyholders owed to the manor. They were not free of the custom of the manor itself. And if they failed to observe the rules of the village, or committed treason or a felony, they, too, could be deprived of their freehold. In that sense, no one, except the lord of the manor, owned anything here. They, as tenants, merely held their tenements. Survival was conditional on obedience. It was a system about as far from the modern conception of the individual and his rights, let alone a welfare state, as it was possible to get.

Estate management, health and safety issues, antisocial behavior, the highways, property law, animal health and welfare, environmental health, planning permissions, local taxation, police issues, rights of way, agricultural practices, land rights and infringements, supervision of property held in common: every one was dealt with by the lord's steward and a jury, or "homage," as it was significantly called, of twelve of the copyholders. The village was not merely an economic unit; it embodied and enacted almost every conceivable dimension of social and political life. This, not England, was a man's country, and political consciousness penetrated to the very depths of village England, a constant and constantly honed practicing of a set of political rules that felt like the frame of life. Economic management, a deal between the members of a community, and moral policing all came together in an arrangement that was essentially corporate. Privacy in such a world was not only scarcely available, but it would also have seemed wrong.

That "custom of the manor" represented an equilibrium of interests between tenant and landlord. The landlord, in fact, could impose only what the tenants would agree to. The way, for example, in which the area of each holding was measured was more responsive to the reality on the ground than to some abstract, imposed rule. Rent was dependent on acreage, but an acre in 1630s was not the precisely defined unit it is today. An acre was simply the area of ground that a plough could cover in a single day. If the ground was heavy, the acre would shrink to match the conditions; and if the soil light, the acre would expand. Everyone knew this, no one would think of altering it, and the conditions of the agreement were all deeply familiar.

Detail was all. No one manor had rules identical to any other. Even neighboring villages in the same valley or on other side of the same chalk ridge, would have quite various habits and requirements. The customs of Great Wishford, in the Wyley Valley, and Barford

St. Martin, in the valley of the Nadder, were "set down in writing" in 1597; a copy of them survives among the Pembroke papers. They were set down jointly because both villages "ever had an old Ancient Custome" that gave them rights in the great old royal forest of Grovely on the chalk ridge that lay between them. Both villages could pasture "all manner of Beasts and cattle throughout all Grovely for all the year" (except "cattle of two Tooth and Goates, and pigs above a yeare old.") "Ever out of mind," villagers could collect fallen boughs twice a day, once in the morning, once in the evening. By "an ancient custom & time out of mind" on Holy Thursday every year, the men of Wishford could collect "One load of Trees"; on Whitsunday the men of Barford could do the same, but only "upon a Cart to be Drawn home with Men's Strengthe." In addition, Lord Pembroke's ranger had to bring them every year, also on Whitsunday, "One fatt Buck, the one half to Wishford, and the other to Barford to make merry withal amongst the neighbours & the ranger is to have from each of the manors of Wishford & Barford one white loaf, one gallon of beer & a pair of gloves or 12d in money for the Whole."

In Burcombe, on the Nadder just east of Barford, "the Custom of this Manor" constituted in effect a memory and inheritance of the duties required of the medieval villains. A sixteenth-century copy of the customs laid down exactly what work had to be done for the earl by each of the copyholders. Each small tenant (with a house and fifteen acres) had to plough and hedge half an acre of barley land for the farmer who had rented the lord's own demesne land; the larger tenants (with a house and thirty acres) had to perform twice that amount of work, with "the same Farmer giving to them their Breakfast." At harvest time, the small tenants had to provide "one sufficient Reaper for one day" or three and a halfpence, the large tenants "one man and one woman for one day or 7d at the choice of the said farmer." Together, the tenants of Burcombe had to "mow and cut down" the hay in the seven acres of the meadow called Westmead (for which more breakfast was to be provided by the farmer), and then, when it had dried in the sun for a day or two, make it into stooks, small drying stacks of cut stems, for which the farmer would provide bread and cheese. Another four and a half acres of hay of Burcombe, which was still in the earl's hands for the horses at Wilton, had to be made by the tenants, for which the lord's bailiff would provide four shillings, four and a half-pence "for and toward the provision of their drink." These were the customs which were "writ and Remember'd."

These old remembered rights, sanctions, and duties were the living inheritance of the Middle Ages. When the castle at Wardour, a Wilt-shire manor belonging to the Pembrokes' neighbors the Arundells, was blown up after a savage siege in the Civil War, all its records were destroyed. After the war was over, both tenants and the steward of the manor inspected the records of Shaftesbury Abbey, to which the manor had belonged in the Middle Ages, and copied out the medieval rules. There was no sense of incongruity in this. These were the rules, and their age was more a guarantee of their excellence than otherwise. Fifteenth- or fourteenth-century codes were to regulate the lives of the people of Wardour in the 1660s. This was normal. Nothing changed.

Everywhere you look in these customary regulations, the memory of the Middle Ages is there. Even in mid-seventeenth-century records, in a country where the worship of the saints and all the practices of the Roman Catholic church were meant to have been abolished for 120 years, the pattern of the year continued to be measured out according to the ancient saints' days. At Chilmark, a few miles west of Barford St. Martin, the common was to be closed off to the copyholders' animals from "Ladyday [March 25, New Year's Day in the seventeenth century, the Feast of the Annunciation of the Blessed Virgin Mary] to the Feast of the Invocation of the Holy Cross [May 3]," when the tenants from both ends of Chilmark common were allowed the use of it until "the Feast of St Martin the Bishop [November 11]," when it was again closed to them and opened to the animals of the neighboring village, until the following spring.

This Christian calendar calibrated the year, its ceremonies and associations miraculously twinned to the seasons. Candlemas, or the Feast of the Purification, on February 2, marked both the halfway point between the winter solstice and the spring equinox, the day on which winter was half over, and the day, forty days after the birth of Christ, when Mary was presented at the temple, the moment at which she also reemerged into the world. It was the time of transition, and the opportunity for bitter peasant prognostication:

> If Candlemas Day be fair and bright,
> Winter will have another flight
> But if it be dark with clouds and rain,
> Winter is gone, and will not come again.

Lady Day, on March 25, the Feast of the Annunciation—the moment at which Christ was conceived—was also the beginning of the farming year, the first hint of spring, nine months before Christmas, and the seeding of the future. Easter, in April, marked the fullness of spring and the culmination of the Christian story, with the fertility of nature finally defeating the darkness of winter. On through the year, as custom after custom makes clear, the people of the chalklands lived in an environment where ancient and inherited signals provided the landmarks for their lives. At Rogationtide, in early May, as the arable crops were just sprouting, the whole village would offer prayers (*rogationes*) for those crops and for their animals, beating the bounds of the village, of individual fields, and even of individual strips within those fields, to establish in the minds of this and future generations exactly where those boundaries were. These weren't always certain, and besides, there was always suspicion that one or two leaseholders might try to encroach on the land of the customary tenants. In 1618, the tenants in the manor court at Heale, in the valley of the Avon, decided to lay down the law:

> Yt is also ordered by the Lord of this Mannor by the Consente of the tenants of this mannor that the homage shall between this and Witsuntyde next stake out all the Tenants' lands of the Mannor, and that they shall then viewe what wronge the Leasehoulders have done to the Coppyhoulders in the feilde, and sett out and stake out the bounds, and shall presente the wrongs att the nexte Courte and by whom the same have been soe donne.

Beating the bounds wasn't some folksy, antiquarian community festival; it was a way of defining the means of survival. But it was also more than that. The land itself was the central mnemonic of people's lives, the map of who they were, the method by which the place and the social relationships within it were known. To plough an acre strip—each "a furrow long" and four rods (sixteen and a half feet) wide—would take a day. This was an arrangement that folded together land, body, property, and time. The body itself would have known immediately and by utter familiarity what an acre meant. The eye could estimate a furlong at a glance. Each strip had a name: Bere furlong, Peashill, Saltacre, Bracelet (probably after "bercelet," meaning a sheepdog), Hatchet acre, Elbow acre, Pyked furlong (after the sometimes strange crooked outline of the strips), and so on. Inherited meaning was folded into the copyhold land like sugar stirred into a cake. No signs or signals were needed; it was simply known, part of what was, time out of mind.

The Pembrokes' cousin, the poet George Herbert, who in the

1630s was the vicar of Bemerton, in the valley of the Nadder between Wilton and Salisbury, gave many overlapping reasons for beating the bounds in May: it was a blessing of God for the fruits of the field; it established "Justice in the preservation of the bounds"; it was a moment for "Mercie, in relieving the poor by a liberal distribution of largess which at that time is or ought be made"; and it was an act of charity and neighborliness, "in living, walking and neighbourlily accompanying one another, with reconciling of differences at that time, if they be any." For Herbert, these were the four dimensions of a village's existence: metaphysical, legislative, personal, and social. The melding of communal action with communal need and communal belief that beating the bounds represented is the clearest of all demonstrations of the depth and multiplicity of meanings in which these places were steeped. Seen from an era of individual rights, the manor system may look like a nightmare of restriction and denial; from its own perspective, however, it was a deliberate and effective mechanism for a multidimensional life in which land was not a commodity but the matrix for existence.

The year rolled inexorably onward: Midsummer Night was celebrated on June 24, six months from Christmas, and holding up a mirror to it. Huge bonfires were lit, boys picked flowers, which they gave to girls, and the girls threw them into the flames to keep themselves free all year of agues and afflictions. The following day was the Feast of St. John the Baptist, the figure who represented not the redemption of the world but the heralding of a new version of it. August 1 was Lammas, or Loaf Mass Day, when the first wheat harvest of the year, baked into a loaf, was brought into church and tenants were bound to present a sheaf of the new harvest to their landlords. By August 24, Bartlemas, or St. Bartholomew's Day (Bartholomew had been flayed alive and was the patron saint of butchers), all pigs' noses were to be ringed; by Michaelmas, the Feast of St. Michael and All Angels, on September

29, all animals were to leave the common fields; at St. Luke's Day, October 18, all lambs are to be counted as sheep; and by Martinmas, the Feast of St. Martin, on November 11, the commons were to be cleared of grazing beasts.

This adds up to an extraordinarily complex map of life lived on the Herbert estates in the sixteenth and seventeenth centuries. These arrangements and patterns represent people's relationship to the land, to history, to the passing of the year, to their neighbors, to livestock, to the growing and getting of food, and even to the universe of which nowadays we have no conception at all. These are the lineaments of the world we have lost. They also describe precisely the world that the aristocracy of England would consistently seek to defend, not only as their property but as the foundation of their existence, as their moral universe.

William Herbert's relationship to this system was deeply ambivalent. He was a new man, who had made his own way in the world and had established himself and his family in a position of enormous wealth. At the same time, as he saw it, he was also heir to the great inheritance of his forebears, the medieval earls of Pembroke. This was the contradiction deep within him, one that would play itself out again and again in the story of this family. Was he a member of the ancient nobility, committed, like Norden's ideal landlord, to the welfare of the people dependent on him? Or was he a ruthless self-seeker, dependent for his standing on his relationship to the crown? Was he a new-made man or the defender of old England against a rapacious modernity? Was he a part of the system or a disruption to it? And how, if these two positions came into conflict, would he behave?

Chapter 4

THE EXERCISE OF
NOBLE AUTHORITY

THE FIRST EARL AS POWER BROKER
1549–1570

The crisis in William Herbert's life erupted in the spring of 1549, as the roads began to dry and people could begin to move. Henry VIII had died two years before and had left the throne to his son, Edward VI, still only a boy of nine. The boy's uncle, Edward Seymour, Duke of Somerset, had become Lord Protector, king in all but name. William Herbert had begun the new reign as Somerset's ally, but their ways had soon parted. Somerset was cold, arrogant, and even priggish. Increasingly he monopolized the boy king and his instruments of power. The atmosphere at court had turned vicious. One of Herbert's allies, Sir William Paget, wrote to Somerset: "Remember what you promised me in the gallery at Westminster, before the breath was out of the body of the king that dead is. Remember what you promised immediately after, devising with me concerning the place which you now occupy. . . . And that was to follow mine advise in all your proceedings more than any other man's."

No sense of communality here; only mutual distrust. The duke, as regent and Lord Protector while Edward VI was still a minor, had issued proclamations to the effect that landowners should return to the old ways of doing things, that they should consider themselves stewards and fathers of their little commonwealths. New men had behaved badly. Enclosures of what had been either open field or common land, either for private gain or for the pleasure a park could afford, ran against this communitarian ethic. In Somerset's hands, the custom of the manor was making a renewed claim against the lordly Renaissance desire for spreading parkland.

In addition, the long history of English radicalism, founded on that element in the Bible that saw men as equal in the sight of God, fed the sense of outrage. If Isaiah could warn, "Woe unto them that join house to house, that lay field to field, till there be no place [left], that they [i.e., the landowners] may be placed alone in the midst of the earth!" it was inevitable that the rioters would demand, "Why should one man have all and another nothing?" What was there to stop the people of Washerne who had been evicted from their houses and had had the seven acres of Lampeland taken from them to reclaim what was theirs in the sight of God and apparently of the Lord Protector?

In April 1549, reports began to come in to the Privy Council in Westminster of peasants creating havoc in many parts of the country. There was nothing new in that: a long tradition of English violence had bubbled away for generations. But there was no doubt that the 1540s were a desperate time in southern England. Not only were there many estates in which the lax government of the abbeys had been replaced by hardheaded modern men, harder-headed than most. The underlying economic situation was desperate, too. The population of England, now at about 2.75 million, had increased by some 35 percent over the previous century. The cost of living had risen by 50 percent in the previous fifty years. In 1545, the harvest had been catastrophic and the economy was still reeling from the aftereffects. The rich, gathering up the pickings from the dissolution of the monasteries, were getting richer, and the poor, their numbers burgeoning against a static food supply, were getting poorer.

On May 25, 1549, the crisis hit home. A Norfolk gentleman, John Paston, wrote to his cousin the Earl of Rutland:

> there is a great number of the commons up about Salisbury in Wiltshire, and they have plucked down Sir William Herbert's park that is about his new house and divers other parks and commons that be inclosed in that country.

It was the people of Washerne taking their revenge. They threw down the new oak palings that Herbert had set up to enclose the deer and exclude the people, and slaughtered what deer they could catch. For three weeks they occupied the ground on the other side of the Nadder from Herbert's new house. They may not have known quite what they were taking on, since in those weeks, as they attempted to rebuild their houses on the old sites—there was a mistaken belief widespread in England that any man who could build a house and light a fire in the course of a day had the right to remain in it—Herbert was away in Wales. There, from his Glamorgan estates, drawing on the "affinity"—the band of his tenants who could be relied on to fight for him when summoned—he marched them back into Wiltshire. Approaching Wilton, he attacked his invading Washerne tenants as if they were an enemy and "slew to death divers of the rebels." News of Herbert's fearsome response reached the young king, who recorded in his journal how the men of Washerne had created trouble and chaos and how "Sir William Herbert did put them down, overrun, and slay them."

The park where Sir Philip Sidney would within thirty-five years wander with the dreams of Arcadia in his head was now restored to wholeness, and if you stand on the lawns outside Wilton House today, staring across the elegance of the park and its gentlemanly accoutrements, you are looking at one of the heartlands of Arcadia: a stretch of landscape in which the people who claimed some rights over it were murdered so that an aesthetic vision of otherworldly calm could be imposed in their place. It is an early, miniature, English version of the clearances on the great Highland estates in Scotland or even of the National Parks in the wilder parts of America: calm, beautiful, and empty landscapes, not because God made them like that but because the people who belonged there were driven off, killed, or otherwise dispensed with.

It is worth pausing for a moment to consider exactly what was done here in the service of Arcadia. Remember the dog chains in the old armory, the bills and pikes, the halberds with which you could spike a man and then cut him. Almost certainly Herbert would have used a sword on his tenants. The favorite and usual strokes in the sixteenth century were not fencing-like thrusts—a slightly later, European development—but rather more woodmanlike slashing and severing: the cutting of the head from the shoulders, the cutting off of an arm or a leg, and the slicing stroke down through the head. This could be dramatic. There are records throughout the Middle Ages of sword cuts leaving the severed halves of the head hanging down to left and right on either shoulder. Sometimes the sword was smashed into the head with such violence that it cut down through a man's torso to his hips, with his body folding apart like a carcass in an abattoir. Skeletons from medieval battles, unearthed and examined, often have multiple wounds: both legs cut off, sometimes apparently from a single sweeping blow with a sword; parts of the skull cut away in several pieces; occasionally many wounds of which any one would have been fatal; bodies left halved.

There is a disturbing echo in this story of the use of a park as a place for a hunt. The king's phrase—"put them down, overrun, and slay them"—is curiously reminiscent of the account of a successful pursuit of a quarry. This was the manly excitement of the hunt taken to its ultimate, a point of view summarized by one Richard Blome, the author of the late-seventeenth-century *Gentleman's Recreation*. Hunting, as Blome described the tradition,

> is a commendable *Recreation* . . . a great preserver of *Health*, a Manly *Exercise*, and an increaser of *Activity*; . . . it recreates the *Mind*, strengthens the *Limbs*, and whets the *Stomach*; . . . no *Musick* is more charming to the *Ears* of *Man*, than a *Pack* of *Hounds* in full *Cry* is to him that delights in *Hunting* . . .

Hunting was universally seen as training for war, or rather, more than that, as a form of nostalgic and pretechnological war that reminded its noble participants of what war must have been like before an awkward, ugly modernity contaminated it. Sir Thomas Elyot, the Tudor theorist of government, had recommended that sixteenth-century Englishmen should use only the javelin in the hunt, because that is what Xenophon had recommended in ancient Greece, and it alone would preserve the nobility of the exercise. James I, a passionate huntsman, would have no gun come anywhere near the parks where he pursued deer, because the use of guns, as he told his son Prince Henry, was a "theevish forme of hunting." Grandeur was antique.

When in the following decade William Herbert paraded through London (the old dowager queen of Scots, Mary of Guise, was visiting), he had with him "a hundred great horses, mounted by a hundred horsemen," their coats lined with velvet, gold chains around their necks, white feathers in their hats, wearing the Pembroke badge of the wyvern, the winged dragon, "and every [man] havyng a new gayffe-lyns in ther hands." That is a word to raise the hackles on one's neck. Was it javelins the men and women of Washerne were hunted with, as Elyot recommended, that summer afternoon in 1549? Was it a kind of pig-sticking? The elision was commonplace in the sixteenth century of any difference between a working man and a brutish beast. Shake-speare's Venus uses a "javelin's point a churlish swine to gore"—and one is left in no doubt that her churlish swine, with his brawny sides, his hairy bristles, and short, thick neck, living in his "loathsome cabin," is a kind of animal Caliban, a dirty commoner, to be gored by the lovely, javelin-wielding elegant men, with feathers in their hats, chains around their necks, and beauty in their faces.

William Herbert's pursuit and slaying of the tenants who had pre-sumed to enter his park represents the most disturbing compaction of the binary worlds of Arcadia and violence: a dreamlike killing of people in a consciously aestheticized place, the reality of human death for once taking over from the playacting of deer death, the heart-pumping chase, the satisfactory conclusion, the restoration of calm.

Having used his Welsh tenants to kill his Wiltshire tenants, Wil-liam Herbert then took the former to war. He was certainly—and from the point of view of his own interests, rightly—excited by it. The summer of 1549 would turn him from a successful adventurer into one of the central power brokers of the Tudor state. He brutally suppressed a Catholic rebellion in the West Country, and emerged from it at the head of an army with which, ominously, he then turned for London.

The crisis rippled on into the autumn. The cold, brusque, rigid, and aloof idealism of the Duke of Somerset, still in London with the king, had alienated most of his supporters in the council: landlords such as Herbert, who had suffered invasions of their parks or enclosed fields; the old nobility who felt themselves supplanted by the new men such as Paget and Herbert; anyone who felt bruised by Somerset's short

temper, arrogance, and obstinacy. It was a grouping fatal for Somerset. Herbert's friend John Dudley, now the Earl of Warwick, was
in Norfolk with another army. Somerset felt caught between the two
of them and retreated with the king to the safety of Windsor Castle.
Again and again, he and the boy king wrote to Herbert, telling him
that the other nobles on the council had tuned against them and imploring him to come to their aid.

Slowly Herbert approached from the west, arriving at Andover, a
mere forty miles from Windsor, on October 8. From there, Herbert
wrote to Somerset a cold, disdainful, and threatening letter, perfectly
aware of the central place he and his army had acquired in the future
of England:

> We have received your letter and lament your dissension
> with the nobility. You required us to repair to Windsor
> Castle. As long as we thought he nobility now assembled
> had conspired against the king, we proceeded with our
> company. But today we heard from the lords that they are
> loyal, which we believe, and that this great extremity pro-
> ceeds only from private causes between you and them. We
> have therefore decided to levy as great a force as we may
> for the safety of the king and realm. Let bloodshed be pre-
> vented by any means. We much dislike your proclamations
> and bills put about for raising the commons. Evil men will
> stir as well as loyal subjects.

It is a hard, cold letter, reliant on the naked power of an armed
force, Italian arquebusiers among them, which had already destroyed
the rebels in the West Country. It is a statement of threat, the violence
in it scarcely an inch below the surface.

Herbert withdrew with his army to Wilton and from there wrote to the Earl of Warwick and the other lords of the Privy Council in London. "We have stayed all these parts, this part of Hampshire, Wiltshire, Gloucestershire, Somerset, Wales and the West, so that [the Lord Protector] can draw on nothing to do any hurt. Let is know what you would have us do, and with what numbers."

This is the foundation level of dominance, the exercise of authority that will later allow the expression of grace. It is about the gathering of power. That casual, proconsular listing of the parts of England and Wales over which they have established their authority is thrown away with the nonchalance of a victor. This is the moment when Herbert became one of the rulers of England. The silverback growls and glares, and the world submits.

Somerset, horrified by the thought of civil war between the nobility and the shedding of still more blood, surrendered to the new power grouping around Warwick and Herbert. He was imprisoned in the Tower. He returned to the Council for a while, but within eighteen months had been executed. His lands, in the most primitive accumulation of spoils, were distributed among the victors, Herbert among them. The Privy Council allowed Herbert to mint two thousand pounds of silver into coin, keeping the difference between the value of the metal and the value of the currency, making him a profit of £6,709, 19s. And rewards continued to flood toward him. During Edward's reign, Herbert received lands worth £32,165 in capital value, including fifty-three manors in Wales, nine in Wiltshire, five in Gloucestershire, two in Sussex, and one each in Middlesex, Devon, and Hertfordshire. And on October 10, 1551, the second son of the illegitimate gentleman from the Vale of Ewyas was created Baron Herbert of Cardiff. The following day he became the Earl of Pembroke.

He had won. He had become what his grandfather had been. He had threatened the throne, defeated the regent, absorbed some of his riches, garnered still more, and had established himself in the position he may always have thought he deserved to hold: not the 1st Earl of Pembroke, as history knows him, but the twentieth, the inheritor of all that medieval dignity. To do so, he had acted not as his son, grandsons, and great-grandsons would do, in defense of the ancient constitution or the ancient social structures on which the well-being of his estates would rely. Rather, he had behaved as the freelance he was, the hired gun, asserting authority through brutish and coldheaded masculinity. Without this exercise of ignoble power, it is perfectly likely that his dynasty would have ended with him. And so when you look at the beautiful boys in their beautiful silks in the Van Dyck painting, or out across the coiffed perfection of the lawns at Wilton, or at any sign of aristocratic elegance, these moments in 1549 are what need to be remembered. Behind the grace and the nonchalance of riches hangs the mask, with the hatchet mouth and hooded eyes, of the man-killing condottiere founder of the dynasty. This particular quarrel with the king had produced money, land, and the prospect of a well-funded future. No idealism here.

At the end of February 1552, William Herbert's wife, Anne Parr, Countess of Pembroke, died at Baynard's Castle in London. She was thirty-six, the mother of two sons and a daughter. She was buried with huge pomp in old St. Paul's, next to the tomb of John of Gaunt, where her memorial described her as "a most faithful wife, a woman of the greatest piety and discretion" and "her banners were set up over her arms set on divers pillars." The earl undoubtedly loved her. When he came to write his own will, despite having married again, he said he wanted to be buried "nere the place where Anne my late wife doth lie buried" in St. Paul's. In a perfectly literal sense Anne had brought legitimacy to the Herberts. If William had vigor and ruthlessness, Anne gave the family grace and courage. When Edward VI regranted the manors to the Pembrokes, it was explicitly "to the aforenamed earl, by the name of Sir William Herbert, knight, and the Lady Anne his wife and the heirs male of their bodies between them lawfully begotten." She was the joint creator of this extraordinary enterprise. A stained-glass window in a Wilton church shows her kneeling before an open prayer book or Bible—no signs of religious imagery in evidence—in a long armorial mantle on which are embroidered the many quartered arms of her distinguished ancestry. It was that Parr-derived inheritance that gave the Pembroke family any legitimate claim to ancient nobility. And she knew it. On her tomb in St. Paul's, the epitaph reads that she had been "very jealous of the fame of a long line of ancestors."

William Herbert, Earl of Pembroke, had become one of the rulers of England, a man without whom no power settlement could be made. He was precisely the sort of figure—independent, dangerous, and unforgiving—whose standing the governments of Elizabeth and the Stuarts would need to erode. His power had been derived from royal patronage, but he had so managed the gift that it had now outgrown its source. Astute buying of lands, the exercise or threat of violence, and the subtle, flickering understanding not only of the best alliance to make but of the moment to desert an ally: all of this had placed him at least partly in control. The Earl of Worcester, the Parrs, his Wiltshire neighbor the Duke of Somerset: all had provided another step up, and at each turn the earl had learned to combine toughness with flexibility, to be the willow not the oak. He knew, in other words, how to run with the fox and hunt with the hounds. The Machiavellian truth of Tudor England was that unless men of Pembroke's substance plotted to remain in power, others would plot to remove them. It was a business principle: either growth in the enterprise or collapse.

The young Edward VI spent time down at Wilton, hunting, getting lost, and being entertained by Pembroke as though he were visiting the palace of an eastern potentate. "The King was served in vessels of pure gold," the imperial ambassador Jehan Scheyfvre wrote to the queen dowager of Spain, "his Council and Privy Chamber in silver gilt, and all the members of his household, down to the very least, in silver. All this plate belongs to the earl, who presented the King on his departure, with a very rich camp-bed, decorated with pearls and precious stones."

Pembroke habitually carried the sword of state before the sovereign. The untrammeled roughness of his Welsh ancestry (he spoke fluent Welsh himself and was educating his son Henry in the language and its poetry) proved an asset at that brutal court. The imperial ambassadors spread the gossip through Europe: Pembroke could speak no other language than English (untrue), could neither read nor write (probably untrue), and stood at meetings of the Privy Council "shouting at the top of his voice," in which mood no one dared contradict him (almost certainly true). The memory of 1549 and his assertion of military power were never far from the surface.

As Edward VI sickened, Pembroke and his ally John Dudley, Earl of Warwick, and now Duke of Northumberland, plotted for a Protestant succession to the throne that would deprive the Catholic princess Mary of the crown. Their candidate, Lady Jane Grey, was Henry VIII's great-niece, and according to the old king's will was to be the next heir after his own children. She had been a girl in the Parr household and had become a passionate Protestant and a Greek scholar there, reading Plato's *Dialogues* in the original for pleasure and denouncing the Roman Church as the home of Satan. According to her parents' wishes but against her own will, she was quickly married to Northumberland's son, submitting only "by the urgency of her mother and the violence of her father, who compelled her to accede to his commands by blows." Her sister, Lady Catherine Grey, was married at the same time to Pembroke's eldest son, Henry.

Once again, Pembroke held the fate of England in his hands. Edward died on July 6, 1553. Three days later, Lady Jane was told she was queen. Pembroke knelt to kiss her hand, at which the sixteen-year-old fell weeping to the floor, speaking of her inadequacy. On July 13, Northumberland left London to capture Mary, who was in Norfolk with an army and with support gathering around her. Once again, Pembroke bent like the willow, sniffed the wind, heard that the people were gathering to Mary's banner in Norfolk, and at this critical juncture abandoned both Lady Jane Grey and Northumberland, his friend and ally. Pembroke got his son Henry to repudiate Catherine Grey. All connections to her were to be severed. On July 19, Pembroke gathered a group of like-minded lords in the great rooms overlooking the Thames at Baynard's Castle and asked them to join him in supporting the Catholic princess even then making her way with her army to London. It was another occasion for shouting. Holding his battle sword in front of him, Pembroke bellowed to the assembled lords, "This blade shall make Mary queen, or I will lose my life." There was no denying him, and the party went out into the streets of London, where they had Mary proclaimed sovereign of England. Pembroke threw his jewelled cap into the air and tossed his gold-filled purse into the crowd.

Mary was crowned queen in October, and Pembroke was there, carrying the sword of state before her. Lady Jane Grey, Northumberland, and his son Guildford Dudley were all eventually executed. Henry Herbert, Pembroke's son and heir, rejected Catherine, Lady Jane Grey's sister, in a series of vicious letters in which he called her a whore.

Once again, Pembroke became the leathered brawn for the new regime, facing down a Protestant rebellion in London in 1554, fighting a series of largely ineffectual wars against the French on Mary's behalf, bringing the spoils back to Wilton, and entrenching his power base ever more in Wiltshire and Wales. Wilton served as a perfect tool in his display of significance. He spent more time there than in London, entertained foreign ambassadors in his exquisite landscape, took them out hunting and hare coursing on the downs, and displayed the vast assemblages of men and money that were the undeniable evidence of his standing.

"The handsomeness and commodities of Wilton, with the good appointment and the good furniture thereof, in all things whereof the better has not been seen," were as impressive as anything England could offer. The most sophisticated Europeans were not entirely taken in. The Venetian ambassador wrote a witty and skeptical account of the strange manners of the English to his masters in the Venetian Senate in August 1554. "The nobility, save as such are employed at court, do not habitually reside in the cities," the Venetian began, his eyebrows raised,

> but in their own country mansions where they keep up very grand establishments, both with regard to great abundance of eatables consumed by them [the ambassador had witnessed the groaningly vast supper and breakfast offered at Wilton to a Spanish marquis and his men] as also by reason of their numerous attendants, in which they exceed all other nations, so that the earl of Pembroke has upwards of a thousand clad in his own livery. In these their country residences they occupy themselves with hunting of every description and with whatever else can amuse or divert them; so that they seem wholly intent on leading a joyous existence, the women being no less sociable than the men, it being customary for them and allowable to go without any regard either alone or accompanied by their husbands to the taverns, and to dine and sup where they please.

This reads more like the description by an Englishman of the pleasures of Renaissance Italy: its slight air of loucheness, the sunshine in their lives, the apparent ease and equality of men and women in the aristocratic milieu. The English by the 1550s had absorbed much of that campagna culture. But here it is clamped to what is also late-medieval behavior, the great gang of the affinity, the display of power, the pre-modern guarantee of luxury through overt threat and strength. When the king of Spain himself arrived at Southampton to marry Queen Mary, the earl went down to meet him with two hundred mounted gentlemen in black velvet wearing heavy gold chains, accompanied by a body of English archers, their yellow tunics striped with bands of red velvet, the livery of the house of Aragon. This is the social and multiple equivalent of the way the earl himself appeared. Here is the fighting body dripping in pearls, velvet, and gold. It is the essence of Tudor England: luxury as the medium of power; power as the under-pinnings of beauty; beauty as the companion of threat.

To a great extent Pembroke came to believe his own propaganda. Where the descent of the crown itself was full of uncertainties and ille-gitimacies, where the claim on power was not a matter of genetic formal-ity but an exercise in politics and force, then the legitimacy of the Pembrokes as magnates who could raise formidable armies of their own was not in question. They had as much right to be sources of power in their own countries as the sovereign did in the nation as a whole. Magna Carta did not mean nothing. Noble power, in an atmosphere where there was so much harking back to the myths of the Middle Ages, to the Arthu-rian romance, must have felt like a reality. In a 1562 survey of his estates, Pembroke's surveyor, after discussing the "free" tenants (those who owed the manor no duties) and the "customary" tenants (those whose lives were ruled by the custom of the manor), asked "which of them could be tallaged [taxed] as serfs *ratione sanguinis nativi*" by reason of their native blood. It was still legitimate in 1560s England to ask whether the ownership of a manor and a piece of land involved the ownership of human beings who came attached to that land as soil-bound slaves.

Pembroke's name in England and Wales was surrounded by a halo of violence and power. In 1556, one Thomas White, arrested and interrogated by the Council, reported a conversation he'd heard secretly one evening in an inn with a man called Ashton. Ashton had said

> he had a noble gentleman able to bring a great part of Wales at his tail. I asked him if it was lord Pembroke. He said, "Tush for him, for he is more feared than loved." I said, Two of the best in England are not able to drive him out of there, being the Queen's friend as you say he is, and she having the trust in him you say she has. He said, all his trust was in his great horses, but with 5,000 or 6,000 footmen, he would wait with stakes sharpened at both ends.

This muttered, half-obscure, secretive talk feels like the last words of the Middle Ages, of great armed power barons stalking the land and holding the central authorities for ransom. That January, Pembroke received a special commission to levy troops for Mary's defense of Calais, a thousand from Wiltshire, a thousand from North Wales, and a thousand from South Wales, by far the largest commission given to any nobleman in the country. He was a figure unthinkable in the modern world, a man too powerful for the state not to use. He had been part of a cabal that had rewritten Henry VIII's will in its own interest. He had helped destroy Edward VI's trusted councillor and protector. He had elevated Lady Jane Grey to the throne and had then destroyed her. Due largely to his support, the English political class had accepted the Catholic queen Mary as she entered London. And he had saved her, by commanding the streets of the city, from the highly dangerous rebellion of Thomas Wyatt and his Protestant bands. Four English sovereigns in a row had, in their different ways, been reliant on Pembroke's goodwill and ability to summon threat.

He had inserted himself like a virus into the body politic of England. This was not so much a quarrel with the crown as a commandeering of it.

Still, for all this potency, the old Wiltshire nobility knew exactly who he was. They treated him as a parvenu. His servants and those of the old lord Stourton, part of the ancient nobility of Wiltshire, brawled in the villages and in the streets of both Salisbury and London over the meaning of *nobility*. The stories were still current in the seventeenth century when Aubrey heard them. Whenever Lord Stourton was returning home from the assizes in Salisbury, his way ran straight past the gates of Wilton. The old man would never lose the opportunity to "sound his Trumpetts and give reproachfull challenging words: 'twas a relique of Knighthood Errantry."

Mary Tudor died in November 1558, and another of Aubrey's stories, hinged to that moment and certainly untrue, nevertheless reveals what Wiltshire thought of this Pembroke: coarse, vulgar, a shifter, an object of ridicule as much as terror, a man in some ways humiliated by his greed for wealth and power.

> In Queen Mary's time, upon the returne of the Catholique Religion, the Nunnes came again to Wilton abbey, and this William earle of Pembroke came to the gate with his Cappe in hand and fell upon his knee to the Lady Abbesse and the Nunnes crying peccavi [I have sinned]. Upon Queen Mary's death, the Earle came to Wilton (like a Tygre) and turnd them out, crying, "Out ye Whores, to Worke, to Worke ye Whores, goe Spinne."

Elizabeth succeeded her half sister and Pembroke apparently seamlessly transferred his allegiance from the Catholic to the Protestant queen. He had been among those who had first acclaimed Elizabeth, but the relationship between sovereign and magnate very quickly shifted. A strained correspondence between them survives from the very first weeks of her reign, thick with a sense of fearlessness on both sides, a prickly manoeuvring but no form of self-abasement. Both Edward and Mary had appointed Pembroke Lord President of the Council for Wales and the Marches, a powerful official in a part of the kingdom that anyway formed some of the Pembroke heartlands. But this queen was to be different. "I have received your letters," he wrote to her from Wilton,

> perceiving your grace has been informed that the counties and marches of Wales (for want of a president and others of ability and reputation resident there) are grown to much disorder and like to fall into greater inconveniences if speedy remedy is not provided. As you are minded to take the presidency from me (which I never sought) I am ready to yield. Where it liked you to have my advice of one or two for that office, pardon me, for the world is such nowadays as if I should meddle I might be thought of some (that have not yet learned to speak well) very partial, having presently both friends and kin there in trouble.

It was a fairly graceless withdrawal, and on August 5, his bastard nephew, also called William Herbert, was to feel the sting of royal power. A letter came from the queen at Richmond to the sheriff of Glamorgan:

> We are informed that William Herbert of Cogan Pill, Glamorgan, has disobeyed several letters from our privy council. Immediately apprehend him and send him hither to the council under safe custody at his own charge.

This William Herbert was thrown in the Fleet prison next to the Thames in London, but all this was a sign of the world changing, of that warmongering Tudor magnate no longer casting any kind of shadow over the central authority of queen, Privy Council, or her sheriff in the wild lands of Wales. Sir Henry Sidney, a royal servant of no great wealth, too poor to be elevated to the peerage, was appointed in his place.

Never in Elizabeth's reign would the queen call on the powerful but dangerous capacity in her great noblemen to provide her with armies. Her avoidance of war was a means not only of saving money but also of preventing the dispersal of power into the hands of those mighty subjects. The subjects themselves were made less mighty, and the story of Elizabethan England is in part one of the emasculation of the nobility, the turning of real warriors into toy warriors, fighters into frustrated lovers, the condottieri of Tudor England into the wan and beautiful princes drifting through the fields of Arcadia, an aestheticization of nobility that buttressed rather than menaced the power of the state.

Elizabeth's was a new form of monarchy, appealing to a wider constituency than the nobles she might have gathered around her, using them but not relying on them. A sign of how this new world was to work had already appeared clearly enough in April 1559. She went one afternoon

to Baynard's Castle, the Earl of Pembroke's Place, and supped with him, and after supper she took a boat and was rowed up and down the river Thames, hundreds of boats and barges rowing about her, and thousands of people thronging at the waterside to look upon her Majesty, rejoicing to see her and partaking of the music and sights in the Thames, for the trumpets blew, drums beat, flutes played, guns were discharged, squibs hurled up into the air, as the Queen moved from place to place. And this continued till ten o'clock of the night, when the Queen departed home.

This was the most elegant form of emasculation, diminishing the nobility by means of a supper party and some fireworks, the defeat of Tudor brutalism by glamour and politics. From now on, the great old magnates of medieval England—the Cliffords, Nevilles, Percys, and Talbots—were left to fester in their huge estates, remote from the levers and rewards of power. And Pembroke, too, was pushed to the margins.

In the late 1560s one last attempt was made by the old earl to influence the state in the way he had at the height of his career. He was keen for the Roman Catholic duke of Norfolk to marry the Queen of Scots, by then a captive in the north of England. Elizabeth heard rumors of this suggestion, Norfolk was sent to the Tower, and Pembroke was arrested. By then two of the old northern magnates, the earls of Westmorland and Northumberland, had raised armies from their affinities in order to release the Queen of Scots from captivity. Pembroke seemed to Elizabeth to have been involved in this reassertion of noble power. For their own purposes, that is what the two earls were claiming. A little pathetically, he wrote to the queen in December 1569:

From my poore Howse at Wilton

My name is moast falselye and wickedly abused by the wicked Protestation of those two traitorous Erles.

I do reverently before God, and humbly before your Majestie, protest that in all my Lief I was never privey to so muche as a Mocion of any Attempte either of these bankcrupte Erles, or of any Mans ells, against either Religion (in defence whereof onelye I am redie to spill my blood) or yet your Majesties Estate or person; and that I am redie against them, and all Traitors to make good with my Bodie when and howsoever it shall please your Majestie to commande: For God forbid that I should lieve the Houre, now in mine olde Age, to staine my former Lief with a spot of Disloyaltie.

There is the willow bent full double. Of course he had never changed sides; of course his only interest was in the validity of the true religion; of course he had never plotted with any other grandee about how they might steer the riches of England into the strong chests in the strong rooms and armories at Wilton. God forbid that anything so impure had ever passed though his mind!

John Aubrey, listening to the Wiltshire gossip about the 1st Earl of Pembroke seventy-five years later—this was a story from his great-uncles, the Brownes of Broad Chalke—heard that "in Queen Elizabeth's time some Bishop (I have forgot who)"—it was in fact the Bishop of Winchester—"was sent to him from the Queen and Council"—actually of his own accord—"to take Interrogatories of him," to ask him some legal and technical details about his landholdings. The bishop, although Aubrey didn't hear this detail, wanted to get back the manor of Bishopstone in the valley of the Ebble, just to the east of Broad Chalke.

So [the bishop] takes out his pen and inke, examines and writes. When he had writt a good deale sayd the Earle, "Now lett me see it."

"Why," quoth the Bishop, "your Lordship cannot read it?"

"That's all one, I'le see it," quoth he, and takes it and teares it to pieces. "Zounds, you rascall," quoth the Earle, "d'ee thinke I will have my throate cutt with a pen-knife?"

It seems they had a mind to have pick't a hole in his
Coate, and to have gott his Estate.

This wonderful story, as if folktales were being constructed even
in sixteenth- and seventeenth-century Wiltshire, has a deep moral and
historical truth to it. This is nothing but the modern, literate, bureau-
cratic state trying to take back from the unlettered warrior, the ancient
earl who depended for his standing on his physical presence, his lead-
ership of men and his native cunning, the lands on which his existence
relied. Here, in a few lines, modernity, legal and lettered, nibbles at the
ancient conditions. The historical truth of the story is that the bishop
attempted to have a private act of Parliament passed, but a covey of
Pembroke-sponsored MPs in the House of Commons saw him and
his bill off. But the emotional and metaphorical truth is not in that account. It is here in the Brownes' memory and in Aubrey's delighted
retelling of it: the sense that the modern world was a clever cheat, the
ancient earl a blind and muscled colossus.

The same anxiety fuels Aubrey's final remembered story of the
earl, which shares the same dreamlike, emblematic quality. As he lay
dying in early 1570, one desperate phrase, the end of all his dreams and
nightmares, was on his lips, repeated again and again: "They would
have Wilton, they would have Wilton." Underneath that armored carapace, and never given voice in the official record, only remembered
here in the gossip of the chalkstream valleys, was a desperate anxiety
over the status and the lands for which he had lusted and fought for so
long. It is a recognition that his noble power, his gathering of armies,
his assembling of crowds of liveried and chain-bedecked followers, his
country of lands and manors, was, in truth, as fragile as a vase.

On December 23, 1567, "remembering the uncertainty of man's
life and to how many perils and casualties the same is subject"—
something of which Pembroke would have been all too aware—he

had made his will. He left £400 each to the poor of the ward around Baynard's Castle, in Salisbury, and in Hendon, near London, where he had yet another house. Apart from a few legacies to his other children, he left everything to his son Henry.

But late on the evening of March 16, 1570, in his apartments in Hampton Court, feeling death coming near, he had his younger son Edward and the Earl of Leicester, son of his old friend Northumberland, whom he had betrayed, come to his bedside. Death had given him a conscience. His second wife was to keep her own clothes and jewels, which would otherwise have gone to Henry. He left his "newest fairest and richest bed" and his greatest jewel to the queen, to Leicester his best gold sword, and to his brother-in-law William Parr, Marquess of Northampton, his second-best gold sword.

Leicester then left the bedside, and the dying earl was alone with his son Edward and the physicians. His dying thoughts are recorded. His second wife, Mary Talbot, whom he had married for her money and connections—she was the daughter of the Earl of Shrewsbury— was to be looked after, to be allowed to stay in Baynard's Castle; his daughter Anne was to be given £500; but more than that, anxiously and insistently, the ordinary men who had been with him and looked after him during his life, were to be cared for by Henry, Lord Herbert, his heir.

> That my lorde Herbert do consider Thomas Gregorie and Tidie with money for their travaile and paines beside that he hath bequeathed to them in annuity that he speciallie do appointe to Francis Zouche and Charles Arundell fit and good annuities for them. That he have special care of Henrie Morgan George Morgan Phillipp Williams Robert Vaughan and Thomas Scudamore and either entertaigne them into his service payinge them their wages beforehand

or else appoint them sufficient annuities That he do enter-
taigne his household and keep them together.

It was his last stated wish that his son should keep his affinity together. Philip Williams was William Herbert's secretary; Robert
Vaughan, his treasurer; Thomas Scudamore, one of the gentlemen
who carried his coffin. Herbert died the following morning, aged
sixty-three, the climacteric, thought to be the most dangerous year
of one's life, being the multiple of the two magic numbers, nine and
seven.

His funeral, on April 18, 1570, was the greatest possible statement
of the man he had become and of the dynasty he had created. The
reverse of a beautiful portrait medal of the earl cast in 1562 showed
a Welsh dragon, or wyvern, by a classical tempietto and carried the
motto "Draco Hic Virtus Virtutem Custos"—This dragon the true
guardian of the virtues. That is how William Herbert saw himself;
the man of violence protecting the good: the humanist inheritance
that Anne Parr had brought to this family, the radical Protestantism
in which, for all the necessary trimming, William and Anne almost
certainly shared a belief, and the people of his lands, whom he had in
part abused but for whom he felt a deep affection.

Two yeoman conductors with black staves led the procession, followed by a hundred poor men, walking "ij and ij," or two by two.
Mr. William Morgan, one of the many Welshmen in London for the
funeral, carried the earl's banner, ahead of "the Defunctes gentlemen
ij and ij," that is, the greatest of his gentry tenants from all those lands
spread across England and Wales. Two secretaries followed, as be-
fitted a man of business, then all the knights and squires who were
beholden to him, then the chief officers of his household (his steward,
his treasurer, and his comptroller). In all of this, it was a funeral indis-
tinguishable from a king's. Another banner carried by his neighboring

Wiltshire knight, Sir George Penruddock, from Compton Chamber-layne, in the valley of the Nadder, who had been with Pembroke fighting the French for Queen Mary; then the York herald with Pembroke's coat of armor, carrying his helm and crest; the Chester herald carrying the shield on which Pembroke's arms were emblazoned; the Richmond herald carrying his sword; and finally the Garter king of arms carrying his coat of arms, accompanied by two "Gentleman Ushers" with white rods. One of these gentleman ushers, dressed up for the occasion, was in fact Roger Earth of Dinton, just across the valley of the Nadder from Compton Chamberlayne, who had been arrested in August 1553, described as "Servaunt to The'erle of Penbroke," and thrown into the Fleet prison for fighting in the streets of London with one of the servants of Lord Stourton. Gentleman usher or brawling member of the affinity: in this life they were the same thing.

The coffin itself was carried by eight gentlemen, some from Herbert's Welsh lands, some from Wiltshire, and eight yeoman assistants, including a ranger of his forests and men from Wyley and Broad Chalke. Further knights and gentlemen, all hooded, processed into St. Paul's, followed by the young Henry, the new Earl of Pembroke, followed by the great of Elizabethan England: the Lord Chancellor, Sir Nicholas Bacon; the Earl of Leicester; Sir William Cecil; Lord Howard of Effingham; and Thomas Sackville, Lord Buckhurst. Finally came the long, long line of the dead earl's yeomen, the copyholders of his estates across the breadth of the realm, and the servants of other noblemen and gentlemen mourners, all of them in black, "ij and ij," for minute after minute through the great west door of St. Paul's.

As a formality, this accumulation of people was the definition of nobility. It was the household in full performance, the affinity in commemoration of death. Everything about this funeral procession enacted the realities of sixteenth-century power: the spread of lands and of people on them; the conspicuous expense of such elaborate obse-

quies; the intimacy with the great of the court and the royal administration; the sense that if this was not, in actuality, a fighting band,
it was not long since it had been. There were men here who had been
with the earl on the bridge in Bristol in 1528; who had helped him destroy the papist images in the 1530s; who had stood with him against
the rebels in 1549; again in the streets of London at the accession of
Queen Mary; again when Thomas Wyatt had threatened the Catholic queen in 1554; again on the battlefields of France, when the great
suits of armor were brought home to Wilton; and who had, of course,
chased with him, day in and day out, across the Arcadian hunting
grounds of Wiltshire.

At the end of it, after "a certain collect" had been read and the chief
mourners had departed, the officers of William Herbert's household
were left alone to see the body buried. "Which officers did put the defunctes staff into the graue and brake each of their own staves and cast
them into the graue with him." The founder of the dynasty was dead
and his authority over.

It had been an extraordinary career, utterly without principle and
single-mindedly violent. William Herbert had favored himself above
all others, except perhaps his first wife, Anne Parr. He had not, until
the very last, attended to the well-being of his people. He had killed
them when they had offended him. He never knew the meaning of
loyalty, either to man or to religion. And his brutality did not conceal
deep inner springs of philosophy or understanding, but rather anxiety
and dread. He had not defended the virtues. He had often opposed the
crown, but only out of self-interest. It may well be that underlying everything that would happen to the Pembrokes in the next eighty years
was the example of this brute, a man who consistently, and without
care, got his own way. They would have been nothing without him.

I'LL BE A PARK AND THOU SHALT BE MY DEER

THE MAKING OF THE PEMBROKE ARCADIA
1570–1586

No earl of Pembroke would ever again enjoy the untrammeled authority wielded by the great founder of the dynasty. On his death in 1570, the long rearguard action began. How would the Pembrokes maintain their standing as powers in the land when the currents of authority were running so consistently against them? How would the Pembrokes survive the Tudor state? From the beginning it seemed clear that the first earl's successor, his son Henry, the second earl, was too weak for the task. He was by inheritance the richest man in England, but his qualities as a man scarcely matched the role his genes had given him.

He had been used by his father as a tool in the advancement of the family. First, in 1553, as part of the great plot to disinherit Mary Tudor and to install Lady Jane Grey on the throne. He had been married to Lady Jane's sister, Catherine, and then, just as rapidly unmarried from her, on the grounds that the marriage had never been consummated. Henry, as an unattractively loyal son, had written cruelly to the poor girl, telling her without any kindness that she had no claim on him. Next, he had been married to the Earl of Shrewsbury's daughter, Katherine Talbot, for her money. Quite smoothly, the willow principle at work, the old man had steered his son around the labyrinth of aristocratic lands and royal influence.

Katherine Talbot died young, and for his third wife, Henry Herbert married the most brilliant woman of her generation. Mary Sidney was so sparkling a catch that according to Aubrey's salacious and voyeuristic gossip, Henry's father, the old trimmer himself, thought she was bound to cheat on him. "The subtile old Earle did see that his faire and witty daughter-in-lawe would horne his sonne, and told him so, and advised him to keepe her in the Countrey and not to let her frequent the Court." As often with Aubrey's tales, this one is impossible. The old earl had been dead seven years by the time Henry married Mary Sidney, but there is a poetic and emotional truth to the tale that goes beyond the simple facts. Henry's personality disappears under his wife's intense glamour. It is she, in alliance with her brilliant and difficult brother, Sir Philip Sidney, who takes up the long quarrel with the crown. Henry shrinks and shrivels in their shadow.

Under the new regime, Wilton turns from being the creation of a canny and potent dynasty maker to the setting and frame for the sparklingly jewel-like presence of Elizabethan England's greatest woman patron and poet. Mary Herbert, Countess of Pembroke, drew around her a dazzlingly literate court. She became the dedicatee, sponsor, completer, and publisher of the greatest prose romance of the age, a distinguished translator of the Psalms, the author of political tragedies, the champion of Spenser, the friend of Shakespeare, and the sustainer of a newly empowered Arcadian vision.

Her father, Sir Henry Sidney, had been an impoverished but distinguished servant of the state. Brought up as a classmate of Edward

VI, he had held the boy king in his arms as he died. Henry Sidney had been unable to accept a peerage because he did not have the income to support the condition, but he was a member of that rising upper-middle band of intelligent, vividly Protestant Englishmen who became the vertebrae of the Tudor state. On her mother's side, Mary Sidney was connected, dangerously, to greatness. Her mother's father was John Dudley, the Duke of Northumberland who had attempted with Pembroke to make Lady Jane Grey queen of England, whom the 1st Earl of Pembroke had deserted at the crucial moment, and who, together with his son Guildford Dudley and Lady Jane Grey, had been executed by Mary Tudor. Mary Sidney's uncles, Robert Dudley, Earl of Leicester, Ambrose Dudley, Earl of Warwick, and their sister, Katherine, Countess of Huntingdon, had been disgraced, imprisoned, and impoverished, but had survived to flower again in the sunshine of Elizabeth's reign. This Dudley inheritance—attuned to power, close to the throne, increasingly attached to the fervent cause of active and aggressive Protestantism both in England and in Europe, thinking of themselves as the core of that interest in England—was Mary Sidney's inheritance. Using the enormous wealth of the Pembrokes, she would make Wilton the heart of that other England, a place dedicated to preserving the country against the erosions of an increasingly powerful court and crown. It was under Mary Sidney's influence that Wilton became the heartland of the English Arcadia.

Her co-champion and co-promoter of the cause was the man who gave this enterprise its name, her brother, Sir Philip Sidney, the author of *Arcadia*, the greatest prose romance of Elizabethan England, which was written largely at Wilton and dedicated to his sister, the woman who was in effect its queen, or as the poet Gabriel Harvey would call her,

> the dearest sister of the dearest brother, the sweetest
> daughter of the sweetest Muses, the brightest Diamant of

the richest Eloquence, the resplendentest mirrour of Feminine valour; the Gentlewooman of Curtesie, the Lady of
Vertue, the Countesse of Excellency, and the Madame of
immortall Honour.

Over two generations in this family, the women whom the bluff,
difficult, and choleric Herbert men married were the ones who
brought the civilization of Renaissance England into the rooms and
garden walks at Wilton. Anne Parr had brought humanist grace to
William Herbert's drive. Mary Sidney brought Renaissance glitter
to Henry's conformity. She had been educated to the highest level:
fluent in French, Italian, and Latin, with a smattering of Greek and
Hebrew. The medieval discipline of rhetoric—figures of speech, the
understanding of decorum, the different forms of language suitable to
different purposes and different occasions—complemented theology
and a reading of the classics. She could sing and play the lute and was
famous for the lace she wove.

She was more than twenty years younger than her husband, and
it was no love match. Mary had been at court two years, since 1575, a
handmaiden to the queen, when her uncle Leicester had arranged her
marriage to the thirty-nine-year-old Henry in 1577. The dowry the
Pembrokes required was an enormous £3,000—Mary's father had to
borrow a large chunk of it from Leicester himself.

As for Henry Pembroke, he seems, if anything, a little overawed
by the massive, remembered presence of his father. As a young man,
he had behaved as required, welcoming as a thirteen-year-old the
Spanish envoys to Wilton with an elegance that was noticed at court,
acting with the propriety his bullying father would have insisted on,
but doing little more in the end than maintaining the role he inherited. No very distinguished image of him survives; nothing compared
with his father's, mother's, wife's, sons', or grandsons' portraits. In the

one picture that survives at Wilton, the man himself seems slightly shrunken inside his clothes. He wears the ribbon of the Garter; he has a little sword; his sleeves are fashionably puffed. Nothing is larger in the landscape than that huge inherited coat of arms. Neither handsome nor authoritative, he looks like a man acting a role with which he does not quite identify. It is inconceivable that this figure could ever have held the future of England in his hands.

Instead, Henry found a role as the agent of royal power in the western provinces where the Pembroke lands lay and where his father had raised armies and decided fates. He became Lord Lieutenant of Wiltshire, Shropshire, Somerset, Worcestershire, Herefordshire, and twelve Welsh counties. He was Lord President of the Council for Wales, responsible, with the sheriffs, for the performance of justice, the preparation of the muster rolls by which the militias were called out, the summoning of those trained bands, and supervision of the military stores. He was, in other words, the local agent of central power, accepting the diminution of the nobility against which his father had railed. The difference between the first and second earls of Pembroke is the difference between a very late medieval warlord and a very early modern official. "My dogs wear my collars," Elizabeth had said. Henry Pembroke was one of those dogs.

The state papers are peppered with complaints about Henry's hopelessness and with his own slightly querulous notes in reply. Local Wiltshire gentlemen badger him to become his deputy. "All men cannot be deputy lieutenants," Henry writes back. "Some must govern, some must obey." The Privy Council in Westminster intervenes. Henry needs more than one deputy lieutenant because he is "for the most part resident in Wales." The Privy Council took to appointing captains of the trained bands in Wiltshire without consulting him. Henry complained, removed the Westminster appointees, and put his own in their place. Without hesitation, the Council told him to reinstate the originals. He was ticked off for the inadequacy of the Wiltshire militia, hopeless in both men and equipment. Henry said that the Wiltshire gentlemen didn't want to contribute money or men. He was told to "be more earnest with them." He was carrying a great name and title, but was he up to the task? England was now at war with Spain; some vigor was required.

Henry, as his father had done, organized the representation of Wiltshire in Parliament, trying to ensure that he always had a body of MPs who would act as his pressure group at Westminster. But even this he allowed to slip out of control. Sir John Thynne, an ambitious north Wiltshire gentleman, cheated and bribed his way into one seat against Henry's wishes and against the candidature of Henry's steward George Penruddock of Compton Chamberlayne, the son of the first earl's great standard-bearer. Henry wrote Thynne a sad and spineless letter:

> I would have all gentlemen to have their due reserved unto
> them, which from tyme to tyme as Parliaments fall out to
> be chosen: now some and then some, as they are fit, to the
> end they may be experimented in the affairs and state of
> their country, not thinking that you meant to be one, for
> that you were last and latelie, . . . if you have a liking to be
> of the house I shall willingly further you to any place I have
> or can gett for you.

This is good behavior, concerned with the balance and regularity of the political community, even treating the gentlemen of Wiltshire as if they were his sons to be educated in the ways of the world, but it is scarcely the correct response to having been outmanoeuvred by a man on the make.

Instead, Henry, when back from his summer expeditions to Wales, plunged into heraldry and bloodsports, the long-standing consolations over many centuries for grandees not quite up to making their way in the political world. "Henry Earle of Pembroke was a great lover of heraldrie," Aubrey remembered,

> and collected curious manuscripts of it, that I have seen and perused; e.g. the coates of armes and short histories of the English nobility, and bookes of genealogies; all well painted and writt. 'Twas Henry that did sett up all the glasse scutchions about the house.

A slightly pedantic nostalgia marked an ebbing of the fire.

Henry had one of the richest hunting establishments in England, an enormous enterprise: Arab stallions and mares, racehorses, horses for "stagge-hunting, fox-hunting, brooke-hawking, and land-hawking." For hounds, the earl had the biggest, the "harbourers," whose morning task was to find "a runnable stag" in its "harbour" in the wood. There were bulldogs, which were put in "to break the bayes of the stagge" at the end of the chase, when the animal had run itself into its final corner; there were also bloodhounds, to find the wounded deer; foxhounds; smaller harriers, "that kind of dog whom nature hath endued with the virtue of smelling, and draweth into his nostrils the air of the scent of the beast pursued and followed," who would put up the hares; and "tumblers," small greyhound-like lurchers, which could be set off to hunt alone and would fall or tumble in catching the rabbits or hares. "His Lordship had the choicest tumblers that were in England, and the same tumblers that rode behind him he made use of to retrieve the partridges." There were setting dogs, or setters—"a certain lusty land spaniel"—which would put up the partridges "for supper-flights for his hawkes." Greyhounds were kept to run in the hare warren, "as good as any were in England."

Henry set up a famous horse race on the downs above Wilton, four miles long from the start, at the Aubrey farm in Broad Chalke, to the finish, by his father's hare warren outside the park at Wilton. He presented a golden bell to the winner worth fifty pounds. The first to win it in 1585 was one of the great glamour men of Elizabethan England, George Clifford, Earl of Cumberland, adventurer, tournament champion, passionate Protestant, enemy of Spain, and practiced robber captain on the high seas. One of Queen Elizabeth's state-sponsored pirates, he once, after a trip to the Azores, arrived back at Falmouth and "unladed and discharged about five millions of silver all in pieces of eight or ten pound great, so that the whole quay lay covered with plates and chests of silver, besides pearls, gold, and other stones which were not registered, elephants' teeth, porcelain, vessels of china, coconuts, hides, ebon wood as black as jet, cloth of the rinds of trees very strange for the matter and artificial in workmanship."

That is the kind of figure with which to fill the rooms of Elizabethan Wilton, a place in which Henry, Earl of Pembroke, is present but not quite dominant. He was too much his father's son and had not absorbed the central place that beauty and glamour had taken in the exercise of power.

It happens again and again in the history of cultures. A generation of severe, rigorous, demanding, and ambitious parents, who establish a form of order and riches, gives way, in the next generation, to a more evolved world, one more intent on fineness than propriety, happy to spend what the parents had earned, indifferent to debt, more interested in display than restraint, more attuned to brilliance and intricacy than mere obstinacy and assertion. The difference between mid- and late-nineteenth-century Britain and between mid- and late-seventeenth-century Holland appeared in the change that occurred between mid- and late-sixteenth-century England. The Wilton that in the 1580s became the dream landscape of Elizabethan England, the heart of a full-blown Arcadia, came out of the armored toughness of an earlier age. Everything William Herbert had done to his tenants and his rivals, his enemies and friends, laid the foundation for a place of the highest and most lightly conceived civilization and literary art. Under Mary Sidney's tutelage, the Arcadian butterfly emerged at Wilton.

Roger Ascham, the humanist and educationalist, correspondent of Anne Parr, had described the men of the first earl's generation, admiringly, as "grave, steadfast, silent of tongue, secret of heart." Perhaps, in his shouting tempers, those words do not quite fit the first earl, but the seriousness and secrecy of purpose, the care with which the willow had to bend with the wind, the self-limitation, the imposition of will: all of that describes the making of the Pembroke fortunes; and all of it was transformed in the following generation into something that was very nearly its opposite.

You can see what happens in the portraiture. The shape of people's mouths, from the tight drawn line in the world depicted by Holbein, the unforgiving straightforwardness of eye and jaw, the sense that each face is a mask over a mind of fixed intent, gives way, particularly in the second half of Elizabeth's reign, to something far less certain. The faces portrayed by the Elizabethan miniaturists turned from that unaccommodating and manly blankness, the defended façade of a calculating mind, to something subtler, more nuanced, and more penetrable, colored by doubt and delicacy, a feminization of the ideal. Men's clothes became gay and brilliant; shoulders were no longer held foursquare to the viewer; a doubting finger rose to the lips; the sobriety and resistance of the difficult years had been left behind. Fineness replaced assertion as the definition of nobility. The wars, threats of war, revolts, and religious struggles engaged in by the makers of dynasties in the years of Henry VIII, Edward VI, and Mary now became play wars in the ever more elaborate shows of tiltyard and tournament, even longed-for wars, wars not as the necessary assertion of social and political dominance but as the fulfillment of personal destiny.

Life for the Elizabethan élite was strung between these ideals: the elegance of an existence without war, increasingly nostalgic for the days of chivalry, combined with a sense that sweetness was not enough, that the world had turned away from manliness and truth and toward the honeyed, jewelled toys, the pearl-embroidered doublets, the glamour houses from which the lights at night glimmered through the branches of the surrounding woods "not unlike the beams of the Sun through the crannels [crevices] of a wall." The medium for any quarrel with authority had moved from the reality of armies and rebellion to the realms of art and elegant display.

The height of this Elizabethan dream-glory was the moment in 1575 when the queen went to visit Kenilworth Castle, decorated by her favorite and sometime lover, the Earl of Leicester, and lit up like a liner sailing through the Warwickshire woods:

> every room so spacious, so well belighted, and so high roofed within, so seemly to sight by due proportion without: by day time, on every side so glittering by glass; by nights by continual brightness of candle, fire, and torch-light, transparent through the lightsome windows, as it were the Egyptian Pharos relucent unto all the Alexandrian coast . . . or else radiant as though Phoebus for his ease would rest him in the Castle, and not every night so travel down into the Antipodes.

At its most self-loving moments, it seemed as if the sun had come to rest in Elizabethan England, to spend the night there, its beams stealing out from the bedroom windows and into the surrounding night, illuminating it like the candles and torches at a feast.

At the end of September 1574, Elizabeth came to Wilton, and Wilton put on its most entrancing show. A full five miles away from the house, Henry Pembroke met her in her carriage out on the beautiful downland grass, "accompanyed with many of his honourable and worshipfull friends, on a fayre, large, and playne hill, having a good band of men in all their livery coates." As a boy, Henry had been there when his father had done the same for Philip of Spain, en route to his wedding with Mary Tudor. Henry knew what to do:

> Men, well horsed, who being placed in a ranke in order, from one another about seaven foot, and about fifteen foote from the highway, occupied a great way; and another rank of the earle's gentlemen servants, about a stone's cast behinde their masters stood on horsebacke in like order. And when the Queen's majesty had ridden beyond the furthermost of the earle's men, those that began the ranke, by three and three, rode another way homeward on the side of a hill, and in like order the rest followed and lastly the gentlemens servants.

This was landscape as theater, the cast cleverly disappearing behind the scenes, only to appear, magically, at the next glorious display. As the queen arrived at the house, riding in through the gateway to the first outer courtyard,

> Without the inner gate the countess with divers ladyes and gentlewomen, meekly received her highnesse. This utter court was beset on both sides the way with the earles men

as thicke as could be standing one by another, through
which lane her grace passed with her chariot and lighted at
the inner gate.

It might have looked like the assembling of the affinity, the great
gathering of the magnate's forces, the reenactment of noble power,
gracefully welcoming a sovereign; but everyone would have known
the reality. Henry was a functionary. His offers to raise his troops
for the defense of the kingdom would not be taken up by the Privy
Council. He received letters from them telling him to attend more
closely to his duties in Wales, was instructed "to reside half the year
at Ludlow"—the headquarters of royal government in the Welsh
marches—an instruction Henry resented "as though I wanted discretion to discharge the like trust which had been committed to all others
[who had held the post previously]; or were unworthie to have any
regard had of my health."

I will not despaier of her Majesties goodness: I haue waited
onlie on her: I haue not by factions sought to strengthen or
by future hoopes endeuered to foster my selfe: and therefore from her Maiesty as I onely dezerwe; so by her Maies-
tie I only expecte to be conforted.

All he really wanted was "some princelie bountie," which he didn't
really need and which never came. In these letters one can see something that might otherwise feel quite intangible: the growth of the
state, the concentration of power in the hands of the crown, and the
converting of the aristocracy into agents of regal power.

Meanwhile, the Wilton show rolled on, with the sugared crust over
the rather different underlying realities. "Her Highnesse lay at Wilton
house that Friday night, the Saturday and Sunday nightes following;

and on Monday after dinner her grace removed to Salisbury; during all which time her majesty was both merry and pleasant."

That final phrase carries within it the expectation that she might have been neither. Elizabeth had been schooled in the same world where the first earl had learned the lessons of survival. Her enormous and defended authority, reserving all options from foreigners and rivals for power, whether in England or abroad, was the great iceberg around which the world of Arcadia was framed. Arcadia looked for openness, mutuality, and a sense of power residing not in the crown but in the balanced organism of the commonwealth, of which the crown was merely the head.

The first earl had been appointed in 1553 to the office of warden and keeper of the park of Clarendon, to the east side of Salisbury, "that delicious parke (which was accounted the best in England)," according to Aubrey, as well as launder, or keeper, of the grazing there and lieutenant of the conies, the keeper of the rabbits. Henry had inherited the post, and the entire party went over there at the weekend. It had been the queen's decision.

> On the Saturday her highnesse had apoynted to hunt in Claryngdon Park. Where the said earle had prepared a very faire and pleasant banquett[ing house made of] leaves for her to dyne in; but that day happened so great raine, that although it was fenced with arras, yet it could not defend the wett, by meanes whereof the Quene dined within the lodge; and the lords dined in the banquet house; and after dinner the rayne ceased for a while, during which tyme many dear coursed with grey hounds were overturned, soe as the tyme served, great pleasure was shewed.

The atmosphere of this hunting party was not the red-cheeked, pink-coated high spirits we might associate it with now. There was something much more consciously elevated about this Elizabethan hunt, a heightening of the world rather than a coarsening of it, as if on the hunting field, or at least in the huge hunting world of the Wiltshire Downs and their long horizons, one could taste some element of an Arcadian reality.

Inside the park, the pursuit and killing of the delicate fallow deer—an animal from the east, which had been kept in parks in Persia when England was little but mud and wildwood, and which had traveled to Europe via Minoan Crete and Norman Sicily—was an engagement with nature on the most refined and feminine of levels. Here, with bow and arrow, is where the women of the household, or the unathletic and scholarly men, would pursue the hunt, often shooting deer that had been driven by men and hounds into convenient corners for them. They might not even engage in the hunt itself, but simply watch as the animals were killed before them.

The hunting park was in that way conceived as a place of delicious femininity, full of an erotic charge, heightened by its sense of enclosure, of a nature shut in but still quite wild. It was never more seductively or entrancingly expressed than by Shakespeare's slightly fat, slightly old, slightly overheating Venus, trying again and again to persuade her lovely young beardless Adonis to enter the sweetness of the enclosure she had to offer. She is lying next to him on a primrose bank.

> Sometimes her arms infold him like a band:
> She would, he will not in her arms be bound;
> And when from thence he struggles to be gone,
> She locks her lily fingers one in one.
> "Fondling," she saith, "since I have hemm'd thee here
> Within the circuit of this ivory pale,

I'll be a park, and thou shalt be my deer;
Feed where thou wilt, on mountain or in dale:
Graze on my lips; and if those hills be dry,
Stray lower, where the pleasant fountains lie."

To that extent, deliciousness was what the park was for. It was a place full of the ambiguities of Arcadia—power and delight, freedom and control, simplicity and sophistication—all overlapping and intersecting in the richest possible cultural landscapes. Every aspect of that Arcadian complex would have been in play when the queen came to be merry at Wilton, and in the rainy enclosures of Clarendon Park. The earl was merely her ranger there, her servant. But he derived huge income from the post, one, anyway, that he had inherited from his father. He was in control but he was there to serve her. He provided the deer for her to shoot at, but the deer were hers anyway, his hounds her hounds, his standing her standing. His need of her was more than hers of him. He might have been surrounded by hundreds of men in his livery, but he wore her collar; she certainly didn't wear his (although she did like to wear, on occasion, a miniature of Robert Cecil, her Secretary in her last years, on her shoe).

And yet, overlying this picture of dominance, which would be less nuanced if Elizabeth had been a man, was a small charged theater of the erotic, of Diana the huntress queen, her taunting and powerful virginity somehow set in play by her role as huntress, a merging and muddling of genders and potencies. James I expressly forbade his queen, Anne, from hunting deer, but a queen regnant was different. She was, in her womanliness, even more removed from those around her than a king would be. Perhaps because of the necessary distance to be kept between male power brokers and her body, any sense of intimacy with her power was stilled at birth. No man could get close enough to be anything less than emasculated in her presence. And that denial of access to power was one of the conditions in which an appetite for Arcadia—which was the absence of tyranny—would thrive.

The Countess of Pembroke's elder brother Philip Sidney was a proud, clever, often slightly touchy, ambitious, well-traveled, fiercely protestant, ingenious, funny, storytelling, highly educated, charming, and occasionally violent man. He once told his father's secretary that he would "thruste my Dagger into yow" because the secretary had been opening the young man's letters. But he was a complex figure, and Dr. Muffet, his friend and the Pembrokes' physician at Wilton, thought Sidney "possessed a gentle, tender disposition." One thing Sidney hated was hunting, thinking it an unnecessary and tyrannical act of brutality. According to his friend Edmund Spenser, he was capable of melancholy but he was also "made for merriment/Merily masking both in bowre and hall."

He had been born in 1554 and was his father's treasured son. As a young man he had swum into the mainstream of English cultural life. Sir Walter Raleigh; Raleigh's half brother the adventurer and explorer Humphrey Gilbert; Dr. Dee, the great mathematician and cartographer of Elizabethan England; the historian William Camden; Richard Hakluyt, the chronicler of English expansionism across the world ocean; Francis Walsingham, the Protestant zealot and spymaster; the poets Fulke Greville, Edmund Spenser, and Edward Dyer— all were part of Sidney's circle, which was literate, literary, politically and materially ambitious, highly Protestant, courtly, and chivalric. Sidney had traveled through Europe, where he had fallen in love with the works of Titian, Tintoretto, and Veronese and had himself painted in the modern Italian style, and across northern Europe, where had conversed at length with Protestant princes and scholars as if he were their equal. It was the training for a life of significance.

But Sidney wasn't much liked at court and was distrusted by the sage heads around the queen for an immoderate turn of mind, a readiness to argument, and an inflated idea of his own importance, derived from his connections to his uncle the Earl of Leicester and from the respectful treatment he had received from Protestant leaders abroad. They saw in him possibilities of an Englishman who might lead England into the religious wars against the Roman Catholic powers of the Continent. Nothing could have been more unwelcome to the queen.

Sidney's life was strung between literature and politics. He was born with a gift for fluency, a rhythmic ease that flooded English sensibility with a new and extraordinarily influential feeling for the beauty of the flowing phrase. Largely through him the current of English poetry and romance turned from the blocky, rough-cut directness of mid-sixteenth-century poetry to something sweeter and more liquid. He thought of himself as someone on whom the service of his country and his faith lay as a duty. He was an elegant man, but pockmarked, his face scarred by smallpox contracted when he was a boy, as his mother's had been. Among the mottoes he would later carry as a knight in the tiltyard was one that said of him, "Spotted to be known." Ben Jonson thought his appearance revolting, "Sir P. was no pleasant man in countenance, his face being spoiled with pimples and of high blood and long."

By his mid-twenties Sidney was already chafing at his failure to be more engaged with a serious career. He took to arguing, angrily, with other courtiers over matters of status and honor. He even spoke forthrightly to the queen herself over her neglect of the dignity of gentlemen such as he at court. By the late 1570s, his frustrations finally led him away from court, where he was unwelcome, and to Wilton, with its delights and consolations. In 1579, an argument over precedence with the Earl of Oxford, who had rudely ejected him from a tennis court at Greenwich mid-game, and over his authorship of a manuscript letter arguing that the queen should not marry a Catholic

Frenchman, led to his banishment to the country. He was already attuned to the power and potential of the pastoral, and in that same year he had given the queen, as a New Year's present, a cambric smock, the dress for a shepherdess—an invitation to the simplicities of Arcadia.

At Wilton, his sister, Mary Pembroke, who loved him immoderately, took him in. Aubrey's strange, half-transmuted, gossipy memories had it that the two of them slept together and that Philip, who would become the fourth earl, was their misbegotten son, named after his father-uncle-godfather. That cannot be true, but the gossip, as ever, addresses a deeper truth. There is something warmer, closer, and more loving in the relationship of Mary Pembroke and Philip Sidney than there ever was between Mary and Henry, the hunting- and heraldry-obsessed earl who'd married her. It was Philip, through his pen, who took up the quarrel with the crown.

There are several versions of *The Countesse of Pembroke's Arcadia*, probably begun in 1578 but revised over several years. The first version was a gentle romance in which an undertone of politics played throughout the pastoral; the second, a more violent and less clear-cut epic; and the third, completed by Mary after Sidney's death in 1587, something of mishmash between the two, perhaps with additions of her own. All of them were dedicated to her. It had begun with a challenge from her to him: she dared him to write a romance in English, something to match the *Arcadia* written by the Neapolitan Sannazaro almost a century before, and which Sidney had bought on his Italian travels. "You desired me to doe it, and your desire to my heart is an absolute commandment," Philip wrote. "Now it is done onely for you, only to you."

Mary had been involved from the start. It was "but a trifle, and that triflingly handled," Sidney wrote with conventional self-deprecation, a "modesty tropos." "Your deare selfe can best witnes the manner, being done in loose sheetes of paper, most of it in your presence, the rest, by sheetes, sent vnto you, as fast as they were done." It was written, then, partly at Wilton, partly in London, perhaps partly at the Sidney house at Penshurst, in Kent.

The first earl's threat to the crown had taken the form of an army ranged up on the London road, with its intention to do violence perfectly clear. Philip Sidney's challenge to the crown took the form, at least to begin with, of a vision of escape. His Arcadia is a land of fertile valleys and rich pastures, where the houses are "lodges of stone built in the form of a star." The inhabitants—and it does not take much to translate this into the circumstances at Wilton—are either great princes or poor shepherds. There is nothing much to do but fall in love and have adventures. Olive trees grow here, and there are sandy beaches by turquoise seas. From time to time the wandering knights might come on a "sleeping lyon" or "a she Beare not far from him, of litle lesse fiercenes," but that is not the dominant tone, which is one of sweetness, conversation, ease in the shade, time for love, some "burning kisses," "sweete kisses," "cold kisses," "many kisses," "kisses oft," and all under "the Palmetrees, (which being louing in their own nature, seemed to giue their shadow the willinglier, because they held discourse of loue)."

This unthreatened, easy perfection was a place where the grief and tension of existence had been eased away and stilled. Sweetness was the face it showed to the world. So often do honey and sweetness appear in Sidney's *Arcadia* that they seem at times a joke. The grass on which the sheep nibble is sweet, the words the princess murmurs through "the cherry of her lips" is invariably sweet and increasingly honeyed. She is, according to the stricken knight, "the sweetest fairnesse and fairest sweetnesse: with that word his voice brake so with sobbing, that he could say no further." Her "breath is more sweete then a gentle Southwest wind, which comes creeping over flowery fields and shadowed waters in the extreme heat of summer, and yet is nothing, compared to the honey flowing speech that breath doth carry. . . . She had no sooner ended with the joining her sweet lips together, but that the shepherd who lay before her recorded to her music this rural poesie":

> *O words which fall like summer dew on me,*
> *O breath more sweete, than is the growing bean,*
> *O tongue in which, all honeyed liquores be. . . .*

It is an Edenic world of wish-fulfillment. A young prince finds himself naked but "this nakedness was to him an apparel." Scene after scene unfolds in the liquid language that became one of the Elizabethan idioms. Handfuls of words pour forth as smoothly continuous as the broad backs of the downs over which Sidney had been wandering. It is all slightly absurd, the mind on holiday. One can only guess what the old earl might have made of it. But, that said, there is also a ballet-like sensation, that this is a realm in which beauty for once might be allowed its freedom. It is the language and the images of youthfulness and re-lease, emerging from under the carapace of a tough-headed, Polonius-like generation of elders, a generation that had been all too insistent for all too long on the proprieties and duties and self-improvements and self-controls to which older generations are chronically prey. This, for all its weakness and oversweetness, is the freedom of writing as if the writing itself were making a new world, discovering a lighthearted en-gagement with some freely invented thing (the models for which Sidney had, of course, read in Virgil and Theocritus, and seen on the walls of the Italian villas and places he had visited a couple of years before).

"Reade it then," he told his sister,

> *at your idle times, and the follies your good iudgement will*
> *finde in it, blame not, but laugh at. And so, looking for no bet-*

ter stuffe, then, as in a Haberdashers shoppe, glasses, or feath-
ers, you will continue to loue the writer, who doth exceedingly
loue you, and moste moste heartilie praies you may long liue, to
be a principall ornament to the family of the Sidneis.

> *Your louing brother,*
> *Philip Sidney*

Not, intriguingly, of the Pembrokes or the Herberts, whose violent, vulgar, grasping Welshness perhaps did not compare with the noble refinement of the Dudley-Sidneys. For something that Sidney revised and struggled over for years, this is the pose of sprezzatura, an assumption of ease laid over a life of hidden purpose.

As Virginia Woolf wrote in her affectionate essay on the *Arcadia*,

> the life that we invent, the stories we tell, as we sink back
> with half-shut eyes and pour forth our irresponsible dreams,
> have perhaps some wild beauty; some eager energy; we
> often reveal in them the distorted and decorated image of
> what we soberly and secretly desire.

Founded on the autonomy of desire, Sidney's Arcadia is fiercer than a mere soft-edged dreaming of a sunlit holiday. He was a disappointed man. To his friend Edward Denny he wrote from Wilton that "the vnnobl constitution of our tyme doth keepe vs from fitte imployments." The queen would not let him have a position at court; nor with the Protestant armies in Europe, where he had been offered the governorship of the Protestant provinces of Holland and Zeeland by William of Orange; nor even in the New World, to all of which he was drawn. The experience of authority in sixteenth-century England was one of either uncertain success or certain humiliation. Arcadia, of its essence, was a place in which to escape authority and enter the world in which desire was king.

Desire, which colors page after page of the romance, is a world beyond power. Both beneath power and indifferent to it, desire was where the self could find an unadulterated and uncompromised being, a form of life beyond the humiliations of hierarchy. Queen Elizabeth's dogs may have worn her collars, but not in Arcadia. Arcadia was beyond the submission to a predefined destiny. It was a form of transcendence into a world of beauty whose essence was freedom. In the romance, there is a deep and pained longing, expressed far more intently than the warblings of shepherds and their oaten pipes, for an age before consciousness, before moral codes, before grief and sorrow, before a man could be disappointed by his life:

> Many times haue I, leaning to yonder Palme, admired the
> blessednes of it, that it could beare Loue without sence of
> paine. Many times, when my masters cattle came hether to
> chewe their cudde, in this fresh place, I might see the young
> Bull testifie his loue. But how? with proud lookes, and ioy-
> fulnes. These beasts, like children to nature, inherit her
> blessings quietly; we, like bastards, are layd abroad, euen
> as foundlings to be trayned vp by griefe and sorrow.

But that desire to escape into the world of desire Sidney knew to be not enough. In his great sonnet sequence, *Astrophel and Stella*, probably also written at Wilton, he dwelt, as any number of melancholic Elizabethan young men would also dwell, on his disgrace with fortune and men's eyes, on the triviality of his life and occupations. His great friend and mentor the French Protestant divine Hubert Languet had written to ask him if it was "honourable for you to be lurking down where you are, while your country is begging for the help and support of her sons." Sidney answered in a sonnet:

> *With what sharpe checkes I in my selfe am shent [shamed]*
> *When into Reason's audite I do go:*
> *And by just counts my selfe a banckrout know*
> *Of all those goods, which heav'n to me hath lent:*
> *Unable quite to pay even nature's rent,*
> *Which unto it by birthright I do ow, . . .*
> *My youth doth waste, my knowledge brings forth toyes . . .*

This is the seriousness of Arcadia, buried inside its sugar. A sense of honor and conscience drove him toward a political life, which he felt it was his duty to take up. The knowledge that he came from a governing family was a powerful force for Sidney. In families like his lay the guarantee of freedom for the country. Only a powerful, crown-denying nobility could keep the country free from tyranny. His brother-in-law Henry Pembroke may have been meekly submitting to the crown's control of noble power, but for Sidney and the many readers of his manuscripts among the élite, that submission was not enough.

No question in the sixteenth century was more alive than the relationship of the crown to the governing class. All over Europe, it seemed clear, ancient limitations on the sovereign, largely guaranteed by an ancient nobility, were under threat. The great struggle for the Low Countries, out of which the glories of the Dutch Republic would come in the seventeenth century, was precisely this conflict between an assertive Spanish state and the old liberties of the Dutch dukedoms that Charles V, the Habsburg king of Spain, had inherited. In Italy, one small principality after another had been transformed from a consultative, self-limiting form of government to one in which the prince, having read his Machiavelli, imposed his absolute will. In France, that same influence had had its play. "Is it better to be loved than feared, or the reverse?" Machiavelli had asked in *The Prince*. "The answer is that it is desirable to be both, but because it is difficult to join them together, it is much safer for a Prince to be feared than loved." Fear and an abandonment of the assumption of good intent, which was behind the layered structures of the inherited medieval custom, were the foundations of tyranny. "It is necessary for him who lays out a state and arranges laws for it," Machiavelli had written in the *Discourses*, "to presuppose that all men are evil and that they are always going to act according to the wickedness of their spirits whenever they have free scope." That was not the custom of the manor. Fulke Greville, Sidney's friend and disciple, had heard Sidney himself bewail the influence of modernity on France, "how that once well-formed monarchy had by little and little let fall her ancient and reverend pillars—I mean parliaments, laws and customs—into the narrowness of proclamations or imperial mandates." That is precisely what Sidney, his uncle Leicester, his father-in-law the spymaster Sir Francis Walsingham, and others of the Protestant party in England feared. A modern, absolutist monarchy would lift England away from "her ancient legal circles" and "our ancient customs and statutes." The custom of the manor, the very mutuality of the ancient workings of the country, was a model of the workings of Arcadia. And the environment at Wilton, for all its self-delusions, was a model of the ideal state. Hubert Languet, the only real person named in *Arcadia*, had in his great book *Against Tyranny*, published in 1579, addressed the central political Arcadian question to a tyrant:

> Just because someone has made you a shepherd for the sake
> of the flock, did he hand over that flock to be skinned at
> your pleasure?

No: the shepherd needed to love his sheep; just as the lord needed to love his tenants, and they him in return.

For Languet, who might have been speaking of Henry Pembroke and his diminished condition, the modern tyrannical state had eaten away at the nobility that was the guarantee of a real freedom and had dressed them up in the fancy clothes of the tiltyard and the tournament:

> You speak of peers, notables and officials of the crown, while I see nothing but fading names and archaic costumes like the ones they wear in tragedies. I scarcely see any remnant of ancient authority and liberty . . . let electors, palatines, peers, and the other notables not assume that they were created and ordained merely to appear at coronations and dress up in splendid uniforms of olden times, as though they were actors in an ancient masque, or as though they were staging a scene from King Arthur and the Knights of the Round table.

Here, already quite clearly articulated but sixty years early, are the phrases that would be used in the English Civil War. The state had put collars on its dogs, and an emasculated nobility felt tyranny creeping across the land. This was not about democracy but the fears of the old ruling class sensing the growing power of the state. An uncontrolled crown would destroy the customs of England. Only with balance, and the organic integrity of a country that had head, body, and limbs in harmony, would England be what it always had been.

This Arcadian heartland is a mysterious place for us: consciously élitist but fiercely Protestant in religion; prepared—just—to countenance the overthrow of kings, but courtly to a degree in manner and self-conception; political in its removal from the political world; aristocratic, community-conscious, potentially rebellious, literary, martial, playful, earnest, antiquarian, English, Italianate, and nostalgic. But this is the essence: Arcadia sees an aristocracy not as an element of a controlling establishment but as an essential organ in a healthy state, a check and balance on the centralizing power of the crown and the true source of authority and care in the lands it owns. The vision of Arcadia is not far from the desire for wholeness that the communities of the chalkland valleys wished to embody in their elaborate and ancient constitutions.

Alongside his written versions of *Arcadia*—they were never printed during his lifetime but circulated in manuscript—Sidney also enacted his vision of courteous rebellion and independent purity at court. Before the French ambassador, on Whit Monday and Tuesday, in the early summer of 1581, Sidney, his friend Fulke Greville, and two other young men, who were prepared to spend their fortunes on the performance, put on a show in the tiltyard in Whitehall. They called themselves "The Four Foster Children of Desire," that word *desire* glowing in the context of Elizabethan show as an acceptable and oblique stand-in for what in the language of Arcadia it really meant: rebellion, or at least self-removal from the structures of power.

They had the gallery at the end of the tiltyard, in which the queen would stand, redecorated and called the "Castle or Fortresse of Perfect Beautie." It was a game of mock rebellion by young men who believed that the queen and court, then considering a French and Catholic marriage for Elizabeth, were neglecting the habits and structures of an older England, even moving toward a kind of tyranny that the land of desire could never tolerate. Sidney had written a speech dense with scarcely concealed meanings addressed to the Fortress of Perfect Beauty:

Forasmuch as her highnesse should be there included, whereto the said foster children layde tytle and claime as their due by discent unto them. And upon denial, or any repulse from that their desired patrimonie, they vowed to vanquishe and conquer by force who so should seeme to withstand it.

This extraordinary pantomime of mock rebellion stands midway between the realities of 1549 and 1642. The same elements were at stake: patrimony; nobility; a crown that seemed to betray the best of a noble inheritance; courteous men in some ways desperately dependent on the crown for their standing, and in other ways proudly independent of it, holding the crown to account, showing no respect, threatening violence. Here was a game whose frisson depended on its approach to reality. The four knights sent a boy to issue their challenge to the queen as she came from chapel. "Without making any precise reverence at all, he uttered these speeches of defiance, from his masters to her Majestie. These foure . . . do will you by me, even in the name of Justice, that you will no longer exclude virtuous Desire from perfect Beautie."

It was, they said, in a breathtaking double bluff, "a plaine proclamation of warre":

If beautie be accompanied with disdainful pride, and pride weighted on by refusing crueltie, then must I denounce unto you that . . . they will besiege that fatal Fortresse, vowing not to spare (if this obstinacie continue) the sword of faithfulnesse, and the fire of affection.

The speech tells it straight. The queen and her government were proud and disdainful. Their cruelty consisted in refusing a place or a role to Philip Sidney and others like him who not only owed the country their duty but had the strength, the independent strength within them to attack that fatal fortress and its hideous obstinacy with the sword of faithfulness—that is, the Protestant religion—and, in an astonishing yoking together of disparates, "the fire of affection," which is to say, Arcadia's burning desire. Here, quite clear, even if buried under ceremony and courteousness like a dramatized version of a jewelled New Year's Day emblem, was the rebellion of the Arcadian lords. Needless to say, this show was so weak and so marginal that it had no effect at all. Any impact would have to wait for different circumstances in the following century.

Sidney's *Arcadia* had argued for action and for giving powerful and glamorous roles to the nobility and their supporters. Elizabeth's reluctance was motivated by a desire not only to avoid war and its expense but to avoid giving her great subjects ideas above their station. Finally, in 1586, after years of pleading and under the command of Leicester, an English expeditionary force, paid for with Dutch money, went over to the Netherlands to fight for the Protestant Dutch against the Spanish. Sidney was appointed governor of Flushing, one of the three ports the English received from the Dutch as guarantees against their paying the costs of the expedition.

It was in a small engagement in that war, at Zutphen on September 23, 1586, that Sidney was wounded. He had left off his thigh armor either, as his friend and biographer Fulke Greville said much later, as an act of theatrical courage, so that he would be no better protected than the other gentlemen around him, or because a lighter armor would give him some added mobility on the battlefield.

So he receiued a hurt by a musket shot a little aboue the left
knee, which so brake and rifted the bone, and so entered
the thigh vpward toward the bodie, as the bullet could not
be found before his bodie was opened.

As the wound became gangrenous, Sidney turned to God. The wound was "a loving and fatherly correction" from the source of loving justice. In the light of this lesson, Sidney promised to "addict myself wholly to God's service, and not to live as I have done. For I have walked in a vain course."

Those words cast a chill over the delights at Wilton. But they were the words of a wounded and dying man. The truth is that as an inheritance, as a dead man, Sidney—and his association with the free-flowing landscape of Arcadia, with its combined vision of Protestant freedom and noble authenticity, in a world away from the corruptions and failures of the court—was more potent than he had been when alive. In death, for England as much as for his family, he became "an Angell Spirit"—the phrase was his sister's—"so rare a iewell of vertue and courtesie."

Theatricality did not desert Sidney in death. His body was taken back from the Low Countries covered with a pall of black velvet. The pinnace that brought him home, right into the pool of London, where his body was disembarked at the Tower, had "all her sayles, tackling and other furniture coloured black and black cloth hanged round about her with Escouchions of his Armes." It was the ship of sorrow and the death of hope. But this image was the guarantee that Sidney's beliefs would survive him. He had made the Arcadian amalgam central to the English nobility's view of themselves as the inhabitants, at least in potential, of a sweet and beautiful world, free of tyranny, whose freedoms were guaranteed by their own independent virtue within it. He had transmuted the quarrel with the king into an act of beauty.

In the reign of his sister Mary, Countess of Pembroke, Wilton would become the focus and reliquary of that ideal.

LITTLE EARTHS
KIND OF PARADISE

Mary Sidney, the glamour queen of a pugnacious Arcadia, took up the cudgels. She gathered around her at Wilton, as her own armory, a company of wits, poets, thinkers, and scientists. She and they made Wilton the center of Renaissance England. Almost the entire family was writing poems. Her other brother, Robert Sidney, who became governor of Flushing on Philip's death, wrote a sequence of poems addressed to Mary. Her son William and her niece, also called Mary Sidney, both became poets. The only silent members of the household were the increasingly ill and curmudgeonly Henry, and Mary's younger son, Philip, both of them devoted to their hawks and hounds.

Mary had not been admitted to Philip Sidney's funeral, and afterward she withdrew to Wilton in her grief for two years. Philip Sidney had made her his literary heir. She was in possession of the manuscripts of *Arcadia*, *The Defence of Poesy*, and the sonnet sequence *Astrophel and Stella*. Over the coming years, from her base at Wilton, she would oversee the publication of all of them. But her role was far more than a keeper of the flame. Before his death, Sidney had been translating the Psalms into sophisticated English lyrics. He had reached Psalm 43, and Mary set herself the task of completing the remaining 107. In doing so, she helped shape the religious lyric of the seventeenth century, steering the atmosphere at Wilton away from the rather flat-footed hunting and hawking to which Henry, her husband, was devoted, and toward a higher, more spiritualized condition. But that heightened world at Wilton was not inert or passive. Its elevated tone was intended to be a model for what a court might be.

"Religion," John Donne, a friend and admirer of both Sidneys, would say in a sermon, "is a serious thing but not a sullen," and the translations of the Psalms that Mary Pembroke would make over the next few years were acknowledged by Donne and others as the most ingenious and richly poetic of any done in English. Donne certainly drew from them, as would George Herbert for the great religious poems he would write here in the early 1630s when vicar of Bemerton.

In the part courtly, part Protestant world of Wilton, the translation of the Psalms was a fusing of those universes. The task of the poet, as Ben Jonson said of translation, was "to draw forth out of the best and choicest flowers, and turn all to honey," and that is what, at least in part, Mary Sidney did with the Psalms, applying the sweetness of Arcadia, its courtly concern for graceful precision and sophisticated invention, to the great poetry of the Hebrew Bronze Age. Religious verse, in her hands, as it would be in George Herbert's, did not exist in a compartment separate from urbanity and courtesy; it was an extension of those qualities, not a denial of them.

The Psalms were thought to be the work of King David, royal poems, and that high religious and kingly standing played its part in the Wilton Psalms. "Hee," Mary wrote later, meaning her brother Philip,

> did warpe, I weav'd this webb to end;
> the stuffe not ours, our worke no curious thing.

She was binding her life in with her dead brother's, both of them in service at a court at which no Tudor monarch held sway, the highest court of which man could conceive. Here, in the Arcadian-Protestant amalgam, is another subtle form of subversion, a demotion, at least by implication, of all the pretensions to greatness that a worldly court might make.

Mary Sidney would have had before her the Psalms as translated by Miles Coverdale in 1535 and distributed throughout the country in the Great Bibles that Henry VIII and Archbishop Cranmer required each parish to hold. Here is the language of Coverdale's Psalm 139, addressing the power of God:

> Yf I saye: peraduenture the darcknesse shal couer me, then
> shal my night be turned to daye.
> Yee the darcknesse is no darcknesse with thee, but the night is
> as cleare as the daye, the darcknesse & light are both alike.

Mary Sidney took that plain and workmanlike statement and gave it a kind of dancing elegance, at the same time elevating and refining its tone, making it courtly, maintaining its seriousness but banishing its sullenness, eliding Calvin with Castiglione:

> Do thou best, O secret night,
> In sable veil to cover me:

Thy sable veil
Shall vainly fail:
With day unmasked my night shall be,
For night is day and darkness light,
O father of all lights, to thee.

"In dancing," Castiglione had written in *The Courtier*,

a single step, a single movement of the body that is graceful and not forced, reveals at once the skill of the dancer. A
singer who utters a single word ending in a group of four
notes with a sweet cadence, and with such facility that he
appears to do it quite by chance, shows with that touch
alone that he can do much more than he is doing.

This is the heartland of sprezzatura, the nonchalance that stems
from discipline and rigor. The apparently effortless movement of the
dancer is just the effect Mary Sidney was aiming for here, not as a form
of worldly refinement but as an aspect of prayer and worship.

The Sidneyan Psalms are far more than a mere sweetening of the
sacred note. They put on a bravura display of different voices and to-
nalities, different verse forms and rhyme schemes, a compendium of
inventiveness that veers from coyness to savagery, from the most styl-
ish of dance tunes to the most unforgiving of homilies. Psalm 52, as
translated by the Geneva Bible of 1587, was a traditional puritan exercise in straight talking to the great of the worldly world:

Why boastest thou thy selfe in thy wickednesse, O man of
power? the louing kindenesse of God indureth dayly.
Thy tongue imagineth mischiefe, and is like a sharpe rasor,

that cutteth deceitfully. Thou doest loue euill more then
good, and lies more then to speake the trueth.

Mary Pembroke had no difficulty in outstripping the Presbyterian divines in the uncompromising attack of her translation:

Tyrant whie swel'st thou thus,
Of mischief vanting?
Since helpe from god to us,
Is never wanting?
Lewd lies thy tongue contrives,
Lowd lies it soundeth:
Sharper then sharpest knives
with lies it woundeth.
Falshood thy witt approves,
All truth rejected:
Thy will all vices loves,
Vertue neglected.

This is the counterpoint of that earlier dancing lightness: the hammering, puritan contempt for the corruption and vanity of power, spoken with the authority of a countess, her own court around her, and the moral strength of her dead martyred brother allowing her no compromise in language or grammar. Truth telling of this kind can largely dispense with verbs and adjectives. The psalm in Mary's hands has become a naked, noun-based charge sheet of worldly failing.

The poets Samuel Daniel, Abraham Fraunce, Fulke Greville, Edmund Spenser, Michael Drayton and Thomas Nashe all became part of the Wilton orbit. They lauded Sidney's sister as the "Arabian Phenix, wonder of sexe," "the inheritor of his wit and genius," the miraculous reappearance of his genius in another guise, "the happie and iudiciall Patronesse of the Muses," of whose patronage, needless to say, these poets were the grateful recipients. The slightly desperate and wayward minor poet and anthologist Nicholas Breton, whose career wavered from one patron to the next, left an account of life at Wilton under Mary Pembroke that at least hints at its combination of courtliness, literariness, and piety. It was the nearest England had ever come to the gatherings of genius around Elizabetta Gonzaga, the Duchess of Urbino, celebrated in Castiglione's *The Courtier.* "Who hath redde of the Duchesse of Vrbina," Breton wrote to his patroness,

> may saie, the Italians wrote wel: but who knows the Countesse of Penbrooke, I think hath cause to write better: and if she had many followers? Haue not you mo seruants? And if they were so mindfull of their fauors? Shall we be forgetfull of our dueties? No, I am assured, that some are not ignorant of your worth, which will not be idle in your seruice.

Breton, for whom life did not always run smooth, had been "a poore Gentleman in the ruine of his fortune," but when Mary Pembroke took him in, he found Wilton to be a "little Earths kind of Paradise." It was everything of which an Elizabethan literary man might dream:

> Her house being in a maner a kind of little Court, her Lord in place of no meane commaund, her person no less then worthily and honourablie attended, as well with Gentlewomen of excellent spirits, as diuers Gentlemen of fine carriage.

Everything was as it should be, "God daily serued, religion trulie preached, a table fully furnished, a house richly garnished, honor kindly entertained, vertue highly esteemed, seruice well rewarded, and the poor blessed relieued." Despite this lavish larding of praise, Breton, for some reason or other that remains obscure, fell out of favor. Such gatherings of dependents in large and highly emotionalized households, as Wilton clearly was, will drift into argument and rivalry. There are suggestions that Breton may have been something of a drinker. His own account blamed "the faction of the malicious, the deceitful working of the enuious, and the desart of his owne unworthinesse." The fateful moment came on a winter's day when, as he described in the third person, he had decided to leave the pressurized Wilton household and go wandering on the downs:

> Taking leaue for a time, to trauaile about a little idle business, in a cold snowy day passing ouer an vnknowne plaine, not looking well to his way, or beeing ordained to the misery of such misfortune [the Calvinist note], fell so deepe down into a Saw-pitte, that he shall repent the fall while he liues.

That's all he says. Had he been drunk? Or sunk into a kind of ridiculous melancholy, not looking where he was going, bringing dishonor on the household? It was certainly the most Sidneyan of mistakes, a wandering man, out on the wide snowy plains of Wiltshire, dreaming of a better world than this. Whatever his misdemeanor, only after a few years of apology and crawling was Breton readmitted to the charmed circle.

Others, more confident in this challenging world, survived more easily. Sir Walter Raleigh's brother, the slightly sinister inventor and "chymist" Adrian Gilbert, joined the household, as did Dr. Thomas Muffet (or Moffet or Mouffet), physician and entomologist, a school friend of Edmund Spenser's, graduate of Basle, a follower of the Earl of Essex, the first man to write authoritatively about the migratory habits of English wild birds, and the editor and compiler of the first English study of insects. His heavily worked Latin manuscript is now in the British Library—one real moth that was flying around the park at Wilton in the 1590s survives squashed between its pages—decorated in the margins with Muffet's beautifully observed drawings of bees, worms, flies, beetles, butterflies, gnats, mosquitoes, the long-legged flies called "shepherds" in Wiltshire, and many, many spiders. These were later reproduced as woodcuts in the 1634 edition of his book the *Theatrum Insectorum*, or *Theatre of Insects*.

Muffet wrote a charming verse tale for his beloved countess about his passion for bugs ("I sing of little Wormes and tender Flies"), but he also turned his hand to some elaborate Latin verses in memory of Philip Sidney. They were written in 1593, on Mary Pembroke's instructions, as a homily to young Will Herbert, the thirteen-year-old heir to this huge cultural inheritance. It was the year he went up to Oxford. The weight of expectation imposed on the boy's shoulders was immense. He would carry the burden of his family's expectations. If the family was to continue to maintain its principled independence of the crown, the duty would fall to him. It is clear that Will Herbert was not entirely happy with the burden being placed on him. Again and again, Muffet tells Will that his uncle, the famous Philip Sidney, when he was a boy, preferred his books to his games. At school "his bedroom was plastered with elegant epistles of choice Latin which he had stuck up on the walls." Twice he became ill through studying too much—a habit of Mary's, too—and when he was at university and then at court, Sidney kept his passions under control. Sloth, greed, self-seeking, and sensuality: all of them this paragon avoided. He was not without lust, but he controlled it.

Muffet did admit that the young Sidney spent far too much on

"Christmas festivities and joustings, at which he was magnificently appointed, and then, with ceaseless liberality, on learned visitors." But he was both modest and regal, and rose by his seriousness as well as by "wit, grace, elegance, learning and influence." Other courtiers—more sidelong glances at Will—"chose to live in clover at home, to hunt wild animals, to follow a hawk, to wallow in every sensual pleasure." Only our hero, it seemed, gave up "love, poetry, sport, trappings, lackeys, pages and carriages inlaid with ivory" for the sake of helping a neighbor country "where without fear he ran into fire as soon as he reached the foreign shore." It doesn't take much to imagine the thirteen-year-old groaning under the propriety of the model being held out to him. Will was the "growing shoot." He was "the flower of the Sidneys." He was given, as his own *impresa*, the motto *Stat messis in herba*—the harvest is in the green stalk. He was the second Sidney, their perfect man in embryo. "Therefore," Muffet, with his eye of course more on the mother than the child, told the boy, "do you embrace and cherish him, your second self."

This sense of urgency in Mary, needing to steer her son and heir toward the otherworldly perfection of her dead brother, was driven, it seems clear, by Will's inclination to the very opposite. He was wandering toward the usual appetites of young men. Even eighty years later, Clarendon, writing his history of the Civil War, thought Will had been "immoderately given up to women." What becomes particularly intriguing, though, is that precisely this set of circumstances, and the very same set of images that Muffet relied on, would repeat themselves within three or four years at another and more significant level.

There have been many candidates for the beautiful, aristocratic, reluctant-to-marry, sexy young man addressed with such overwhelming passion in the first 126 of Shakespeare's *Sonnets*, but none fits the circumstances as closely as Will Herbert: from a family of immense standing, which was of famous beauty in both men and women; with the initials W.H., those given by the publisher's dedication of the *Sonnets* in 1609 to "The Onlie Begetter of These Insuing Sonnets"; of exactly the right age (born in April 1580) for an early middle-aged Shakespeare (born in April 1564) to fall in love with in the late 1590s; with a history behind him of his parents commissioning poets, whom they had known professionally, to urge him on to virtuous paths; seen as the "green shoot" of the family, with the next generation's harvest latent in him, imagery on which Shakespeare memorably drew; and, as it turns out, with a wild and amorous nature but a deep reluctance to marry, exactly the subject of the first seventeen sonnets.

The Pembrokes had almost certainly come to know Shakespeare in the early 1590s, when he was writing for a touring company, of no great success, subsidized by Henry and known as Pembroke's Men. Shakespeare had also written *Venus and Adonis* and *The Rape of Lucrece* for another aristocratic patron, the Earl of Southampton. It would be entirely appropriate, and even resourceful, for Mary Pembroke to turn to this brilliant, youngish court poet to address her increasingly wayward son. The first seventeen sonnets—more conventional than the rest, "sugared," as they were described at the time, in a Sidneyan way—clearly form a group. Repeatedly playing on the same themes, they urge the young man to marry, to extend his line through children, not to let age destroy his beauty but to further it in children, an extension of the gifts his famous family has given him. The imagery plays around Will's *impresa*, "Stat messis in herba." Just as the harvest lies latent in the bud, the passage of the year erodes the beauty of the spring.

> When I doe count the clock that tels the time,
> And see the braue day sunck in hidious night,
> When I behold the violet past prime,
> And sable curls or siluer'd ore with white:

When lofty trees I see barren of leaues,
Which erst from heat did canopie the herd
And Sommers greene all girded up in sheaues
Borne on the beare with white and bristly beard:
Then of thy beauty do I question make
That thou among the wastes of time must goe,
Since sweets and beauties do them-selues forsake,
And die as fast as they see others grow,
And nothing gainst Times sieth can make defence
Saue breed to braue him, when he takes thee hence.

The setting is polite Arcadia: it is courtly and contained; the herds mill around the house; the woods are shady and the fields produce their harvest. The world turns on its Virgilian axis. This is Wilton, if beautifully animated by that vision of the barley sheaves on their funeral bier, white and bristly in the paleness of high summer, and suddenly shocked by the fruitless summoning of the "wastes of time" amid all this fecundity.

It is also a celebration of the defiance of Time's scythe, the victory of marriage and progeniture over the shadow of age and death. Shakespeare's sonnet, for all its local beauties, is driven by a need to defy time because the family corporation required it. This sonnet, which, along with the other first sixteen, is patronage poetry, involving no disturbance to any social or sexual hierarchy, was perhaps delivered, it can be conjectured, to Will Herbert, perhaps at Wilton, perhaps with the indulgent overseeing of his mother and father, on April 8, 1597—there is a great deal of spring imagery in these first sonnets—which was the heir's seventeenth birthday. Shakespeare had taken up where Thomas Muffet had left off, playing a decorous role as prompter of virtue. The poems feel like what they were: a commission, a birthday present, a paid-for imploring, dedicated to the understanding that only by the complex of marriage and negotiation, of getting and begetting, can a person defeat his own mortality. That in effect is the voice of worldliness, of a good deal well done. The poems are driven by the understanding that this family could maintain its dignity and potency, its wealth and significance, only by the individuals within it submitting to the corporate ideal. If these assumptions are true, Shakespeare was co-opted for a moment as a bit player in the long Pembroke struggle to win.

Still, Will Herbert would not conform. In 1595, marriage had been proposed between the young Will and Elizabeth Carey. On September 25 of that year, the Carey parents were to visit Wilton, where "great preparacon was made for them," but they never came. Will had by then met Elizabeth, and the match was broken off "by [William's] not liking." Henry was in no position to force his son into a marriage he did not like and cancelled the engagement. Sir George Carey was enraged "that lord Pembroke broke off the match between Lord Harbert and his daughter."

Next, Bridget de Vere, the daughter of the Earl of Oxford and the granddaughter of Lord Burghley, was suggested. The families manoeuvred toward each other. Burghley sent Mary some special medicine from London, and she wrote to him in her increasingly convoluted style:

> *Yowr Lordships fine token is to mee of Infinight esteem, and no less in regard of the sender than the vertu in it selfe. It is indeed a cordiall and presious present. Not unlike to prooue a spesiall remedy of a sadd spleen, for of lyke effect do I alredy find what so euer is of likely success proceeding from the cawse whence this proseeded.*

That might have been the way to address someone fifteen or twenty years earlier, but the late Elizabethan world had moved on to a quicker and more impatient rhythm. Mary wrote another letter of almost equal inflatedness to Sir Robert Cecil, Lord Bughley's son. "To bee silent now finding so iust cawse to be thankfull were a wrong to yow and an Injury to my selfe whose disposition hath euer held yow in very worthy regard . . ." In her Wilton outpost, it looked as if Mary Pembroke, still only thirty-six, had begun to lose touch with the ways of the world. The whole Pembroke enterprise was starting to look shaky.

Burghley was also worried. His granddaughter Bridget was only thirteen, but there would be no consummation of the marriage until Will had come back from his travels. Would Bridget stay with the Pembrokes then or with her parents? The money was to be discussed by their agents, but the principles were clear. He would give a jointure equal to the dowry, plus a good allowance every year. Oxford himself was keen "for the ionge gentelman as I vnderstand he hathe been well brought vp, fayre conditioned, and hathe many good partes in hym." Again, though, the match came to nothing. Henry Pembroke, increasingly ill and short-tempered, had, it seems, insulted Robert Cecil, perhaps suggesting that the rather recent descendant of impoverished Welsh farmers, as the Cecils were, should not have the pretension to become Viscount Cranborne. The fact of the Herberts' own bastardy was by now well buried.

Mary Pembroke had to try to make good the damage and wrote to Robert Cecil in her high Elizabethan style.

> Sir I vnderstand report hath bin made vnto yow of sum speech
> that should pass my Lord (not in the best part to be taken) tuch-
> ing Cramborne. My desire is yow should be trewly satisfied
> therein, and that in regard of truth and the respect I beare yow,
> for otherwise I woold be silent. I protest unto yow the report was

most vntrue; and upon myne owne knowlidg, word, and honor,
do assure yow ther was not any word spoken at any time to which
yowr selfe bin present yow coold have taken any exception.

Yowr frend as wellwisshing as any M. Pembroke

It was no good. The wickedness of court, its life juice of malice and gossip, had broken her designs.

Lewd lies thy tongue contrives,
Lowd lies it soundeth:
Sharper then sharpest knives
with lies it woundeth.

Henry, now chronically ill, was desperate to see his elder son married before he succeeded to the earldom. If he were unmarried and under twenty-one at Henry's death, the Pembroke estates would fall into the Court of Wards (then in the hands of the Cecils), and his wardship would be sold off to the highest bidder, who would in turn suck from the Pembroke fortunes as much as he could in the few years that remained before Will turned twenty-one in 1601. Still another marriage, to a niece of Charles Howard, Earl of Nottingham, was suggested, half arranged, and then failed to materialize, in the summer of 1599.

Meanwhile, in Herbert's life, another eruptive passion broke loose. From those first seventeen sonnets, Shakespeare's sequence suddenly comes alive with the reality of his love for this beautiful and feckless young man. Shakespeare, feeling aged himself, is rendered powerless in his presence: "Some say thy fault is youth, some wantonesse," he pleaded, pitiably subject to Will's grandeur and carelessness. "How many gazers mightst thou lead away, / If thou wouldst vse the strength of all thy state? / But doe not so, I loue thee in such sort, / As thou being mine, mine is thy good report." The poetry leaves behind the formal, dancelike qualities of the Petrarchan world with all its reliance on the inaccessible girl of unimpeachable beauty, and replaces her with some of the great truth-telling, homosexual, often brutally misogynistic, willfully complex, and psychologically agonized love poems in the language. It is as if the lid had been lifted on the Elizabethan world, the formality taken away, and the reality exposed to air. The fuel for that poetry was not only love, lust, sex, and desire but also the pains that came in the wake of that desire, a longing for Arcadian peace, a place of resolution beyond the torments of daily existence, beyond all conflict, but also a recognition that time, death, and mortality had their place in Arcadia. *Et in Arcadia ego*. Far from urging the boy to a life of heightened virtue, Shakespeare fell in love with him as he was, as both the embodiment of delicious and beautiful sexual delight and the object of a love that went far beyond the worldly manoeuvrings on which the directors of the family business were intent.

Everything in the *Sonnets* drifts into the metaphors of hierarchy, land, inheritance, the law, the court, the embroiled nature of life, as if life itself, in the modernity that swept from one negotiation to the next, was at the same time the great webmaker and the great eroder. Time digs furrows in our brows. Life and time remove from us the happiness we thought we had. Even the things that seemed for a moment unapproachably ours are rubbed down and worn away. "Like as the waves make toward the pebbled shore, / So do our minutes hasten to their end."

The great and life-affirming paradox for Shakespeare is that only in the place made by the poem itself, in the actual written poem, can love and beauty remain impervious to time. Only there, in what the poet can do, can things of value be safe. Love itself can hurt, but there is a pervasive sense throughout the long sequence of the *Sonnets* that the poem, in its jewel-like existence, is itself the Arcadian space, the place in which hurt cannot occur and where perfection is removed from the erosions of weakness and time. The three words that appear more often than any other in Shakespeare's *Sonnets* are "*fair*, *kind*, and *true*." As a fugue on these themes, the sequence is a longing for goodness in a treacherous world. It is a realm in which grace has a chance, where truth can be spoken and love remain true. The poem itself is a park.

That itself is a Sidneyan idea. In the most famous paragraph of the *Defense of Poetry*, written by Sidney at Wilton, he makes precisely this Platonic claim: only in art can perfection be found, and Nature must regard the perfection of art's forms with envy:

> Nature never set forth the earth in so rich Tapestry as diverse Poets have done, neither with so pleasant rivers, fruitful trees, sweet smelling flowers, nor whatsoever else may make the too much loved earth more lovely: her world is brazen, the Poets only deliver a golden.

The poets alone can deliver a golden world. It is perhaps impossible now to read some of these poems as they might have appeared when their first manuscript copies were read by the beautiful boy of distinguished lineage to whom they were first addressed. But if they do not illuminate the life of William Herbert, which they might, they at least illuminate for sure the world in which he lived, thought, and felt.

This may be an unexpected turn for this story but it is perfectly integral to it. The Pembrokes' quarrel with authority begins in military strength; transmutes into the literary complaint of the *Arcadia*; takes a high-minded and religious turn in the hands of Mary Sidney; and in the putative love affair with Will Herbert described in Shakespeare's *Sonnets* becomes even more otherworldly, a challenge to the ordinary world not by confronting it but by removing oneself from it, looking for victory in unbridled retreat. That love affair is in many ways a teenage phenomenon. In the 1590s, even after his father's death in 1601 and right up until Elizabeth's death two years later, William Herbert, 3rd Earl of Pembroke, continued to behave badly and willfully. He quarrelled with his father and mother. He had an affair with Mary Fitton, one of the queen's maids of honor, made her pregnant, acknowledged he was the father, but refused to marry her. He was thrown into prison and then banished to Wilton, where he bewailed his rustic fate. Even by the time the queen died in March, Pembroke was still only twenty-three years old.

But he would not remain the wayward young man of the *Sonnets* for the rest of his life. As age gathered around him, as his waist thickened and time dug furrows in his brow, his careless, self-indulgent youth would come to seem like an interlude in the long story. In the heart of early-seventeenth-century England, and right up until 1630, when he died, Will Herbert would become one of the most admired men at court, the champion of everything his family had believed in and an upholder of the idea that dignity and significance did not in the end come only from the crown.

TWO INCOMPARABLE BRETHREN

THE CAREERS OF WILLIAM, EARL OF PEMBROKE, AND
PHILIP, EARL OF MONTGOMERY
1601–1630

Along with hundreds of other peers and gentlemen, both William Pembroke and his younger brother Philip Herbert hurried to meet the new Scottish king as he made his way south through springtime England in May 1603. Philip was four years younger than his brother and as they settled into adulthood, each began to play the complementary pair to the other. William was the older and the richer, the more established, increasingly the more political. He championed anti-Spanish and anti-Catholic policies, as Sidney had done. He was driven by a growing awareness of his inheritance as the heir to the Sidneyan tradition, which looked back to more glorious days under Elizabeth. Then, they told themselves, the great men of England had stood for a heroic Protestant clarity against the Spanish, and for ancient communal practices of hospitality, for the custom of the country, the law of the land, and the Ancient Constitution, in a way that the modern world of James's court, disturbingly attracted to a foreign absolutism, seemed to be leaving behind. William was a poet, if not a very good one, and, like his mother, the patron of an enormous range of writers, fostering the literary heirs of Sidney and Spenser. The inherited idea of another more perfect country was allied in both sons to a growing interest in the English colonies of the New World as a place where a vision of Arcadian perfection could perhaps be made real. Both Herbert brothers were among the most substantial investors in the Virginia Company.

Philip was the more glamorous, lighter on his feet, dedicated to the delight and charm of the king and his court, a passionate huntsman and gambler, needing to make his way in the world, hungrier than his brother, no litterateur, but agile and beautiful, and a champion in the tiltyard, at the staged fights known as "the barriers," and in the elegantly performed allegorical dances of the masque.

In these two, known at the time as the "incomparable brethren," the quarrel with the king takes its subtlest and most subterranean form. Both brothers, for their entire adult lives, were inhabitants of the court. Both received offices and riches at the hands of both James and Charles I. Both became deeply integrated with the workings of the court. But for all that, first in William and then, only later, in Philip, a clear sense of distance opened up between them and the roots of royal power. They were at court but not of the court; they were favorites but only for a while. They behaved gracefully as courtiers should, but not humiliatingly. They could not be part of the grossly self-indulgent culture that began to develop around them.

The Herberts were a complex amalgam. No family was so identified with life at Whitehall, its entertainments and extravagances, its glory and honor; and no family carried in its sense of itself so powerful an inheritance of noble, aestheticized, principled independence from the crown. The two tendencies were folded in with each other, in their own family history, in their political and social assumptions, in their pride in themselves as great magnates in Wales and Wiltshire, and in their recognition that the crown, like it or not, was the source of virtually all modern wealth. They were, like the grandees in Shakespeare's *As You Like It*, lords dressed as foresters, Arcadianists of the real world, the incomparable brethren, the Earls of Paradise. These two currents in their lives ran at full bore for thirty years. To understand their Arcadianism, one must first understand the courtly world in which they lived, moved, and at times seemed utterly absorbed.

Philip Herbert's place as the second son seems to have liberated him from the burden of melancholy that affected his brother. When he first came to court, he charmed and shone, and when James arrived in England, the royal eyes alighted on him. As Edward Hyde, Earl of Clarendon, the Pembrokes' Wiltshire neighbor and later the historian of the Civil War, would recall, the beautiful young Philip Herbert had made an early impact, in a court suddenly liberated from the formalized antiquity of its predecessor:

> Being a young man, scarce of age at the entrance of King James, he had the good fortune by the comeliness of his person, his skill and indefatigable industry in hunting, to be the first who drew the king's eyes towards him with affection; which was quickly so far improved that he had the reputation of a favourite.
>
> He pretended to no other qualifications, than to understand horses and dogs very well, which his master loved him the better for (being, at his first coming into England, very jealous of those who had the reputation of great parts), and to be believed honest and generous, which made him many friends and left him then no enemy.

Philip may have been the more robust, less troubled, and less complex of the two brothers, but there is no sense of William, Earl of Pembroke, living in his shadow. James made William a Knight of the Garter as soon as he arrived in London. Pembroke had been in disgrace during the last years of Elizabeth, for the pregnancy of Mary Fitton. That shame was now lifted and there is no doubt of a real warmth and intimacy with the king. At the coronation in August 1604, delayed because of the Plague the year before, the Venetian secretary in England, Giovanni Scaramelli, after watching each of the earls kneel before the newly crowned king, had seen "il Conte di Pemruch, giovane gratioso," a handsome youth

> who is always with the King, and always joking with him, actually kiss his Majesty's face, whereupon the King laughed and gave him a little cuff.

That moment provides a sudden bridge between William Herbert, earl of Pembroke, the serious man of court and state business, and the "Mr W.H." who would not marry and who drove his poet to distraction.

William was already vastly rich from his Pembroke inheritance, but Philip had to play the favorite to gain his fortune. In the summer of 1603, James made him a Knight of the Bath (which meant what it said: each candidate was given a purifying bath the evening he was knighted), and in Whitehall, on December 27, 1604, he was married to a girl he had fallen in love with, Susan de Vere, daughter of the Earl of Oxford and sister of the Bridget de Vere William had turned down in the 1590s. Susan was beautiful and entrancing.

The king loved nothing more than the wedding of one of his chosen young men. A riotous party followed, at which "many great ladies were made shorter by the skirts," whatever that might have meant. Silver and gold plate worth £2,000 was given to the newlyweds. The king gave them £10,000 worth of land at Shurland in Sheppey, in Kent. The party rolled on deep into the night. Finally, Philip and Susan were put to bed in the Council Chamber, where "there was sewing into the sheet, casting of the bride's left hose, and twenty other petty sorceries." First thing the next morning, "the King gave them a *reveille matin* in his shirt and nightgown, and spent a good hour with them in the bed, or upon, choose which you will believe best." The distance that Elizabeth had maintained from her court, her virginal horror at the marriage of any man or woman close to her, had disappeared with this regent. The king was now cuddling in public and in bed his favorite and his favorite's bride.

A river of money now came both the Herberts' way. William Pembroke was made Warden of the Stannaries in Cornwall, Steward of the Duchy of Cornwall, and Lord Lieutenant of the County of Cornwall, every one of those appointments bringing patronage and payments in its train. Philip was given a half share in a license to export thirty thousand undressed cloths duty-free every year. In 1605, the doting king made him Earl of Montgomery, the title named after a castle and county in the Herbert heartland in Wales.

William Pembroke had inherited the great estates garnered by his grandfather and had also married a hideous Talbot heiress with enormous riches, having, according to Clarendon, "paid much too dear for his wife's fortune by taking her person into the bargain." It was Philip, the happy beneficiary of a love match, who was in need of financial support. To the horror of royal Treasury officials, the king granted him revenue from the crown in the amount of £2,000 a year for sixty years, plus a pourboire of "200l. a year as our free gift." This was favoritism in action, a draining away of crown assets into the pockets of the minions who would so radically threaten the well-being of the crown in the years to come.

The king paid off £44,000 in debts incurred by the Earl of Montgomery and two other favorites, and asked Montgomery to collect £20,000 due to the crown from lands that had been confiscated from Roman Catholics, on which he was given a 50 percent commission. In the summer of 1612 a Roman Catholic, Sir Henry James, refused to swear the oath of allegiance to the king because it conflicted with his attachment to the Roman Church. Without a flicker, the Earl of Montgomery "begged Sir Henry's goods and lands, worth 1,600l or 1,700l per an," and received them. The mechanism was different from the way in which the 1st Earl of Pembroke had collected his estate, but the effect was the same: a redistribution of money and power into the hands of those who got themselves close to the body of the king.

Nor was William Pembroke immune to such gold digging. In 1618, his mother-in-law, the ancient, widowed Countess of Shrewsbury, was said to be "almost out of her mind, with a dread of being poisoned." No thought was given to the old woman's mental health. More important was that Pembroke and her other powerful son-in-law, the Earl of Arundel, "beg the protection of her estate"—meaning the control of her lands and money—"and will enjoy the fruits of it if she do not mind," which in the seventeenth century meant "if she does not notice." A third, less important son-in-law, Lord Ruthin, and his wife, Elizabeth Talbot, were cut out of the arrangement. It does not look, at this stage, as if either Herbert—William or Philip—was maintaining much independence from the crown.

No portrait survives of William, the third earl, as a young man, as he was when Shakespeare fell in love with him, but there is a portrait of his brother, with the same reddish-brown hair, the same "pritty sharpe-oval face" they inherited from the Sidneys, painted soon after Philip had become a Knight of the Garter, on April 23, St. George's Day, 1608. In the painting, probably by William Larkin, Philip wears the badges of his recent elevation: the pearl-embroidered garter below his left knee, matched by the wide satin sash under the other. He wears the garter collar around his shoulders, and hanging from it, the enamelled jewel of St. George wielding a sword studded with diamonds, the green dragon crouching at his feet. Philip's own sword swings from a hanger around his waist; his cuffs and ruff are of lace, halfway between the Elizabethan cartwheel and the loose lace collars of the cavaliers;

and a beautiful coral bracelet encircles his left wrist. His hand drops carelessly from the pommel of the sword behind him; the other hand is at his hip, holding a hat emblazoned with a cloud of ostrich feathers.

The broad scarlet ribband and the scarlet velvet mantle of the Order of the Bath are laid over his doublet and hose of a satin that has been embroidered with silver thread in damascene stripes. Lace pom-poms decorate his high-heeled shoes, his hair is loose and unaffected, his chestnut reddish beard light, his lips feminine, his eyes intent and watching. There is no depth or complexity in his expression. There is even a kind of naïveté in his face, as there is in this portrayal of worldly glory. This is the sort of materialist, enriched, pleasure-loving, world-enjoying figure against whom the Puritans railed. He is the Jacobean court. Everything here is new, so new in fact that the creases are still visible in the velvet and on the satin lining of the outer mantle. He is a bride dressed for a wedding, but what he has married here is no husband, but status, the Garter, riches, glory, himself.

This is perhaps the greatest portrait painted in Jacobean England, and its beauty consists, at least in part, in its heightened worldliness, its frank enjoyment of the gifts the world has to offer. It is, perhaps, a portrait of luck. This is no ancient noble. His brother, not he, has inherited the ancient Pembroke title and the vast spread of lands in Wiltshire and Wales. But James has made Philip a peer, too, simply because James loved the verve with which Philip went about his hunting and gambling, his life. It is a portrait of success.

By the time William, the elder brother, first appears in a Daniel Mytens portrait of about 1616, he has left behind his wayward and passionate youth. He has become the noble politician, the patriot, the man who was maintaining the meaning of old England against the corruptions of court favorites. In the political and aesthetic ecology of the time, William, in his recessive patience, occupies the opposite niche to his brother's wonderful flamboyant display. In young Philip, at the peak of his courtly success, one sees the Jacobean courtier like a peony in full bloom. He has done well by courting the sovereign. He can make no claim to independent power because he is the sovereign's creature. Without James, he would have been merely Mr. Philip Herbert, not this jewelled, pearl-decked, coral-braceleted, and gartered hero.

Against Philip's verve and risk taking, William acted the judicious statesman. A famous incident occurred at court on September 17, 1608. William had been playing cards with Sir George Wharton, a wild young courtier, who was to die the following year in Islington at a duel with a young Scot, who was also killed. On this occasion, Sir George, presumably losing at cards, also lost his temper, at which Pembroke told him,

> Sir George, I have loved you long and still desire to do so, but by your manner in playing, you lay it upon me either to leave [cease] to love you, or to leave to play with you. Wherefore, choosing to love you still, I will never play with you more.

That is the voice of this tradition, looking back to Sidneyan sweetness of temper, a balanced composure, and an opting for long-term love over passing diversion. Wharton did his best to maintain the argument, but Pembroke refused to be riled and tried to make peace. But Wharton was uncontrollable. Out hunting with the king in Surrey the next day,

> Sir George spurred his horse with all speed upon [Pembroke], which was observed by the earl of Montgomery who cried out, "Brother, you will be stricken." The earl thereupon received Sir George with a sound backward blow over the face which drove him almost back upon his horse's croop. But company being present, they galloped

again till in the end the stag died in Bagshot town, where Sir George comes up to the Earl offering him a paper, protesting there was nothing in it unfit for his lordship to read. The earl said, "Sir George, give me no papers here where all they may see us who know what hath passed; but tell me, is not the purport of it to challenge me."

"Yes," said Sir George.

"Well," said the earl, "this night you shall have answer."

His answer was to send Wharton his sword by a messenger and ask him "to take the measure of the Sword, for the earl would not take one hair's breadth of advantage at his hands." They were to meet, alone, the following morning. William Pembroke's life might have ended there, but the king had heard of the argument and by his command no duel was fought.

Status anxiety, a man's honor endlessly under negotiation, a rivalry between Scots and English, a tense world in which tennis games, the hunting field, the racecourse, gambling, women, your relationship to the king, the chair one was given at dinner—all provided arenas in which offense might be taken and violence done. The king's habit of showering honors on his favorites and selling titles to the rich, whatever their background, served only to exacerbate the sense among the old aristocracy that the bonds of society, the old certainties were under threat. A frenzy of dueling and gambling overtook the court, as though honor and luck had constantly to be demonstrated. Courtiers would bet on which of their footmen could run fastest from St. Albans to London, on whether the king of Spain would turn Protestant (long odds there), and of course on horses, cocks, and dogs. At every stage, offense waited in the wings. Of the two brothers, Philip, in the less established and more vulnerable position, was more likely to turn to violence. Even though he had a lifelong habit, which would finally erupt in a fateful contretemps on the eve of civil war, of hitting his fellow courtiers, he had no greater reputation for violence than any other. The culture had turned febrile.

William Pembroke was rich enough and secure enough not to need to engage in this posturing. The illegitimacy in his ancestry had long been forgotten. Without any effort, he could act the easy dignified noble of ancient lineage and vast wealth, independent of the sometimes desperate market in favors and standing at court. He was known in particular for his generosity. When the Lieutenant of the Tower, Sir Gervas Elways (or Elwes), was hanged for his part in the famous murder of Sir Thomas Overbury, the Elwes estate, worth more than £1,000 a year, came to Pembroke. But without hesitation, William gave it away to Elwes's widow and children. Ben Jonson described how his "noblesse keeps one stature still, / And one true posture, though besieged with ill." That dignified, unshowy self-possession is how Mytens painted William, and it is exactly the tone of Clarendon's later portrayal:

> As he spent and lived upon his own fortune, so he stood upon his own two feet, without any other support than of his proper virtue and merit; and lived toward the favourites with that decency, as would not suffer them to censure his master's judgement and election, but as with men of his own rank. He was exceedingly beloved by the court, because he never desired to get that for himself which others laboured for; but was still ready to promote the pretences of worthy men; and he was equally celebrated in the country for having received no obligations from the court, which might corrupt and sway his affection and judgement.

In that way, the two incomparable brethren were aligned on either side of the great cultural fault line of the age: William, the earl, standing on his own dignity and ancient wealth, loved in the country, able to look the succession of favorites in the eye without fear or favor, a hero for passionate Protestants and intellectuals, a man of words; Philip, of no great intellectual dignity, delightful where his brother could be "accounted melancholy," fascinated by the visual and physical aspects of culture, a creature of the very court culture of which William remained at least in part skeptical and removed.

For both William, Earl of Pembroke, and Philip, Earl of Montgomery, the tournaments or barriers that were held at court, and the dazzlingly expensive masques that were part of the same culture of courtly theatricality, were some of the principal stages on which this complex of attitudes could be displayed. In the usual interfolding of inheritances, much of Jacobean court culture derived from the Sidneyan court-critical world. The *Arcadia* itself is full of the fantasia of Elizabethan medievalism, knights in armor that was "blew, like the heauen," shields showing "a greyhound, which ouerrunning his fellow, and taking the hare, yet hurts it not when it takes it." Others were "armed in a white armour, which was al guilded ouer with knots of womans haire, which came downe from the crest of his head-peece, & spred it selfe in rich quantitie ouer all his armour"; some "all in greene, both armour and furniture, it seemed a pleasant garden, wherein grew orange trees; which with their golden fruites, cunningly beaten in, and embrodered, greatly enriched the eye-pleasing colour of greene." On his shield, the green knight had "a sheep, feeding in a pleasant field, with this word, *Without feare, or enuie.* And therefore was called the Knight of the sheep." His opponent "was all in milke white, his attiring els, all cutte in stares." Even now one can sense the shudder of romance that these images of a purified, distant, idealized, meaning-drenched world sent through the Elizabethan and Jacobean imagination.

As descendants and carriers of that tradition, the Herbert brothers appeared in tournament after tournament and masque after masque. It was a world that was from the beginning deeply connected to the imagery of Arcadian and rural retreat. *The Masque of Blackness*, in 1605, in which Susan de Vere and Pembroke's cousin (and mistress) Lady Mary Wroth both danced, opened with a curtain showing a hunt making its way through the woods. In that masque, as in the many that followed over the next thirty-five years, the pattern unfolded of disorder turning to order, or sometimes of order falling into disorder followed by an even more cosmic level of order. This was the story with which for decades the court, at quite enormous expense, consoled itself. Everything would be all right in the end. There was a higher and a better reality, removed from the grubbiness of the everyday, and none were better qualified to embody it than these dancing nobles. Nobility was fineness, and they were the vehicles for it. It could take any number of forms—medieval or classical, martial or pastoral, exotic or ancient—but the story was always the same: the lives they were leading, and the people they were, held within them the possibility of distinction.

So high were these ideals—the masques were not exactly stories, but glittering enactments of the nobility latent in this world—that money was irrelevant. In the wedding masque called *Hymenaei*, staged on January 5, 1606, in which both Susan, Countess of Montgomery, and Philip, Earl of Montgomery, danced their parts as masquers, one John Pory, a poor Greek scholar, looked on in amazement:

> The men were clad in Crimzon, and the women in white. They had every one a white plume of the richest herons feathers, and were so rich in jewels upon their heads as was most glorious. I think they hired and borrowed all the principal jewels and ropes of perle both in court or citty.

As citizens of Arcadia, they had their hair "carelessly (but yet with more art than if more affected) bound under the circle of a rare and rich coronet." Naturalness was virtue. The sequins and silver thread sewn into their costumes glittered under the massed candlelight. The metal-thread lace—silver for the great, copper for the lesser masquers—chevronned all over the costumes, caught the highlights from the candelabra. All this combined with the glamour and exoticism of Inigo Jones's Italian-derived costumes to amaze the court audience among whom the masquers, at the climax of the performance, would descend to dance, blurring and even erasing any boundary between the imagined, perfect world of the masque and the world of the court itself.

Alongside the masquing came the tournaments, twenty-seven of them staged at court between 1604 and the moment when the tradition came to an end in 1622. Philip Montgomery was often the star. On June 1, 1606, four Knights Errant of the Fortunate Islands (the king's cousin the Duke of Lennox and the earls of Southampton, Pembroke, and Montgomery) issued a universal challenge: "To all honourable Men at Arms, Knights Adventurers of hereditary note and exemplary nobleness, that for most maintainable actions do wield either sword or lances in the quest of glory." They had "four indisputable propositions" to defend:

1. That in the service of Ladies no knight have free will.
2. That it is Beauty maintains the world in Valour.
3. That no fair Lady was ever false.
4. That none can be perfectly wise but Lovers.

It was pure Philip Sidney, even if denuded of its political burden. At the barriers staged for the knighting of the young Protestant Henry, Prince of Wales, on Twelfth Night 1610, Philip Montgomery won the prize. The show began against a Jonesian backdrop in which medieval

and classical architectural elements were jumbled together, portraying "the fallen House of Chivalry" where Chivalry was "Possessed
with sleep, dead as a lethargy." Inevitably, the antics of Philip and
the other youngbloods of the court restored it to full life. No expense
was spared. The skills of trumpeters, silk merchants, painters of the
shields, chariot makers, bit makers, and cutlers were employed to
work the silver velvet into caparisons for the horses; to make dresses
for pages and grooms; to devise subclassical, mannerist designs for the
helmets descended from Cellini, with cumulus clouds of ostrich feathers above them; to build tents like caves or castles; to prepare lamp
bearers dressed as centurions; and even at one point to introduce an
elephant covered in its own jewelled cloth and castle, which trundled
around the tiltyard too slowly for any sense of drama to survive.

The masques were, for all their materiality, an escaping of the material world. There was a bewitching fluency in Jones's designs, a sense
for the first time in English draughtsmanship that the dross of existence was being left behind. These entertainments were not dramas,
just as the almost obsessively repeated hunting expeditions were not
acting out anything except reality. As the hunt was theatrical but not
fictional, and as the park was a kind of dreamland but one that could
be owned, the masque was a theater of the real, a making visible of the
highest of ideals.

But this community of honor was not mere playacting. It had its
political dimension. Even in the first decade of James's reign, a political and cultural grouping began to form around the Pembrokes, and
the Sidneys, that was opposed to the cynical, passionless, unidealis-
tic managerialism of the Cecils. This informal opposition cherished,
if perhaps underground, a resistance to autocracy and a belief in the
possibilities of an Arcadian ideal. It was deeply retrospective. In the
early years of James's reign, after his brief honeymoon was over, there
was a feeling that the great moment of Englishness had gone. Sidney

was dead; Leicester and Essex, his heirs, were both dead; Elizabeth was dead; and who had they all been succeeded by but simpering minions and a Scots king, "the cold northern breath," as the poet Michael Drayton, a Pembroke client, described him. For Drayton, only among people like Samuel Daniel and Sir William Alexander—both also Pembroke clients—was there any continuity, any hope for the virtue of England. There you could find "men from base enuy and detraction free / of vpright harts and humble spirits." The freewheeling materialism of Jacobean England, the vivid corruption of the court, the opening of the royal shopping center, Britain's Bourse, on the Strand, drove these cultural conservatives into an embattled place where purity was longed for. Much of the hope focused on the young Henry, Prince of Wales, who promised to be a martial champion of English virtue, unlike his soft, peace-obsessed, degenerate, boyfriend-dabbling father.

Pembroke might have become the natural leader of this party, but at least as a young man in his twenties he did not have the drive. "For his person he was not effectual," Francis Bacon said of him, and his political programme suffered from drift. Others claimed the center of royal attention and policy. None was more successful than a young Frenchified Scots page called Robert Carr, who managed to break his leg at a tilt in front of a solicitous King James, who nursed him to health and taught him Latin while lying on his sickbed. Carr soon climbed on to the escalator of Jacobean favor: a knighthood, the viscountcy of Rochester, the earldom of Somerset, manors, lands, and the scattering of golden pennies that in the words of Thomas Dekker, the great satirist of the age, made "spangle babies of them all." Finally, in July 1614, the king made Robert Carr, Lord Chamberlain, the man in charge of the royal household, the hinge between royal favor and royal favorites, "because he would bestow a place so near himself on the friend whom he loved above all men living."

The rise of the Robert Carr, Earl of Somerset, was a defeat not only for Herbert interests—Montgomery was at the same time quietly eased out of the glow of royal kindness—but for the Protestant interest as a whole. Carr was closer to the pro-Catholic, pro-Spanish interest at court. The fortunes of the Sidney-Herbert party were at low ebb. But Robert Carr, Viscount Rochester, Earl of Somerset, was to experience a fall as rapid as his rise. He arranged with the king for Frances Howard, Countess of Essex, part of the fiercely pro-Spanish Howard family, with whom he had fallen in love, to be granted a divorce from her husband, the Earl of Essex, on the publicly humiliating grounds that the poor earl could not get an erection when in bed with her. The trial was fixed, the Earl of Essex exposed to ridicule, and the divorce granted. Carr then married Frances himself. At their wedding she appeared with "her hair long over her shoulders in brazen token of her virginity."

At the very center of national life, this kind of scandal did lasting damage to the prestige of the crown and court. It was everything Arcadia—not to speak of the enormous puritan constituency and the knights of the shires—most deeply despised. The divorce and remarriage was scandal enough, but the two Carrs then plotted the murder of Sir Thomas Overbury, who had been a close friend of Robert's but who had advised him not to marry Frances Howard. Overbury was a reproach and an annoyance, and James sent a reluctant William Pembroke to persuade him to go abroad as an ambassador. Overbury refused and instead was sent to the Tower. There, Frances Howard arranged with the lieutenant of the Tower, Sir Gervas Elwes, to send Overbury poisoned tarts and jellies. He ate them and died an agonizing death. Philip Montgomery, who had been accused a few years earlier of trying to seduce Frances Howard himself, was sent to her by James and she confessed all to him. Or so it is said: no written version of the confession was ever produced. Both Carr and his wife were sentenced to death, but were pardoned by James and lived the rest of their lives in ruin, first in the Tower and later in the country, uncommunicating, in separate wings of the same Northamptonshire house.

In recognition of the moral crisis at the court, Pembroke, unstained by this scandal, was in December 1615 made Lord Chamberlain in Somerset's place. Ben Jonson dedicated his book of *Epigrams* to Pembroke, as "THE GREAT EXAMPLE OF HONOUR AND VIRTUE" in a court that was as degenerate as the Roman court on which Martial's Latin epigrams, Jonson's model, had poured their "wormwood and sulphur." Among Jonson's barbs was Epigram XV, "On a Court-Worm":

> *"All men are worms": but this no man. In silk*
> *'Twas brought to court first wrapped, and white as milk;*
> *Where, afterwards, it grew a butterfly:*
> *Which was a caterpillar. So 'twill die.*

The collapse of Carr's gilded wings was the moment for Pembroke to enter what he might have considered his inheritance. He had already hatched a plot to insert a pliant and amenable favorite in the king's heart as a way of exerting even greater control over the fount of all patronage. A "great but private entertainment at supper" had been held the year before at the Pembroke house of Baynard's Castle, in London, attended by several Herberts and their friends and allies, including the brutally severe Archbishop of Canterbury, George Abbott. As their candidate for royal love, the Pembroke dinner party had settled on an impoverished but exceptionally beautiful twenty-two-year-old Northamptonshire man, who had traveled in Italy and was cultured charm itself, a master of the dance and the hunting field: George Villiers. In August 1614, he was a guest, not by chance, at a house party in Northamptonshire where the king's eye fell on him. By April 1615,

Villiers had arrived: he was appointed Gentleman of the Bedchamber, knighted by James, and given an annual pension of £1,000. By August, the plan had succeeded beyond all possible dreams: Villiers and the king slept in the same bed at Farnham Castle, then in Hampshire, where the king was on his annual summer journey through the shires. This, in itself, did not necessarily mean that their relationship was sexual, but Buckingham's later description—of "the time which I shall never forget at Farnham, where the bed's head could not be found between the master and his dog"—can leave little doubt.

The prizes for Villiers came rolling in: the Order of the Garter, a barony and a viscountcy, an earldom, a marquisate, and eventually a dukedom—all of Buckingham—a title that, it was suggested at the time, even by the king, carried some sexual implication. Lands, manors, and appointments all followed, not only for Villiers but for almost everyone he knew. His mother became Countess of Buckingham; his lunatic elder brother, John, Viscount Purbeck; his younger brother, Christopher, earl of Anglesey; his brother-in-law Earl of Denbigh; and his half brother, Edward, a knight and the vastly profitable position of Comptroller of the Court of Wards. "He loved Buckingham," James told his Privy Council, gravely sitting around their table in Whitehall, with Buckingham himself on his chair among them, "more than any other man." James liked to call his favorite Steenie, short for Stephen, as it was said of St. Stephen in the Acts of the Apostles that "all that sat in the council, looking stedfastly on him, saw his face as it had been the face of an angel." This love was only appropriate for a king, James insisted. "Jesus Christ had done the same as he was doing . . . for Christ had his John and he had his George."

The Herberts were left in the wake of this Villiers coup. Philip Montgomery kept up a friendship with Villiers, based on their joint enjoyment of courtly pleasures. They danced together in the masques (performing in January 1617 to an audience that included Pocahontas, the Indian queen) and hunted with the king. In 1618, Buckingham became godfather to Montgomery's son. But a growing distance developed between Pembroke and Buckingham.

Although part of a single court, they represented two sides of the great cultural divide opening up in early-seventeenth-century England: the old aristocracy against the new; a Protestant inheritance against Spanish-loving modernity; propriety against glamour; integrity against corruption; chivalric medievalism against self-promoting, money-gathering absolutism. To some extent, Buckingham simply made Pembroke look old-fashioned. Pembroke's attachment to his tradition, to the Elizabethan-revivalist "patriot party," as it was called, the party in effect of the country, which saw England not as a crown and a people but as a patchwork of manorial estates, with a deep suspicion of courts and their favorites—all of that seemed out of date in the context of Buckingham's high-glamour, internationalist, ineffably charming appeal. For Buckingham, the old aristocracy, with its fantasies of goodness rooted in the old social structures, was an irrelevance. But to that ancient aristocracy, of which Pembroke was the leader, Villiers himself, the archangel of beauty and power, the smooth facilitator in the market for titles, monopolies, and office, was the embodiment of wickedness. Philip Montgomery hung uncertainly between the two of them.

The coming of Villiers polarized the Arcadian inheritance. Around Pembroke clustered a group of writers, poets, and playwrights who maintained a steady and constant stream of nostalgic, Arcadian, anti-court literature, dreaming of a better time when England was whole. In those fantasies, lords were always kind to their people, and friendship, unlike the bitter rivalries of court, described the relationship between men. "Friendship on earth we may as easily find," Sir Benjamin Rudyerd, a Pembroke client, wrote,

As he the North-East passage, that is blind.
Sophisticate affection is the best
This age affords, no friend abides the test.
They make a glorious shew, a little space
But tarnish in the rain like copper lace.
So by degrees, when we embrace so many,
We courted are like whores, not lov'd of any.

The world was in decline, and only in Arcadia, the place not of cheap copper but of real silver, not of show but of truth, not of whoring but of love, did any virtue remain. Eclogues, pastorals, and Arcadias poured from the pens of these poets. *The Shepheards Pipe*, *The Faithful Shepherdess*, the *Queen's Arcadia*, *The Shepherds Hunting*, the *Shepheards Sirena*: one after another they emerged to imply or state the wickedness of modernity. English pastoral Protestant comedy, Italianate pastoral tragicomedy, ancient British pastoral tragedy, Italianate English romantic pastoral comedy, Virgilian Georgian civic pastoral romance, native pastoral satire—Arcadianism surged out of England in response to the modern wickedness of the courts.

William Browne, in residence at Wilton and the author in 1616 of *Britannia's Pastorals*, wrote bitterly and angrily of the differences between the reality of Buckingham's Britain and the dream of pastoral. There had been enclosure riots, poverty, famine. The lords, for their own pleasure, were destroying the ancient landscape of custom. Copyholders who had been in their houses and lands for years were being dispossessed.

The country gentleman, from's neighbours hand
Forceth the'inheritance, ioynes land to land,
And (most insatiate) seekes vnder his rent
To bring the world's most spacious continent

This was in a poem dedicated, with permission, to William Herbert, Earl of Pembroke. The upstart alien Stuarts were irrelevant compared with the profoundly British Welshness of Browne's patron:

> *Cambria is a land from whence have come*
> *Worthies well worth race of Ilium.*

Next to that rooted heroism, the court, which should have been the source of such life and goodness, was nothing but a sink of iniquity and the home of sterility and desolation.

> *What wreck of Noblesse, and what rape of honor,*
> *Hath laboring Tyme brought forth (to humane dearth)*
> *Whose Womb, a Tomb; whose Byrth a liveles Earth.*
> *What Howse, or rather hospitable Court*
> *(Erewhile a Receptable for resort*
> *Of all Estate) is that which seemes so vast*
> *With desolation, emptiness, and wast?*

In the mind of this school of poets gathered around the Pembroke interest, England was a wasteland of wrongness, and to that wrongness one name could be attached: Buckingham.

The tensions between Pembroke and Buckingham were those that would break into civil war in the 1640s. Was the crown to show respect for the ancient habits and practices of England, for its deep structure of manors and lords, whose relationship was one of head and limbs, equivalent to the relationship of king and Parliament? Or was it to abandon that organic structure and set up instead an effective, authoritarian government, much as was happening all over Europe, which treated the country as a whole as landlord would be treating a manor if he abandoned the copyhold system and turned it all over to leases and commercial rents? Was the crown to consult the nobility and gentry in Parliament? Or was it to ignore them? Was it to collude with the wicked Catholics of southern Europe? Or help the beleaguered Protestants, England's natural allies, of the north?

Pembroke's relationship with Buckingham for many years drifted toward a crisis. It was not merely a matter of two court grandees manoeuvring for advantage. They had squabbled over the appointment of minor functionaries at court, with Pembroke asserting his right as Lord Chamberlain, and Buckingham using his influence as the king's favorite. But large-scale ideological differences came between them, too. Buckingham had no inheritance; he was the ultimate creature of the court and of the moment; the glamour of Spanish prestige, sophistication, and style attracted him; his interest was in monopolizing and extending royal power in England. Pembroke was his opposite: acutely aware of his place at the head of a powerful, half-nostalgic, half-subversive movement in England that needed to protect the "pattern of manors" against the depredations of a hungry court and state. His task was to defend that world against greed and corruption. He was the heir to the Sidney inheritance: the independence of a self-respecting nobility; the location of that nobility's meaning and source of significance in the land over which it held sway; the sense that in that connection there was an authenticity and value that the world of the court would erode; fixedly Protestant and anti-Spanish, always looking for the ways in which the royal administration was either drifting toward Rome and Catholicism or simply failing to defend the Protestant interest in Europe; highly literate and with a high-minded view of its destiny; a patriotic position that could contemplate the possibility of civil war. There was nothing contradictory in its close service to the crown over several generations and the possibility that one day, if the crown failed to uphold the custom of the manor, the way in which England had always regulated itself as a form of balance, it might desert the crown in favor of the health of the country.

Pembroke had long cultivated a position in Parliament, which he could use to fight his battles at court. At least twenty MPs, and on occasion half as many again, including Benjamin Rudyerd and the young Edward Hyde, later to be Earl of Clarendon, depended on his patronage and could be expected to speak out in favor of this agenda. He also controlled the proxy votes of several peers. On one occasion, under the great new Palladian coffered ceiling of Inigo Jones's redesigned chamber for the House of Lords, Pembroke was reported by the letter writer John Chamberlain as having cast four votes on one side of a question and four on the other, an act of supreme, patriotic balance. Unfortunately, this marvellous story cannot be true because Pembroke only ever controlled five proxies in the House of Lords, but it is a signal of the role he played in England's political imagination in the 1620s: a man of power because he was a man of balance.

Pembroke's program always insisted on unity, on making the king responsive to Parliament and vice versa. The well-being of the body required the head and limbs to be in active equilibrium. The surging ambition and power control of the Duke of Buckingham was like a hectic in the blood. Unfortunately, the power struggle on the mainland of Europe between the Catholic Habsburg empire and the new Protestant states could not provide an environment of calm and ease. Throughout the 1620s, English domestic politics were riven by the insolubly difficult questions of alliance and aggression within that shifting European political-military-religious storm.

In the 1620s English foreign policy became embroiled in marriage proposals first with Spain and then with France; in war first with Spain and then with France. All four of those policies were more or less catastrophically handled. The prestige and financial position of the crown and of Buckingham in particular crashed under the impact of expensive failure and national humiliation. This was not how it had been in the great days of Elizabeth, when England, the Protestant hero country, had defeated the great Spanish Armada.

Pembroke played around the edges of these disasters, never dictating policy but working consistently to maintain a position that was anti-Spanish, anti-Catholic, and anti-Buckingham. His freedom of manoeuvre was severely restricted by the deep affection that both James I and, in his turn, Charles I had for a man who, uniquely in English history, became a favorite of two kings in succession. If Pembroke was to maintain his own position at court, he could not attack Buckingham openly. When a Privy Council vote was taken in the summer of 1623 to approve Charles's proposed marriage to a Spanish princess, Pembroke was unaccountably ill with kidney stones in Wilton. His brother Montgomery stood in for him. But Pembroke had not been that ill. Three weeks later, the king was down at Wilton for some hunting.

When James died in March 1625, Buckingham was so distraught that he took to his bed. The new young king took Montgomery and Pembroke along with him to Buckingham's sickbed, and the four of them spent three hours talking together. But the underlying differences among them were too powerful for such palliatives to work. Pembroke told the Venetian ambassador, who had begged him to be reconciled to Buckingham for the sake of European Protestantism, that internal enemies must be dealt with before external ones and that the cause they both had at heart would be better served without Buckingham than with him.

Buckingham was the enemy within, and by the spring of 1626, Pembroke was ready to attack the favorite. Through his network of patronage spread across the whole of the West Country, Pembroke, in alliance with the fiercely Calvinist George Abbott, Archbishop of Canterbury, had assembled his team of MPs. As Parliament gathered that year, the Pembroke party had Buckingham in its sights. A disastrous attack on Cadiz, of which Buckingham had been in charge as the Lord Admiral, a recent revelation of his sympathy for Roman Catholics in his own family and beyond, a growing disgust at his self-enrichment and his singular intimacy with the late king—all were weapons in Pembroke's hands. His squad of MPs were not slow to attack. "Affairs are not guided by the public counsel," it was said in Parliament. "Was it good for the state that all things should be guided by the Duke's single counsel?" No money, they said, would be granted to the king by the Parliament before these worries had been addressed.

Leading the charge, Dr. Turnour, the member for Shaftesbury, Pembroke's nominee in one of the constituencies his grandfather the first earl had acquired and where most of the people voting would have been Pembroke's tenants, asked whether,

> by common fame, the general cause of evils in the kingdom was the Lord Admiral, whether his being Admiral was the cause of the King's loss of his control of the Channel, whether unreasonable gifts to the Duke and his kindred were the cause of impairing the king's revenue, whether the multiplicity of offices held by the Duke and his dependents was the cause of the ill government of the kingdom, whether recusants were increased because his mother-in-law and father-in-law were known papists, whether he was a cause of scandal through sale of offices and whether his being lord Admiral was the cause of the ill success of the Cadiz action.

It was a bruising list, perhaps drawn up by Pembroke himself in the form of attacking questions that he often used, and it was undoubtedly designed to destroy the duke. The crown was desperate for money from Parliament with which to wage war on the French. But the young king Charles would not surrender his beloved Steenie and instead dissolved Parliament. Moneyless, divided from the kingdom, and with a war to fight, but with his favorite at his side, Charles now turned to the solution that, perhaps more than any other single act, pushed England on the road to civil war.

He decided to demand directly from the people the money that their representatives in Parliament had refused to grant. In July, letters went out to all the justices of the peace requiring the men of property "lovingly, freely, and voluntarily" to subsidize the war. The request was greeted with silence, and that summer almost no one in England paid up. In September, the king decided to levy a "Forced Loan." This was a euphemism for a compulsory tax, for which there were rare and extraordinary precedents but never on the scale now required nor in such bubblingly dangerous political circumstances. Under threat of being summoned to the Privy Council, the gentry of the country paid £250,000 into the royal coffers. Some refused and "very many gentlemen of prime quality," in Clarendon's words, were imprisoned for that refusal to pay, one of them Sir William Coryton, a Cornish MP who was one of Pembroke's key clients. In a famous case, Coryton and four other knights challenged the legality of what the crown had done to them. To the shock and surprise of the ancient constitutionalists in England, they lost the case and were returned to prison. The gap between the two tendencies in English life represented by Buckingham and Pembroke, between an authoritarian government and a government based on balance and consent, had grown wider than it had ever been. "Could it be imagined," Clarendon wrote, "that these men would meet again in a free convention of parliament, without a sharp and severe expostulation and inquisition into their own right, and the power that had imposed upon that right?" Writing in the 1650s, on the far side of a terrible civil war, Clarendon thought that this forced loan and the imprisoning of the gentlemen was the source "from whence these waters of bitterness we now taste have flowed."

In June 1626, perhaps at the prompting of the king and perhaps drawing on some earlier approaches, Buckingham and Pembroke started to achieve some kind of reconciliation. Pembroke would not have wanted a rupture in the state. The entire foundation of his life was a belief in organic unity, in a binding of king and country, and he began to make arrangements with Buckingham that would restore that unity. Pembroke was to become Lord Steward of the Household, a post he had long desired, the lynchpin of any administration, controlling and auditing the king's finances. His brother Montgomery would replace him as Lord Chamberlain, the officer who organized the running of the household. In an era of personal monarchy, these positions were at the center of the political nation. As a balancing gesture for Buckingham, his own allies, the earls of Carlisle and Holland, became Gentlemen of the King's Bedchamber, and the earls of Salisbury, Dorset, and Bridgewater became privy councillors. It was an attempt to reintegrate the fissure that was opening in the court and that the events in Parliament that year had been widening.

Both sides benefited, with the Pembrokes establishing themselves at the heart of the administration and Buckingham drawing legitimacy from his connection with the leader of the patriot party. The Venetian ambassador put it succinctly: Buckingham had gone in for the arrangement "to gain the Lord Chamberlain's faction." The seal was to be put on it with money and marriage between the two families, with Buckingham's daughter Mary to marry Montgomery's son Charles.

The deal was done and the legal documents settled and signed on August 3, 1626. The two children, who were seven and four, "played together before the King, calling one another Husband and Wife. My lord Montgomery is promised great things to raise his House and Fortunes." The same day, Pembroke became Lord Steward, and Montgomery, Lord Chamberlain. And on the same day the queen's French attendants were suddenly commanded to depart, Samuel Pepys's future father-in-law among them. This no doubt was also part of the deal to reduce the influence of Catholicism on the court. In less than ten days, Pembroke was moving to assert real physical control. On August 12, 1626, he wrote to William Boneman, the king's locksmith:

> *Too much liberty having been given for making keys of his Majesty's Privy Lodgings at Whitehall, he is to take off the locks and make them in such sort that the former double keys may be quite shut out, but without interfering with the King's, Queen's and Lord Chamberlain's treble keys.*

In the next session of Parliament in 1628, Pembroke called off the attack on Buckingham, but affairs went no better for the duke. The disastrous campaign at La Rochelle and the Isle de Rhé had blackened his name still further. The commons then called on the king to consider "whether, in respect the said Duke hath so abused his power, it be safe for your majesty and your kingdom to continue him either in his great offices or in his place of nearness and counsel about your sacred person." But Charles would not abandon him, and again the session of Parliament was brought to a close. Buckingham equipped himself with a bodyguard. His personal astrologer was torn to pieces in a London street. Finally, in August 1628, in Portsmouth, an enraged ex-soldier called John Felton murdered him, stabbing him from behind. Buckingham was able to shout "Villain!" and pull the knife from the wound before staggering back dead. Felton said later, when asked for a motive, that he thought by "killing the Duke he should do his country great service." It was one conclusion of the long debate between court and country, custom and corruption, Pembroke and Buckingham, which had held England in its grip for so long.

For all the elaborate alliances, Pembroke had remained hostile to his old enemy. After the assassination, he wrote to the elegant self-indulgent old courtier and diplomat the Earl of Carlisle (a man who had spent "over £400,000 in a very jovial life") that "the king our master begins to shine already. And I hope this next session to see a happy agreement between him and his people." Every element of Pembroke's statement—a dawnlike glowing of light, happiness, agreement, an Edenic togetherness in the nation—reflects a kind of Arcadian optimism, the conclusion of the sort of plot on which masque after masque had relied for decades.

But it was hope without foundation. England, in the words of Izaak Walton, had changed from what they thought it used to be, "that garden of piety, of pleasure, of peace, and a sweet conversation," into "the thorny wilderness of a busy world." Demons had been loosed at every level, fuelling widespread distrust of royal government at every level. The joint enterprise of England was under threat, and trust in the ancient constitution had been eroded.

The parliamentary opposition that Pembroke had fostered was not radical; it was defensive, set up to oppose the power-acquiring, independence-enjoying instincts of the new crown and its new counsels. England would have loathed Buckingham whether Pembroke had encouraged the country in that or not. But his orchestrating of the campaign against him and his championing of the anti-Buckingham cause had done nothing to diminish the hatred. Felton's downward strike with the knife at Portsmouth was in that sense an intimate part of this long story, a blow for the country.

William Pembroke did not long survive his great rival. He "departed this mortall life at Baynard's Castle, the 10th of Aprill 1630." He was fifty years old, the victim of apoplexy "after a full and cheerful supper," and £80,000 in debt, much of it to his own household officers. One of them, his steward, Sir Thomas Morgan, the seventh son of a Welsh squire, who had been knighted at Wilton in 1623, built for himself what remains William Pembroke's most poignant memorial: a great Jacobean house, posing as a toy castle and bearing the Pembroke arms, at Ruperra, in Glamorgan, the center of the ancient Herbert estates. Morgan, as steward and controller of the Herbert household, had acted for Pembroke in the function Pembroke had acted for the king. What Wilton had been to Whitehall, Ruperra was to Wilton. Now burned and in collapse, Ruperra's toy towers and toy battlements are some of the last remaining vestiges of that honorable and chivalric ideal to which William Pembroke had devoted his life, an image of late-medieval perfection brought into a modern world that would neglect and ruin it. Clarendon called William Pembroke "the most universally loved and esteemed of any man of that age." He was buried in Salisbury Cathedral, where, in 1644, a royalist trooper, Richard Symonds, quartered in the town that "wett, cold, and wyndy" October, saw his memorial:

> Upon the south pillar next the lower steps of the altar hang
> the atchements [a coat of arms in a black lozenge-shaped
> frame, which would previously have hung over the great
> door at Wilton], sword, and golden gauntlets of William
> earle of Pembroke . . .

That sword and those golden gauntlets, perhaps from the tournaments and barriers in which he had fought as a young man forty years before, were relics from a previous age.

SO MUTABLE
ARE WORLDLY THINGS

ANCIENT COMMUNITIES AND THE THREAT OF MODERNITY

What was happening beyond the gilded viciousness of court? As Pembroke and Buckingham battled for the soul of England, what was the reality in the Pembrokes' Wiltshire chalkstream valleys? And to what extent did this sophisticated dispute—between the Pembroke vision of an ancient organic community and the Buckingham ideal of a modern, efficient, centralizing state—reflect a conflict and tension within the body of England?

It so happens that a great deal can be known about the Pembrokes' world, the world that surrounded the family in the great Van Dyck portrait, because in the early 1630s Philip Herbert, who in 1630 succeeded his brother as the fourth earl, had his estates meticulously surveyed. No map survives, even if one had been made, but a set of enormous written documents were preserved from those surveys, recounting the names, family relationships, and tenancies of hundreds of people in the chalkland valleys. An extraordinarily detailed picture emerges from them: the shopkeepers, millers, clothiers, smiths, "husbandmen," cheats, and laggards who were the earl's tenants and dependents; the houses, yards, and barns these people occupied; the earl's "Lands, Woods, Meddowes and pastures," the marshes, orchards, warrens, "lawns," bottoms, bowers, breaches, hedges, coppices, crofts, furzes, lanes, moors, and ditches that made up the estate; the farm animals that were such intimate co-occupants of these places; and the extent to which the great estate, with its own manorial courts, its own police system, its own punishments, and its own deeply embedded hierarchies, was its own, self-reflective world. It is, in other words, the foundation of the whole Pembroke enterprise, the "country of lands and mannours," as John Aubrey described it, for which, over the generations, the Pembrokes had been striving against the centralizing power.

In Broad Chalke, for example, the village arranged on either side of the Ebble, where John Aubrey would later delight in its tunable bells, there were thirty-six copyhold tenants in September 1631. The first to be named were Thomas Randoll, fifty-seven, and Avice, who was two years younger and was probably Randoll's sister. They lived together, in a single-storey house of four rooms, with storage lofts over the rooms, but it was not an isolated dwelling. The house was surrounded by a "4-room" barn, a stable, a cow-house and "other houses fit for husbandry." It was, in other words, a small farmyard, just off North Street on the north side of the village, above the line of clay where the springs bubble up and run down through the meadows to the river. The Randolls had kept everything in good repair, as they were required to, and next to the buildings they had a backyard, called "a backside," a small orchard, and a vegetable garden. Below them, on the wet ground by the river, they had a half-acre "close of meadow or pasture" called the East Close—a small hedged field that they would either have kept closed for hay, to be cut and made in July, or, if they had calves or a thin "rother," a cow due to go out to grass, they would have grazed them here in the spring. "It is the pasture lards the rother's sides," Shakespeare's Timon says, "the want that makes him lean." Above the house and yard stretched the open fields in which the Randolls had their arable strips: fourteen acres in the East Field, ten acres in the Middle Field, and eleven acres in the West Field. On these fields, after the barley and wheat harvest had been taken, and on the fallow fields, the Randolls had the right to pasture three horses, four cows, and a calf. Above that, on the chalk, they could keep eighty sheep with the village's communal flock.

Everything was fixed. There was no idea that the enterprise should grow or change. This was how it was, an ingeniously interlocked system that had been like this for a long time, and no one could see why it should not continue like this forever, just as it seemed to have come out of a distant past "time before mind." Their father, John Randoll, had entered into this agreement with the Pembrokes in 1596 and had named Thomas and Avice as the two other "lives" in the copy. The Randolls were entirely secure here for as long as they lived. In 1596, John Randoll had given the earl twenty pounds as entry money to the property, quite a high "fine" as it was called, the equivalent of the annual stipend for a vicar, and had agreed a rent of eighteen shillings a year, about the annual wage of a servant girl, or the price of about ten turkeys. In effect, the copyholder bought a lease on which the rent was both low and fixed as long as the three named people remained alive. It is a measure of life expectancy in early modern England that three lives were thought to be the equivalent of twenty-one years. The Randolls had done well: in 1631 they were thirty-six years into their copyhold and still going strong.

The rest of the village repeated much of this pattern: the copyholders occupied neat small farmsteads lined out between the arable fields and the wetland by the river. The house of the old lady Goody Dewe was here, from whom Aubrey would later hear about Edward

VI getting lost while hunting. She lived on the south side of the river with her husband, Bartholomew (sixty-six years old in 1631), and their two sons, Thomas and John, their house one room smaller than the Randolls', but otherwise similar in all its arrangements and appurtenances.

There were signs of optimism. A fifteen-year-old boy, William Lawes, and a ten-year-old, John Penn, were both named as lives on copyholds. There can have been no expectation there of an early death. And there was no sense that women were excluded from the system. Widows continued to have unassailable rights in their properties after their husbands died; and a pair of sisters, Anna and Mary Fish, occupyied one ten-acre farm on the north side, off High Lane. Anna was married, but her husband had no part in the tenancy, and it was Anna herself who would become a member of the "homage," or jury, of the manor court.

It isn't difficult to imagine how beautiful a place Broad Chalke must have been on a summer day in the 1630s. Its interlocking of private property and common interest, the sheer neatness of the relationship of downland fields, meadow, river, and village, laid like a tapestry sampler across the dip of the valley, the presence of the animals as an extra layer of life in the village. "A farme without stocke," John Norden had said, "is like a piece without Powder, or a Steeple without bells": all of that exudes a sense of health and coherence. "About Wilton and Chalke," Aubrey mused in his memory, "the downes are intermixt with boscages that nothing can be more pleasant, and in the summer time do excell Arcadia in verdant and rich turfe and moderate aire. . . . The innocent lives here of the shepherds doe give us a resemblance of the golden age." There was a real financial basis for this sunny view of life in the downland villages. Between 1540 and 1640 inflation affected all goods—the price of timber tripled, building materials went up two and a half times, metals doubled in price, and textiles went up by 150 percent. But at the same period, prices for farm produce in southern England rose by a factor of four or five. It was a good time to be in farming.

The Pembroke estate made sure that through an increase in entry fines it relieved the tenants of some of that profit, but the three-lives copyhold meant that the fixed annual rents were very soon out of date. In 1631 one old widow, Anne Witt, was living in a four-room house in Broad Chalke, with the usual barn, cowhouse, orchard, and garden, and thirteen and a half acres of arable strips, according to an agreement made by her now-dead husband seventy-one years before, in 1560. Anne Witt was paying a very low, uninflated eleven shillings, sixpence rent a year. The village as a whole in the 1630s was undoubtedly experiencing a wave of well-being on which tenants and landlords both rose.

From the list of possessions made upon householders' deaths, one can begin to visualize the way in which these copyholders lived. In the Pembrokes' village of Wylye, on the north side of the Grovely ridge, one of the copyholders, William Locke, died in February 1661. At the time of his death he was eighty-two. As with the other copyholders, his house, with three rooms and lofts above them, was on the street side of his backyard, which was surrounded on the other sides by a barn, a cowhouse, and stable, and a separate kitchen. Much later buildings are now on the same site, opposite the Bell Inn, but are arranged exactly as those in the seventeenth century.

The bay size of the Lockes' timber buildings, constructed probably using small oak trees roughly adzed to shape, would have been about fourteen feet square. Both house and barn would have been single-storey thatched buildings about forty-two feet long and fourteen feet wide. Less room was devoted to human habitation than to buildings designed to keep the farm enterprise going. But the Lockes were clearly living in comfortable conditions, even with some pretension to them.

The house had a room called the "hall," with a dining table and a side table, three chairs, three joiner-made stools, and a pair of cushions. William had six tablecloths and two dozen napkins with which to make the room elegant; as well as six pewter dishes; two candlesticks, also in pewter, which can take a high polish; two saltcellars; and sixteen silver spoons. In the smallest possible way, there is a dignity of self-possession here, of a man and his family conceiving of themselves as living an honorable life. Upstairs were two bedrooms, plenty of sheets and pillowcases, blankets, pillows, bolsters and hangings for the beds, and a rug, a good set of towels, and two chamber pots.

Alongside these best rooms were the harder-working parts of the farmstead. It was a crowded and busy place. In the cowshed was a cow and a bullock. Three pigs lived in the stable and five shillings' worth of poultry pecked their way about the yard. There was a hay-stack here—the winter food of the stalled cow and bullock—with some peas stored with it, two woodpiles—one very large, worth ten pounds, and one small—and a stack of timber, maturing, which had been cut into planks and posts. There was also a "wheat-rick" in the yard, the corn still in the ear, waiting to be threshed on the threshing floor in the barn and then stored in the "old garner"—the granary, which was also somehow within the barn. Threshing equipment, ladders, sacks for flour and winnowings, "and some other baggs" were all kept here, too, along with the barley, part of it threshed when Locke died, part still waiting to be threshed.

This sense of the busy, small-scale farm enterprise invaded large parts of the house, too. The hall was flanked by the buttery on one side (barrels, five pounds of lard, a meat safe, a cheese press, three flitches of bacon, a flagon, and "other small things") and the brewhouse (a furnace, vats, pails, bowls, iron bars, hooks, and halters), a place in which more washing was done than any beer brewed. Unmentioned, but certainly here, were the willow baskets in which the washing was taken to the line to dry, perhaps out in the vegetable garden or in the orchard beyond it

The kitchen had all the equipment needed for cooking over the wood fire: chains, hooks, pots, kettles, skillets, spits, forks, frying pans, dripping pans, "and other lumber." In the loft above it, which must have been warm and dry, the Lockes kept their wool equipment: a pair of scales, some "liden waits" and "one pair of way beames," ninety pounds of wool worth four pounds, ten shillings, as well as still more "other lumber." The state of attics in the seventeenth century was not very different to that in any other period.

Beyond this dense concentration of carefully gathered, materially significant, and valuable objects—no mention of a book, a painting, or a musical instrument—was the land: a vegetable garden, an orchard, a set of little closes, and the twenty-seven and a half acres in the common fields. Only ten acres of wheat was sown in them when William Locke died in February. A third of the land had been left fallow, as usual, and the barley for the other third, once it had been threshed in the barn, would be sown by Locke's heirs in the spring, as usual. Locke had three pounds' worth of hay "in the fields," his contribution to the communal hay stack on which the communal flock was feeding during the winter, and "two dozen of hurdells" with which to fold the sheep on the arable (tillage) that would soon begin to sprout. It is a depiction of an exactly ordained life, of a rootedness.

Of course this is not the whole story. The village was both a sustaining and a fierce, demanding, exclusive, and excluding organism, but what was here undoubtedly feels good. The poorer families are scarcely mentioned. Some families right in the middle of the village were sharing these small houses and barns, which can't have been easy. Ralph Street and his son John, farming a mere three acres, lived in "a dwelling house, sometimes called the stable." There was a tiny cottage of two rooms, with a little garden and orchard, right out on the eastern edge of the village, called the Hermitage, for which the annual rent was four shillings, the price of a dozen candles. Strikingly, and unexplainedly, this is the earliest known figurative use of *hermitage* in English (the next was in 1648). Was it a joke? There are certainly other half-jokes in seventeenth-century Wiltshire place-names. Out on the open ground on the other side of Broad Chalke was a cluster of houses called "Little London." The seventeenth-century hovels belonging to the landless laborers who lived here have gone now, but judging from equivalent places in Wiltshire, called sardonically Little Salisbury, Ireland, Scotland, or Cuckolds Green, this would have been the living place of the poorest of the poor, Broad Chalke's own slum, single-roomed hovels of only ten or twelve feet square, some even ten feet by eight, in which families would attempt to maintain their lives. The floors were often no more than straw on mud. Transient laborers and their families, often, as the place names imply, from the poorer margins of the British Isles, clustered at the edge of these elaborately instituted villages like dogs at a camp.

Although necessary and tolerated as the source of casual labor for those copyholders who were too old or infirm to do the farmwork themselves, villages such as Broad Chalke loathed and despised the slum dwellers existing on the margins of their pretty villages. Hundreds of petitions were made by parishioners to have these sheds and their contents removed, often "by reason of the soyle"—the dung— "for the said Cottage so built doth stand unto a watercourse, which watercourse runneth into a well which is used by the most parte of all the Inhabitants to fetch there water. And further the Children [living in the hovel] have a Loathsome decease called the White Scurfe which is infeccious." Villagers often wanted such human styes pulled down, but this example, from a 1628 petition of the parishioners of Melksham, in the north of Wiltshire, is significant not only for the villagers' policing the village's physical and moral health, but also for the proper procedure they went through to do so. They didn't simply demolish the house but also applied to the justices to agree to let this sick, poor family have another house in a better place:

> *We th'inhabitants of the said parish whose names are under-written, Knowing that he hath lived as an honest and poore man . . . and pittying his Distressed estate in regard of himselfe, his wife and Five small children who are likely to perish through want of harbour, do hereby Signifie both our contents unto his disyres, and that we conceave that it wilbe a worke of greate mercy to satisfie his humble request.*

That is the manor working as it was meant to, as a social organism that nurtured the weak while carefully protecting the communal resources and well-being of the village itself. It was a quality of rural life that George Herbert would also celebrate in the 1630s.

At Broad Chalke, in addition to those copyholders, was a single tenant of the demesne farm—that is, the land the lord in the Middle Ages used to keep for himself. In 1631, he was Anthony Browne, a gentleman, John Aubrey's great-uncle, the source of endless stories which his great nephew would greedily write down. His deal with the Pembroke estate was not by copyhold at all, but by indenture, a modern rental agreement, which was an almost purely financial transaction between him and the earl. In 1601, he and his wife had bought the lease, which was to run for the rest of his life, for forty pounds. On top of that, he had to provide the lord every year as rent thirty quarters, or very nearly a ton each, of wheat and barley, slightly less of oats, twenty-four geese, twenty-four capons, which were castrated cocks, and one hundred pigeons. By a separate contract, for which he had to pay rent of twenty pounds a year, he had some extra bits of grazing and the "warren of conies," whose meat Aubrey would come to love so much—the highly profitable fat rabbit farm—on the downland to the south of the village.

Here, already, is a sign of the transitional nature of these arrangements. The key money to be paid upon getting into the lease was a straightforward amount of cash; the annual rent was meant to be in kind. But instead of the pigeons, cheeses, capons, and rabbits, Browne in fact gave the earl thirteen pounds, fourteen shilling, eightpence a year. Only the grain he owed continued to be paid in kind. The wheat, barley, and oats would have gone to the earl's barns and granaries at Wilton: ten quarters filled a cart, and so every August, seven or eight cartloads would have made their way out of Anthony Browne's yard at what is now Manor Farm in Broad Chalke, across the Ebble at a wide ford, into the northern part of the village, past the farmyards of the Laweses and Randolls and then up the long, dusty, white chalk track, climbing three hundred feet to the top of the downland ridge, before dropping to the valley of the Nadder at Burcombe, and turning east through South Ugford and Bulbridge, joining the tens and maybe hundreds of others creakingly bringing the rent to the lord's store at Wilton.

It was part of the agreement between the earl and his tenants that in delivering rent in kind "to the Capital mansion house of His lord at Wilton," they should take "meat, bread, & drink, at the Lord's cost whensoever they come." The summer carts gathered outside the barns, the carriers and laborers from the downland villages sitting on them in the midday sun, the refreshments provided by the earl's men, overseen by the steward or more likely his deputy: all of this was a perfectly real financial relationship in action in the early seventeenth century, but it was also a Virgilian scene, working to the rhythms of Arcadia.

Something else is also in play here. The same document, preserved in the Pembroke papers, that describes the meat, bread, and drink that will be given to those bringing the rent to Wilton also says that the tenants of the land "out of their Benevolence, or good will, shall every

Open grassland on the Down above Broad Chalke *(top)*; burred oaks in the ancient hunting forest of Grovely Wood *(above right)*; and *(above left)* the clear-running waters of the Ebble: the ingredients of the Pembrokes' Arcadia.

The deer around the Ranger's Lodge in Grovely Wood *(above)*, as drawn by the first Earl's surveyors in the 1560s; the hay harvest *(right)*, one of the pinch-points of the community's year; and the community flock *(above right)*, folded at night in temporary, hurdle-fenced enclosures, so that the dung could enrich the soil.

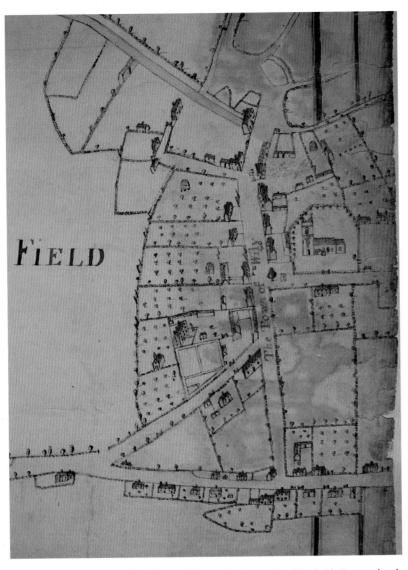

The Pembrokes' village of Wylye: each house has its yard or "backside," an orchard, and one or two closes. There are haystacks and stacks of unthreshed grain. Stocks stand in the village square. It is a place of control, as neat as a sampler.

William Herbert, 1st Earl of Pembroke *(left)*, perhaps painted to celebrate his elevation to the Garter in 1548, when he was about forty-two: a hybrid of Renaissance prince, medieval magnate, and man on the make.

A drawing by Hans Holbein *(below left)* of a woman of about twenty, perhaps Anne Parr, wife of the 1st Earl: clear-eyed, Protestant, cultivated, bringing grace and refinement to her husband's unbridled aggression.

The 1st Earl of Pembroke *(below)* as one of the great Tudor power brokers, an English condottiere, on a medal cast for him in 1562, when he was fifty-six.

Tudor Wilton *(above)* encased the remains of the abbey in a pedimented courtyard house, as drawn on the vellum rolls of the 1st Earl's 1560s survey.

OPPOSITE: Henry, 2nd Earl of Pembroke, failed to achieve his father's dominance and was overshadowed by his wife, Mary Sidney, "the sweetest daughter of the sweetest Muses, the brightest Diamant of the richest Eloquence, the resplendentest mirrour of Feminine valour." Her brother, Philip Sidney *(opposite below)*, at his most powerful: carried to his burial in St. Paul's in February 1587. As the revered author of the *Arcadia*, Sidney was far more powerful than when alive.

William, 3rd Earl of Pembroke *(left)*, carrying the staff of Lord Chamberlain, painted by Daniel Mytens in about 1615, when William was thirty-five. A man of balance, dignified, the cultural heir to his uncle Philip Sidney. His racier younger brother Philip *(below left)*, made Earl of Montgomery by James I, painted by William Larkin soon after becoming a Knight of the Garter in 1608, aged about twenty-four.

Philip's second wife, Lady Anne Clifford *(above)*, wears in her ear a single pearl suspended from a black thread, in memory of one of her dead children: "Having many times a sorrowfull & heavy heart, I may truly say I am like an owl in the desert."

Inigo Jones's drawing of a backdrop for *The Shepherd's Paradise (above)*, performed by the queen and her ladies in 1633, may well be a sketch of the new Wilton then being designed by his associate and pupil, Isaac de Caus. De Caus's huge new garden at Wilton *(below)* appears lightly drawn in Inigo Jones's design, occupying the middle ground between the sinuous colonnade of parkland trees and the formality of the Palladian villa in the distance.

The great wedding portrait of the Pembrokes at Wilton, painted by Van Dyck in
late 1634 or early 1635. At the top left, the dead children of the family float on clouds.
Below them, the three youngest brothers—William, John, and James—look up to
that heaven. In the center, Lady Mary Villiers, the bride in white. Two steps above
her, the boy she is marrying, Charles Lord Herbert, and his younger brother Philip,

with whom she is in love. Holding center stage, Philip, Earl of Pembroke and Montgomery, and his wife, Lady Anne Clifford. On the right, the earl's daughter Anna Sophia and her husband, the highly glamorous Cavalier Robert Dormer, Earl of Carnarvon. Life for the Pembrokes would never again seem as complete.

OPPOSITE: The fifty-year-old earl, looking tired and run down, and Lady Anne Clifford, his wife, aged forty-four. His left hand loosely holds the Lord Chamberlain's staff of office. Her gesture may signify that she cradles the ghost of a dead child in her arms.

The two young Herberts—Philip, aged thirteen, and Charles, fifteen *(above)*—both about to embark on a grand tour to Italy, dazzle in silks, a balanced pair of assertion and withdrawal.

The twelve-year-old heiress, Lady Mary Villiers, daughter of the assassinated Duke of Buckingham, brought a £25,000 dowry to the marriage, the equivalent of 2,000 years of a Wiltshire shepherd's wages.

OPPOSITE: Anna Sophia Herbert and her husband, Robert Dormer, Earl of Carnarvon, both aged about forty-four. Anna Sophia holds the pearl of a living son, their heir, Charles Dormer, between the fingers of her right hand. He openly dabbles his fingers with hers.

The 2nd Earl of Carnarvon, aged about twelve in 1644 when painted by the young Peter Lely, a year or so after his father's death in the first battle of Newbury. Lely gives the boy clothes and a stance that echo his father's in the Van Dyck wedding portrait. Behind him, what were once Arcadian boughs are now shattered by war.

year carry Houseboote [timber for repairs] & Fireboote [firewood]"
to Wilton's capacious stores. "Benevolence" and "good will" are, of
course, code for no payment. This is another imposition for which a
free lunch would have been scarce recompense. Arcadia continued to
have steel in its core.

Browne had a very pleasant setup in Broad Chalke: a house with
fifteen rooms, a big barn next to it, a cowhouse, stable, and pigeon
house, a carthouse, a garden, and a one-acre orchard. He had 34 acres
down in the valley, much of it sweet, rich, grass-growing meadow,
about 270 acres in the arable fields, of which a third was left fallow
each year, 80 acres sown with wheat, and 100 with barley; and the
right to keep 1,200 sheep in the communal flock up on the downs. This
was a serious enterprise on a different scale from that of the copyholders.

But this was more than just business: this was the also the working of a community, and Browne would have found himself intimately
entwined in the life of the copyholders around him. Manor Farm in
the seventeenth century was surrounded by a positive nest of obligations and duties inherited from the Middle Ages, the obligations owed
by custom, time out of mind, to the lord's farm, of which Browne was
now the tenant.

First, in June or early July, the copyholders had to wash and shear a
thousand sheep and then mow and make the hay in the meadow down
by the Ebble called Long Meade, which was four and a half acres in
extent. At harvest time, in high summer, late July or August, the "customary tenants" had to find thirty reapers, for a day, to cut and bind
Mr. Browne's corn. Most of them would have "found" themselves to
do the work. They then had to find thirty carts and wagons plus the
teams of horses or oxen to pull them, to carry the corn from the fields
and into the barns.

In return, Browne had obligations toward the community. First, there was the vicar. He was to get "6 akers of the best wheate which he can make choice of out of 80 akers." One can imagine that scene well enough, the parson touring the fields, Mr. Browne, perhaps, guiding him toward the slightly less than best, the parson knowing already exactly where the best was to be found. Once he had made his choice, Mr. Browne had to "reape and carrie the same home into his Barne for him." After the harvest and up until Martinmas, on November 11, Browne then had to provide the vicar with grazing for sixty lambs, then weaned from their mothers, for free. He had to give eight bushels of wheat to the chief forester of Cranborne Chase (from whom he received two acres of wood each year, for firewood and with which to make sheep hurdles, cut from the earl's coppices in the chase), and Browne's note says that he was meant to pay more wheat and barley to the underforester "Which Corne hath been demanded but hath never been paid by me hitherunto."

While the customary work was being done by the tenants, Mr. Browne, standing in for the lord of the manor, effectively acting for him in this tiny community, gave meat and drink to the reapers while they were doing their hot days' work in the fields. More meat and drink was provided for the men carting the sheaves back to the barns. While they were cutting the grass and making the hay down in Long Mead, Browne gave the reapers a ram and eleven gallons of beer to be divided among them. The ram, in many of the chalkland villages, had a strange custom attached to it. The animal would be placed in the middle of the field, the tenants around the edge. If it remained quietly there, they could keep it. If it escaped or wandered off, it remained the lord's. What was this? An entertainment? A piece of theater? A dramatization of the potency of lordship and the impotence of tenancy? In the *Surveior's Dialogue*, John Norden had his freeholder, while discussing the virtues of freehold, tell the surveyor, "It is a quietnesse to a man's minde to dwell upon his owne: and to know his Heire certaine.

And in deed, I see that men are best reputed that are seized of matter of inheritance: Leases are but of base account." But dwelling upon one's own was not available to the vast majority of the population. Maybe the lord's escaping ram, a taunting form of largesse, was a means of telling the copyholders exactly where they stood.

Browne also had to provide the customary tenants with good food at Christmas. A quarter of beef (which meant what it said: a quarter of an animal) was to be shared out among the tenants on St. Thomas's Day, December 21. On the same day, he had eighty-four pounds of wheat baked into bread and distributed to his neighbors, plus sixteen gallons of barley baked into "horse bread" for their animals, and a large expensive cheese (costing four pounds, sixteen shillings) cut up and distributed around the village. Two one-year-old pigs, called "Composition Piggs" by Browne, meaning that they were payment instead of tithes owed to the church, were given to the parson every year.

In his own accounts, Browne calculated his yearly income from the meadow grass, the wheat and barley, and the sheep at about £272, and his annual costs at £127, but he gave no monetary value either to the work he received freely from the copyholders or to the food and supplies he gave them each year. All of that was beyond money, merely the mutual obligations of an ancient community, each part reckoned intuitively to balance the other. And he wrote a note to this effect in his papers:

> I doe accompt these Customarie services are but equally
> valuable with what Custom they reseve [receive] from me
> in Lue [lieu] thereof.

This was the nature of the Wilton universe. It was, for the beneficiaries, a model of conservative wholeness, a set of economic, agricultural, and social arrangements that reflected the ideals of Arcadia itself: full at least of the possibilities of an integrated society; with no expectation that anyone would do any better than any other; with a level of mutuality that urban, commercial, and courtly life could scarcely tolerate (but nevertheless longed for); and that instituted the lord of the manor as a king in his own domain.

It was a system that provided the political classes with a metaphor for the country: England itself was a manor, with the principle of inherited and customary law at its heart; where its sovereign lord, according to the ancient constitution, was powerful only in response to the law as it had been handed down and only in consultation with the representatives gathered not in the manor court but in parliament; where a tyrant would ignore that mutuality but a king would recognize it as the identifying quality of this society.

This was the ideal and these the principles to which figures as diverse as Philip Sidney, Shakespeare, John Norden, George Herbert, the Pembrokes, and the gathering of poets whose lives and writings they supported at Wilton had all appealed. It was "a countrey of lands and Mannours," one of the limbs of the body of England.

In many ways, even in the 1630s, the system was operating at full strength. The copyhold, the customary terms on which families held their properties from their landlords, came to be seen as such a valuable commodity, a meal ticket for thousands of yeoman families, that again and again in the inventories you find "the iron-bound chest," the chest with four locks, "the stronge chist," "the greate chiste," which stood in the copyholder's bedroom and was the first thing to be saved in case of fire or flood. The wattle-and-daub walls of the houses themselves could easily be broken through with sledgehammer or axe, but these defended boxes shielded the papers on which entire families relied for their existence. Robert Furse, a Devon yeoman, had written a long account of his family and their belongings in the 1590s, telling his descendants that what he had set down "will be to those that come after you, gret quyttenes perfyt knowledge, and a trewe menes to understond all there evydenses and tyteles." Quite as much as the elaborate devices of the cultural élite, these copies and the strongboxes in which they were held were the vehicles of the culture, the means by which an organized past was transmitted to the present, a dam against the mutability they all felt and all feared.

Copyhold's place in the law was an underpinning of the continuity people craved. The great jurist Sir Edward Coke, saw the situation of the copyholder as a form of freedom guaranteed by law:

> Copyholders stand upon a sure Ground, now they weigh
> not their lord's displeasure, they shake not at every sudden
> blast of wind, they eat, drink and sleep securely, (only
> having a special care of the main Chance viz) to perform
> carefully what Duties and Services soever their Tenure
> doth exact, and Custom doth require: then let the Lord
> frown, the Copyholder cares not, knowing himself safe and
> not within any danger.

This approaches a kind of Arcadian center: a version of freedom which was dependent not on rights but on duties and in which any-one's good was dependent on everyone's good. People were essentially not individual but social. Although many manors, including the Pem-brokes', allowed the lord to set the entry fine at whatever level he wanted, there is no strong evidence that the Pembrokes abused this position. In fact, the ideology to which the world of Sidneyism had attuned them would certainly have set their minds against exploiting their copyhold tenants, even if the ruinous costs of life at court brought pressures on them to do so. One sign that they did not is the astonishing level of debt one seventeenth-century Pembroke after another was prepared to enter into. With annual incomes approaching £25,000 through most of the century, none of them died owing less than £40,000.

Needless to say, there was an argument on the other side. Copyhold, with its elaborate burdens, its binding of the copyholder to an
unending series of mutual, community-based duties, was thought by
many to be full of encumbrances. It was innately conservative. Even
the surveyor John Norden complained of the old yeomen that "they
only shape their courses as their fathers did," spending their lives in "a
plodding kind of course." In this light, the tenurial fetters of copyhold
were not the means of maintaining a community but a way of hamper-
ing the freedoms of freeborn individuals. Both landlord and tenant
could see it that way and, in many parts of the country, although not
on the whole on the Pembroke estates, there was steady drift away
from copyhold to a straightforward leasehold, a pure money arrangement, one in which each participant was a player in the rental land
market and in which any notion of community came as an optional
add-on, not as an integral part of how and where people lived.

In the Pembroke valleys, there are clear signs that community was
continuing to work. A statute passed in the reign of Elizabeth had required that any new house should have four acres of ground attached
to it, a way of guaranteeing a means of self-sufficiency and of no burdens encroaching on the charity of the village. This was all very well,
but it meant that the poor, particularly in an era of land hunger, were
unprovided for. There was not enough land to go round, and if there
was not enough land, there could be no more houses. The poor were
driven on to the roads and into the cities, where they would beg. A
steady stream of petitions was made to the justices for such cases. In
Ramsbury, where the Pembrokes had one of their smaller houses, a
petition came to the justices at the quarter sessions in 1639:

> A poore man but of honest life and borne and bred in
> Ramesburie aforesaid one whom in regard of his povertie
> it hath pleased some of the worthy officers of the Right

> Honble the earl of Pembroke to confirm and bestow upon
> him a little platte of ground to erect and build a howse fitt
> for habitation in and upon the same.

It is a sign of the system working well that the earl and his steward had agreed to provide Lionel Ounter with a piece of ground, but a house could not be built on it without the permission of the justices of the peace. The villagers of Ramsbury wrote to them that spring:

> Commiserating this poor man's penurie and desirous to
> further his future good we do in most humble wise desire
> ye worships that you would be gratiously pleased to grante
> this poore man full power and licence to erect and build
> a Cottage or dwelling house in or upon the said Platte of
> ground and he according to his bounden dutie will continu-
> ally pray for yr prosperous estates long to endure.

It remains an intriguingly integrated system: royal justice hears an appeal by a village committee (acting according to the custom of the manor) on behalf of a poor homeless man, for whom the lord of the manor has provided a plot of ground, all framed in the language of obedience and hierarchy, even with certain phrases mimicking the language of the litany ("in most humble wise" "his bounden dutie"). This is not what a market-based system would have done.

One of the central points about custom as a governing principle of village life was that it should be agreed between the copyholders of the manor, gathered as the "homage." Custom did not have to be of any great age. Custom was simply what the village did as a village. As long as those of the homage considered that something might be a custom of the manor, then it could become one. Customary tenure was in that way not pure conservative rigidity but an adaptive organic system.

In 1632, the people in the Pembrokes' manor at Wylye decided that they wanted to introduce the newfangled technique of the floated meadow, and they did so using the instruments of communal decision making they had inherited from the Middle Ages. The floating of meadows was a method by which river water was led out over the low-lying grass fields next to the banks, bringing enriching silt down on to the meadows and a seed rain of various grasses to thicken the sward. The comparative warmth of the flowing river water, at something like fifty-five degrees Fahrenheit, would keep the grass growing when the frost would stop it in an unfloated meadow. The costs of setting up the sluices and channels, the gates, banks, distributor channels, and flow systems for these meadows were high: fourteen shillings an acre up front and then a maintenance payment of two shillings an acre thereafter, "the same to be paid at the feasts of St Thomas the Apostle and the Annunciation of the Blessed Virgin Mary yerely by even and equal proportions." The flooding of the meadows provided an early bite for the sheep, more hay in summer, making a bigger flock possible, which could manure a larger extent of arable ground. Because of such obvious advantages, large stretches of the valleys of the Ebble, Nadder, Wylye, and Avon rivers were converted into water meadows in the seventeenth century, with much of the work encouraged by the earls of Pembroke and their stewards, who recognized of course that the value of the estate itself, as well as the incomes of the copyholders, would be increased by the improvements. But the decision to make those improvements could only be made communally, because the land of every tenant in the village would be affected by them.

So at Wylye an agreement at the manor court was made on September 10, 1632,

> Which said agreement all the said parties at this courte
> desired to have entered in the rolles of the courte of this

mannor and that thereupon an order should be made for the
byndinge all said parties to perform this agreement upon
paynes and penalties to be therein expressed, being a business conceived to be very behoofefull and beneficiall to all
the inhabitants of this mannor.

As smoothly as the clear waters of the Wylye itself, the ancient
community of the manor at Wylye was sliding on to an enriching,
technological, and modern future.

Happiness finds it difficult to make its way into the records, but
for all that, an undoubted and even rather subversive note of well-
being and gaiety flows through these valleys. There was unlawful
drinking and playing at quoits, game playing on the Sabbath, dancing, and music. Particularly in the upstream villages of Broad Chalke
and Fovant there remained a high proportion of Roman Catholics, repeatedly listed as not going to church, and even of one man, in 1636,
Edward Lucas of Fovant, a gentleman, for keeping a schoolmistress
in his house (Sarah Overton, a spinster) for at least three months,
"in order to teach his children Popery." The fact that so much of this
starts to appear in the court records in the seventeenth century may
be a symptom of an increasing puritan confidence in taking to court
the minor delights and naughtinesses that until then had gone unpun-
ished. When, after the Civil War, the Parliamentary Committee for
Sequestrations came down to these valleys to discover who had been
on the king's side and who, therefore, might have their property confiscated, all kinds of informants came creeping out of the woodwork to
snitch on the ways in which their neighbors had been going in for unnecessary delight and even "injoiinge itt." The vicar at Bemerton, Dr.
Thomas Lawrence, did "permit William Bowlton to play upon his In-
strumt (beinge a Treble[?]) at his the sd Doctors Howse and did pmit
dauncinge on the Saboth day in his presence and hee did not forbid itt."

Edward Poore, described as a yeoman, had seen him "dauncinge and bowlinge and kittlinge upon the Sabioth daues at Bemerton." *Kittling* means "tickling" in Scots, but probably means "playing at skittles" here. The priest, they all said, liked to do this with his children.

There is one piece of evidence, apparently almost unique from these valleys, of a song written and sung by a spirited young woman from a house next to the Ebble in March 1631, which describes that other, unspoken life below the level of official arrangements of what people bought, owned, sold, earned, and spent. It is almost the only equivalent of that world of jokes and laughter, storytelling and amusement that filled the parlors and drawing rooms of the great house at Wilton. In Stoke Farthing, a hamlet just downstream from Broad Chalke, a carpenter called Thomas Holly, one Saturday afternoon, saw Edward Penney, the son of the man who had the demesne farm, a big place with a separate room for the servants to live in and two huge ten-bay barns, coming toward him. Penney gave him "a certeyne writting in paper wch was made in verce." Holly could neither read nor write himself and he took it to John White, one of his neighbors, a thirty-two-year-old husbandman—a proper member of the homage, who according to the earl's surveyors, kept his house in good repair—to tell him what it said. White read it out to Holly and to two other of their neighbors, the old Walter Whitemarsh and the big farmer himself, John Penney, who hadn't been able to read it himself. The homage of the village was, informally and ad hoc on a Saturday afternoon, gathering to deal with a small crisis. (Only one of them could read, but the ability to read gave him no particular status.) Walter Whitemarsh tooke "the certeyne writting in paper" away from John White and kept it himself.

Clearly the meeting had decided to do something about it because ten days later, the document was produced before the justices in Salisbury. The author of the verses had been identified. She was the thirty-eight-year-old Jane (or Joan) Norrice, the wife of Harry, and the copyholder herself of a very small farm in Stoke Farthing, with an acre of orchard and garden and sixteen acres of arable land in the common fields. The farm wasn't in good repair, and the Norrices were clearly hovering on the margins of the respectable community, and this "certeyne writting in paper" did Jane Norrice's standing no good at all. The fact that this poor, small, middle-aged woman farmer could write verses and sing them meant nothing. The power of the manor, translated into court Latin in Salisbury, was disturbed that she, Jane Norrice, "made, fabricated and wrote in the following English words from her own ill will a false, scandalous and obscene libel." The poem is in fact a funny account of how the tiniest of chalkstream villages had wickedness going on underneath its proper surfaces:

> Rouse braue spiritts boyes and why should wee be sad;
> for I haue newes to tell yow the whiche will make yow glad
> [If]* yow a wench doe want then vnto Stoake draw nigh sir,
> and there for a small [?groat]† a nightes lodgin yow may
> by sir
> Singe boyes drinke boyes why should [we] not bee merry
> at Stoake you may haue spoort and play vntell that yow be
> wery;
> Firste to begin at vpper end and soe the street goe downe,
> enquire for the Well‡ wench at the end of the towne;
> and There yow may be sure to speed§ yf periman¶ be not
> there,

---

* Illegible in original.
† Illegible. A small amount of money?
‡ Or Wells, the town in Somerset.
§ Succeed.
¶ The pear man?

customers shee hath but few be cause shee is but scrose* Ware
but yf yow will a fine wench haue then vnto Buttwills goe;
but her I thinke without tellinge yow doe already knowe;
for lately shee hath been ut court for to make her purgation†;
but firste shee to the taverne went to drinke wine with the
passon‡;
but yow happen there to miss to shufgroots§ then resort,
and there tis a greate chaunce that yow may haue somme
sport:
or ells with goodman lotes wife¶ whom bitehard they doe
call sir
wich is a resanable one if not the best of all sir;
but if all these doe happ to miss wich straunge they should doe all,
at next door dwells the old puncke** the wich will never faile;
besides the other mans wife which is the old puncke daughter;
for yf that shee should honest be were it not a straunge matter;
now to conclude and make an end, noe more I will now name;
because I will be faultles and be yond of blame;
for though a man be cuckold made he must not now speak
of [it]
least that he play at butwills and soe be made [to] pay for it:
Singe boyes [drinke boyes why should we not bee merry
at Stoake you may haue spoort and play vntell that yow be
wery;]
Finis.

---

* Scrow: dogeared, used.
† Compurgation: to be cleared of a charge in court on the sworn evidence of others.
‡ Parson.
§ A game, shove-groats, like shove-halfpenny.
¶ Lot's wife was turned into a pillar of salt in Genesis.
** Whore.

Henry Norrice, husband of the singer and composer Jane, when asked about his participation in the libel, said he knew nothing of it. It was all her work. And what can one say? Tantalizingly, it is not quite possible to make out who in Stoke Farthing Jane Norrice was teasing. Who lurks behind the nicknames? Who was the salty shriveled-up old dame called Lot's Wife "whom bitehard they do call"? There are three widows who were copyholders in Stoke Farthing at the time. Ann Penney and Eileen Bryne were both too rich and too big as farmers to qualify, and so maybe Lot's Wife was Margaret Savage, her "bitehard" nickname perhaps having some connection to her real surname? But the others soak back into the soil, and we are left with the wit and wickedness of Jane Norrice herself, quite independent of old Harry, possibly married before—she was also known as Jane Clinton—and with a gift for the sly dig and the startling punch line, entertaining all the like-minded others in Stoke Farthing on a cold Friday night in the tippling house in the village, sending up the proprieties, life leaking out from underneath the carapace of control and suppression within which an English village survived. Was she herself, I wonder, the fine wench at Buttwills, who "without tellinge yow doe already knowe"?

A few years later, just up the road, in Broad Chalke, another late-winter party fell afoul of the law. It, too, played games with the proprieties, teasing the structures of religion and government. A girl called Jane Lawes was examined on oath by one of the justices, who happened to be John Penruddock, of Compton Chamberlayne. She told him that

> on St Iohn his day last att night she was invited to the Myll
> in Broad Chalke to a daunceinge match where there were
> divers of the younge men and maidens of ye parishe where

as she saith, she saw noe abuse offered or incivility comit-
ted by any dureinge the time of her beinge there.

That was all, a dancing match, which may not mean a contest here,
but simply a gathering, a dancing party in the mill, which apart from
the church was almost certainly the largest-roofed space in the village. It had been a good party and had gone on all night, until after
the candles had burned out, and it was then that others did not have
quite such an innocent view of what happened. Joan Deane, another
villager, was questioned on oath and she said that

> on St Iohnes day last she was invited to the myll as aboue-
> said where there were many young men and maides att
> daunce and about two houres before day the candles
> beinge burnt out she heard some of the maides cry out, but
> whoe they were that did cry out or did cause them soe to
> doe she knoweth not beinge in the darke and sittinge by
> her brother and when a litle time after she and [her brother
> and] her sister went home about the break of day. and more
> she saith not.

A third girl was interviewed, Mary Randoll. She too had been

> att the myll at broad Chalk on St Iohns day at night where
> there were divers of the younge people of the said parish att
> daunce and beinge vp in a chamber she saith yt she heard a
> cryeinge out sometimes of some of the younger women, but
> who they were she knoweth not but saith that one Thomas
> Wise who termed himselfe to be the Bishoppe beinge vp in
> the chamber, with diuers other young men but what they
> did she knoweth not by reason the candles were out and yt

they were lockt in, and could not gett out before it was day, but she her selfe had noe wronge offered vnto her, but she saith that she heard divers report that Catherine Sangar of knoyle was sett vpon her head and was bishopped but by whom it was done she knoweth not and more she saith not

One more girl, Aves Gerrett, was to be questioned under oath, but under her name the record is blank. Thomas Wise was a shoemaker and a friend of Edward Targett, the miller, who was there with him that night in the dark upper room of the mill, along with Thomas Deane, a tailor from the village, and Henry Pen, a husbandman. Were they raping the girls? Were they playing? What kind of crying out was it? What exactly does "bishopping" mean? This was 1640, a moment at which religious tensions were running spectacularly high. Broad Chalke had a long and strong tradition of Catholicism, of families named and fined for decade after decade as recusants, but this is scarcely about church politics. It is surely something on the boundary, where teasing, drink, bullying, sex, and the physical dominance of men all intersect. These girls would have had to continue to live in the village, and their silence, their retreat into the candleless dark, is as articulate as any words uttered in court.

Nevertheless, throughout these Wiltshire villages, there are signs of strain and tension; of the underlying presence of cruelty and violence; of an inability to keep the wholeness of the vision whole; of shepherds not as calm philosophers but as anxious, unsocialized, curt, and peremptory outsiders; of these villages as organisms that could not quite keep their mechanisms properly oiled; of early-seventeenth-century England as a place of reluctant commitment; of the men increasingly unwilling to fulfill the unpaid tasks that the government of their manors, the parishes, and the county required of them; of a conflict between ambitious, developing landlords and those whose ancient communal rights were threatened by the developments proposed. The great positive statements of a John Norden about the beauty of a communal world were made against a background in which that communal world was coming under strain. It was a time of technological improvement, of a modernizing market system, of a burgeoning population and an uncertain food supply, of an increasing number of vagrants and beggars, when there was a sense that the old structures were not holding up, that people were frantically on the move: a survey of Wiltshire inns in 1686 revealed more than twenty-five hundred beds available for travelers in the county. Even the small town of Wilton itself had room for more than fifty strangers to spend the night there. England had begun to shift.

Increasingly, a national market was eating away at local practices. But even at the highest level, the workings of the market itself were seen, quite explicitly, as the great enemy. The government, at its various creaking levels of administration, attempted detailed forms of control that would make any modern administrator blanch. The Privy Council, the most powerful political committee in the country, entirely appointed by the sovereign, was intimately involved with, for example, what bakers could and could not do. No one, the great lords of the Privy Council insisted, could be a baker or a miller unless they had been an apprentice baker for at least seven years. Only farthing, halfpenny, and penny loaves could be baked, the size of each set down. A baker could sell thirteenpence' worth for twelvepence—the baker's dozen—but only to victuallers and innkeepers. Outsiders who came to sell loaves where there was already a baker had to make their penny loaves three ounces heavier in order to protect the business of the local man. With the extra weight of bread he compelled to include, the incomer's margin would have disappeared and his business would have

been unviable. The fundamental basis of market behavior—a better product or a lower price—was ruled illegitimate. Spice cakes, which carried about them an air of the Middle Ages, popery, and wrongness, could be sold only on Good Friday—the ancestor of the hot cross bun—and at funerals, consistently the most conservative of all human ceremonies.

One method of ensuring that people did not behave as rational economic beings was the public informer, a mainstay of Tudor and early Stuart economic and social policy. Food supply, farming methods and timings, moneylending, the terms on which an apprentice worked: all of these were subject to government control, but the government had no inspectorate. The tax system was radically out of date, inefficient, and corrupt. It could never have paid for an army of inspectors, and so it encouraged people to set up as freelance informers for profit. There were even "informing syndicates," usually with managers in Westminster, where the courts were, and agents in the regions where people were offending against the rules of the regulated market. About two thirds of those cases brought to court from Wiltshire were the p[roduct] uct of professional informers or their subagents working the W[iltshire] markets.

A grisly tour was made of Wiltshire towns and vill[ages] autumn of 1605 by one Roger Cawdrey of London, yeom[an] up with a fat collection of indictments at the Excheque[r] got back in November. The crown was usually ha[ppy] with the informer, a 50 percent commission on [the] had a long list of Wiltshire men and women [who were] offending against the drink regulations: J[ohn] had been selling claret and sack and al[e at his] dwelling house, where he had no licen[se] others were guilty: William Smith[ ] berlyn for the same offense, Joh[n]

This strain, and the attempt to control behavior that was bubbling up from the deepest levels of society, was symptomatic of a deep shift in the way the country was working: away from any kind of self-sufficiency and toward a growing reliance on the market. The closed world of the manor was coming apart, but government control and the ideology that directed it were taking time to adapt to changing realities. Increasingly, people were breaking the rules. At the quarter sessions in Salisbury in January 1634, several men—including William Penny, one of the earl's copyholding tenants at Bower Chalke, near Broad Chalke—were "presented" for marketing offenses both in Wiltshire and in Dorset. They were trading in sheep, but the offense was described to the judge as if it were a sin against the Holy Ghost:

> They and every of them are great enemies to the woale publique of this county, in that they continually go from Faire to Faire, and from markett to markett, from Sheepefould to Sheepefould, from one man to another, where they buye continually great numbers of sheepe; as for example one Saterday to the markett at Blandford Forum, the Wensday following sell the same again at Wilton: Nay they and most of them will buye one day and sell the same the next, nay, buy and sell in one and the same day, insomuch that our Fayres and marketts, are generally and for the most part furnished by these sorts of jobbers and ingrossers who take up all the cobbs [a stall made with hurdles] and pens there that other men viz. Farmers and yeomen who doe not trade as they doe must sell their sheep in Common fields abroad in regard they cannot gett penns for them. Some of the before named have not been ashammed to brage and boast that they have sould this year last past 6,000, 5,000, 4,000 and 3,000 sheepe, some more some lesse, wch is contrarie

to the lawes and statutes of this realme, wch wee desire by
this Honble Court to be reformed and amended.

The court papers, as so often, contain no record of what the
justices decided, but it is clear that the real wickedness for the
seventeenth-century Englishman was working the market. Making a
corner in wheat, or even failing to sell at a low price and waiting for
a higher, was a criminal offense. "Forestalling" (buying by private
treaty before grain reached the market) and "regrating" (buying at
one price and selling at another), the foundations, in other words, of
simple market behavior, were not only frowned upon but thought to
be morally offensive. In 1630, all justices were sent a copy of a Book
of Orders that described the price at which everything was to be sold.
Those who hoarded "pinched the guts of the poore to fill and extend
their own courses, taking advantage by the dearth of corne to make it
more deare." The Book of Proverbs had made it clear: "He that hoar-
deth corne the people will curse him; but blessing shall be upon the
head of him that selleth it." In case after case, informers told the justices of "Private barnes," secret stores, places in which the spirit of
communality had been broken.

Among the commodities flooding on to the market was land itself.
Sale of crown lands under Elizabeth had raised £817,359. In the first
six years of his reign, James I squeezed another £426,172 out of the
royal estate, all of it pouring onto the land market. John Norden in
1607 had never known so much land passing from hand to hand, a
symptom, it was thought, of the end of martial behavior among gentlemen. "The gentlemen which were wont to addict themselves to the
warres," Thomas Wilson wrote in 1600, "are nowe for the most part
grown to become good husbands [farmers] and knowe well howe to
improve their lands to the uttermost as the farmer and countryman,
so that they take their fermes into their handes as the leases expire,

and eyther till themselves, or else lett them out to those who will give most." That final phrase has the air of a death knell about it. "Those who will give most" are not those whose ancestors have tilled the ancestral acres, nor those whose first concern is the well-being of the community, but those for whom the relationship to the land is founded on money and the market.

It was all a cause for anxiety. Thomas Wilson found "great alteracions almost every year, so mutable are worldly things and worldly mens affaires." Those who were best sited to take advantage of the boom, particularly in the south of England, and particularly those who were sitting on a copyhold rent that had been fixed when prices were much lower, were outstripping those in the rest of the country who might have thought themselves socially superior.

> A knight of Wales
> A gentleman of Cales [Calais]
> A laird of the north countree
> A yeoman of Kent
> Sitting on his penny rent
> Can buy them out all three.

Everywhere, though, there are signs of this world breaking down, of communality disintegrating and the authorities attempting, often brutally, to shore it up. The roads were awash with men, women, and children who had fallen out of the social network of manor, village, and town. The vagrancy statute of 1598 had ordained that any rogues, vagabonds, or sturdy beggars over the age of seven who were found "begging, vagrant, wandering or misordering themselves" were to be whipped and sent back to the parish of their birth. Over-population, recurrent food crises, repeated cyclical collapses in businesses, such as the cloth trade, that were dependent on fickle foreign markets, the influx of the poor from the margins of the British Isles: all put immense strain on the conventional distinction between the impotent or God's poor (the old, young, or crippled) and the impudent or Devil's poor, who were considered capable but lazy. In a recession, or in a situation of chronic underemployment that lasted from decade to decade, there was little that whipping would do to address the real problem.

The scurf of unwanted humanity blew around the lanes and streets of Elizabethan and Jacobean England. Upright citizens, closely held within the confines of their customary manor or the chartered town, regarded this flotsam with disgust, as masterless and ruleless. They "have not particular wives, neither do they range themselves into Families: but consort together as beasts." Sometimes a vagrant woman was spared punishment if expecting a child or her body was crippled or ill. But the level and extent of punishment remains disturbing.

In Devizes, in April 1609, five men and a woman charged with petty larceny were sentenced to be publicly whipped in the market place "till their backs do bleed and then discharged." The next year, Thomas Elye was "burnt in the hand" with the letter *F* to mark him as a felon. A poor woman called Agnes Spender was whipped for deserting her child. Benjamin Salisbury was burned on his left shoulder with the letter *R* to mark him as "an incorrigible Rogue." In January 1617, William Farret and Elizabeth Longe were whipped "by the Tythingman until their backs doe bleed, and this to be done at the comon metinge place under the Elme in Wylye neere the Church."

The story of William Vennice, a husbandman or small farmer of Barford St. Martin, just below the beautiful reaches of Grovely Wood, can stand as an example of how life could go wrong in the Arcadian valleys. "Omitting and forgetting my prayers unto the Lord," he told the justices in the spring of 1627, he became a prey unto the Devill who with his allurements and enticements fell into the terrible and fearful sin of adultery with one Joan Hibberd of the same parish, who being my wife by promise before God and ourselves in private, sithence being ruled or as it seemes, over ruled by her mother she utterly denies it.

Vennice brought the statement of his neighbors in Barford as witness that he and Joan—or Jane: the names were interchangeable—had even been to Salisbury to get themselves a marriage license from a justice there. But he didn't win his case. Joan had given birth to a child, his, and the court told him he had to give her ninepence a week until the child was ten. Joan refused to marry William Vennice and was sent to a House of Correction for a year. William "shallbe well whipped on his naked back from his girdle upward until his body doe bleed and that the Tythingman of Barford do yt or cause yt to be done without delaye within a fortnight after Easter next."

If anyone still imagines that cruel and unusual punishments were not a part of English life in the early seventeenth century, they should read the case of a widow called Katherine Peters brought before the Wiltshire justices in 1623. She and a woman called Alice King, whose sister Joan King also lived in Barford St. Martin, were accused of stealing some washing that had been laid out to dry on an orchard hedge on July 16 of that year. Katherine Peters's accusers said she admitted to stealing the holland sheet and the tablecloth, which they later found in her basket. She said she had found them lying under the rabbit warren fence. When the case came to trial, Peters refused to plead and so was sentenced to the punishment known as "de peine forte et dure." She was

to be brought to a close room and there to be laid upon her back naked from the middle upward her legges and

armes stretched out and fastened towards the fowr corners
of the room, and upon her body to have so much waight
and somewhat over then she is able to bear, the first day—
she requiring food—to have three morsels of coarse bread
and noe drink, the second day drinke of the next puddle of
water, not running, next the place she lyeth and noe bread,
soe every daye in like manner until she be dead.

Katherine Peters's infant son was taken from her before her punishment and death, and lived as a charge on the parish until 1641, when
he turned seventeen.

Bad behavior—or at least behavior that rubbed and worried at the
tender edges of this fragile society—is what summoned the fiercest
of reactions. At Broad Chalke in 1610, the leading men of the village
decided they had put up with enough of "the Manifold & Continu-
alle Misdemeanors of one Robt Came of our sayed parish." Obse-
quiously, and in the language that the world of hierarchy required,
they approached the Justices of the Peace. Robert Came had, in
seventeenth-century terms, gone half mad. Instead of living quietly
with his neighbors, conforming to the custom and requirements of the
manor, he was now

wholy given to Contention & to raise strife & enmitye
betweene Neighbour & Neighbour practisinge nothinge
more then to breed brawlinge and discord Wherene hee im-
ployethe all his time and his Whole endevores For havinge
made away all his goodes and house & Nowe doth Idlely
and in lasines he giveth himselfe altogether especially to
this sayed trade of life as your Worships by our information
followinge may Vnderstand

They felt "dayly Mollested disquieted & disturbed" and started to lay out some of the details of the case "Omittinge others to avoyde tediousnes of troublinge your Worshippes Which are these that Followe." Came had accused a woman of being a whore, and a neighbor of wanting to sleep with his wife (who was said to have been complicit in this); made speeches that he hoped would start a riot; accused another neighbor of theft; hit his uncle in the village street with a flail; torn up and then burned a hedge that belonged to old Bartholomew Dewe; and fomented arguments between neighbors. Worst of all he was the tithingman, the village policeman, and

> although it belonged to his office to see yat such thinges should be reformed and to complaine of such persones as vsed any vnlawfull games himself Would be the Chieff man to vse them most especially on the Saboathe day playinge out Eveninge Prayer most comonly and alsoe to fight and brawle to breake the king Maiesties peace Contrary to his office and the lawes of this Realme.

Was this madness in the Broad Chalke tithingman? Or was it simply the human spirit breaking out of the overwhelming supervision, the instituted control system of the English village?

There is another case, just over the down from Broad Chalke in the valley of the Nadder, from a couple of years before, that makes much of this clearer. John Penruddock had heard this case, too. Marie Butler, a young unmarried woman from Barford St. Martin, courageously gave evidence about a terrifying night the previous winter. It was exactly the same time of year as the party in the mill at Broad Chalke,

a boute St Iohn day att Christmas last, one Richard Hurst
came vnto Bartfoord St Martin to her Masters house one
Iohn Carpenter and there did solicite this examinate to haue
the vse of her bodie, hauing formerly often promised her
marriage and there vpon they coming from a dancing toge-
ather wch was att Bartfoord aforesaid, hee perswaded her
to goe home with him to her Masteres house, and when she
was neare her Masteres house he desired her to goe in wth
him into an out house, where they vsualy tie there beast,
wch she agreed vnto and there hee had to doe wth her,
wch was the first tyme and after aboute a month befoore
ouer Lady Day last, hee came to Bartfoord to her Masteres
house, her saied Master and dame beeing from home, and
there he had the vse of her bodie, and she verily bee leeueth
that she was then beegotten wth child by the saied Richard
Hurst, and she farther saieth that hee hath diueres times
since promised her marriage and more she saieth not.

Cruelty to and exploitation of the poor and the weak appears again
and again in the records, often with poignant clarity. There is an un-
dated appeal in the quarter sessions records from a Ramsbury pauper,
Thomas Seald:

I am a pore man and have noe releufe out of the parrish of
remsberie hether I come to have some relefe but I cane have
none and I desire your worship that you wold helpe me to
sume relefe Being I have noe munie

A note on Thomas Seald's appeal says: "Recommended to the over-
seers [of the poor—small-time parish officials] & on their neglect the

next Justice to bynd them over." Royal justice again ensures, or attempts to ensure, that the community looks after its own. But there is no hint that Seald would get any charity until his own parish gave it to him.

John Bevin of Brokenburrough, near Malmesbury, came with an even more pathetic tale:

> Now the Church wardens & overseers have throwne yor peticoner & his wife out of theire house & will not suffer them to rent that or any other, by reason of this their Tiranous dealinge your peticoner and his wife hath bin constrained to dwell in a hollow tree in the streete a moneth aleady to the great hazard of their lives they being anncient people.

Perhaps the elegant denizens of Sidney's Arcadia might have dreamt of living in the trees that seem to speak of love. Attempting to do so over a Wiltshire winter in the street at Brokenburrough might have been a rather different proposition.

In 1631, John Dicke, a shepherd from Imber, had been thrown out of his house—the shepherd was not a copyholder and would have had no rights to any property once his employment had come to an end—and his "landlord having use for the house he dwelt in hath taken it into his own hands to make him a stable by wc meanes yr por Supplyant is dismist of a house & could not get any roome nor house in ye parish." The landlord had evicted the shepherd not because he wanted to live in the building himself, nor for another employee, but to house his horse. Again, the community had stepped in: "the neighbours gave him a place to build a poor cottage but some enemies doth threaten to pull it down to the great spoyle and undoing of your Wor Supplyant."

Inevitably the pressures of work and of coping with the stresses of the farming year would combine on occasions with sheer neighborly vindictiveness. In 1633, Robert Feltham, a Pembroke tenant at Fovant, wrote to his friend and ally James Hill, who was, at the time, with the Bishop of Salisbury on his regular tour of the diocese to check that the people were behaving as they should. The visitation was, of course, another chance for informers to reveal to the authorities just what their enemies had been doing wrong.

Feltham had got behind with his ploughing, the weather having been bad, and had been caught doing the work on a saint's day by a couple of churchwardens from the village. The wardens were under pressure themselves from a fourth villager, Hercules Candill, who had been thrown out of his pew in the church, the so-called Maiden Seat, and was angry about it.

M[aster] James Hill I moste hartily com[m]end me unto you with many thankes for divers cortesees formerly receavid at your hands so now at this time presuming farther on your favoure somuch as to take note that if our Churchmen John Gervis & laurence Strong of Fovant doe present my self with others for goinge to plough uppon S[aint] Marks day which then being a time of grete necesite by reason of the weet wether & being much behind was the more pressious for husbandmen nevertheles for my part I intend to make no coustome of it nether did the lik in all my life for which matter I would intret you to stande my frend it maybe staide untill I doe speake with you next. For Hercules Candill hath thretned them if they doe not present us he will present them for he doth it in mallis he bears to John Gearvis for dismissing him his Mayden seat wherein he had no right. This one busines shall reveng another

although it doe himselfe no good. So I leave you to gods moste
holy protettion.

> *Your loving Frend Robert Feltha[m]*
> *To Mr James Hill his very*
> *loving Frend now being at the*
> *visitatacion deliver*
> *these I pray you.*

This letter is a small model of the Wiltshire valleys at work. Church and church obedience are central to the workings of the society. Mutual supervision stimulates a habit of blackmail. The churchwardens would probably have let Feltham's indiscretion with the plough go—he was not the only guilty one—but a malicious desire for revenge in Hercules Candill disrupted the acceptance of failing within the village. Favors were called in, grudges worked out, obligations fulfilled, and pleading was the substance of life. Arcadia? Not exactly. This was undoubtedly an integrated society. These are not the complaints of an atomized, individualized loneliness, but the social stress is palpable. Here is something of the reality that Sidney's self-occluded gaze had drifted over in his daydream of perfection. It was Arcadia, but Arcadia for real, with all the drawbacks that communality must inevitably impose.

Chapter 9

ELIZIAN FIELDS
AND AYERY PARADISES

The Perfecting of Wilton
1630–1640

The story has at last returned to the great Van Dyck family portrait at Wilton, which takes its place in a period that, at least on the surface, had been full of contentment. England in the 1630s then, Lord Clarendon would later write in his silky Augustan phrasemaking, had been "the garden of the world," blessed with "the greatest calm and the fullest measure of felicity that any people in any age, for so long time together, have been blessed with," enjoying "a full, entire undisturbed peace," glowing in "the general composure of men's minds." Compared with the situation in Europe, where Germany in the Thirty Years' War, was "weltering in its own blood," Great Britain was a haven of civility. Scotland was at peace, Ireland had been "reduced to profitable husbandry," England was rich, "flourishing with learned and extraordinary men," where government revenue was higher than ever, the navy stronger, the king "the greatest example of sobriety, chastity and mercy that any prince hath been endowed with." England was "a pleasant promontory" from which the general grief of Europe could be surveyed.

After the death of William, 3rd Earl of Pembroke, Wilton and its world became the property of his brother Philip, Earl of Montgomery. In the eyes of many, Philip scarcely measured up to the great tradition. He may have been named after Philip Sidney, his godfather, but he was no poet, no politician, and no great speaker. He was gruff where his brother had been steady and dignified. He had a reputation for violence. He was addicted to hunting. He wasn't very clever. More than that, though, he was a court man, a friend of Buckingham and of the Villiers clan. The Pembroke adherents were all full of one question: Would Philip, the 4th or 23rd Earl of Pembroke, maintain the tradition? Would he fight for the dream of a better England against a crown at whose table he had supped for decades?

The answer to that question lies in two parts: during the 1630s, Philip Pembroke served his king; only after the catastrophic turn of events in 1642 did he turn against him. He would become the rebel earl, and the grounds on which he rebelled were precisely those on which his family had based their position for so long. The Pembrokes had a dignity not to be slighted. They believed in the organic wholeness of the ancient constitution. The behavior of the new men—with new counsels surrounding Charles—supplanting the ancient nobility, was not to be tolerated. The rebellion, when it came, would be a profoundly conservative act.

Little of that appeared on the surface in 1630. When Philip inherited Wilton, he looked like a king's man to the core, and without hesitation, in public, the serious men who had gathered around his brother began to apply the pressure. A sermon was delivered at Baynard's Castle in late April 1630, preached on the life and legacy of the earl who had just died. It was the work of a Jacobean divine called Thomas Chaffinge, born in about 1581, of whom little else is known. The words of his sermon, "The Iust Mans Memoriall," ring out like a summons to seriousness, a sudden revelation, under the surface of court intrigue, money and manipulation, of an intense and radical Protestant agenda. It was a pointer to the fact that this family was not merely, like the Earl of Carlisle, let alone the Duke of Buckingham, engaged in self-enrichment and self-promotion. The Protestant inheritance from the time of Philip Sidney remained a moral imperative for them. Chaffinge's sermon, in magnificent, old-fashioned Jacobean language, reads like the voice of their consciences speaking.

In the printed version, Chaffinge began with an "Epistle Dedicatory," addressed to Philip. Seventeenth-century England sanctioned truth telling, whether from the dwarf fools who played at court and who even went on diplomatic missions or from preachers; divine authority allowed them to step beyond the bounds of deference. Chaffinge addressed Philip directly:

> My Lord, let me take the boldenesse to tell you, that the
> eyes of the world are fastned on you; you cannot bee hid,
> your actions are not done in a corner, notice will be taken
> of all your Counsels, and your Counsellors, men are big
> with the expectation of you; and blame them not that they
> should be so, especially of you, who (besides others of your
> illustrious stock and linage well known) have had so pious
> and religious an *Aeneas* to your Brother, and so famous and
> valiant a *Hector* to your Vnckle.

This was the burden of inheritance: to have William Pembroke, the wise moral statesman, as a brother and Philip Sidney, the warrior on behalf of virtue, as an uncle was both a spur and a goad.

> Let the Piety and goodness of the one, and the valour and
> Cheualry of the other, serue as so many siluer watch-bels

in your eares, to waken you to all Honourable and Noble
atchieuements.

There was an implication here, not stated, but clearly understated,
that Philip was not good enough. He had the genetic background, he
could certainly be charming, but did he have the moral backbone?
Was he not an indulger of physical and material passions?

> You liue in the face of a glorious Court, where your eyes
> are daily fill'd, as with Magnificence, so with Vanity; yet
> you shall doe well, otherwise, to cast them aside from such
> Gorgeous Spectacles, and sticke them in the shrowds and
> winding-sheetes of the dead. Nothing shall more humble you
> then this, and so nothing lift you neere Heauen then this . . .

That was the puritan paradox: never more elevated than when self-
abasing, and never more heightened than when dealing with the great
of the world, whose elevation was exceptionally fragile:

> None is your Peere now, but your Peere; yet the time shall
> come, when you and I shall be fellows; in the common bag
> of mortality, the Rooke in Checke-mate with the King.
>   The theatres and scaffolds of the greatest eminency,
> whereon you great Potentates, and Grandees act your
> seuerall parts, either stand leaning and reeling on the
> quick-sand of Mutability, and Inconstancie, or else lie open
> and obnoxious to the wind of Disfauour, and Disgrace.

Anyone listening to this, with the memory in their mind of what
happened to the Duke of Buckingham, would have experienced a shim-
mer of schadenfreude, a form of aesthetic and moral pleasure at the con-

ventions of courtly life being so ruthlessly stripped away. The life of worldliness at court would always be anxious at its own instability; both God and Arcadia provided a refuge from it. That elision of categories is exactly what Chaffinge then embraced, drawing on the botany of the Bible, looking around him at the next generation of Herberts gathered in Baynard's Castle, and from the sound of it, knowing exactly the look and atmosphere of Wilton. William, the dead earl, was not dead.

> He seems to liue (as it were) multiplied in an Honorable Brother, and many a sweet Nephew; and O may the dew of Heauen still lodge vpon those branches; let them spread forth as the Vallies, as Gardens by the Riuers side, as the Trees of Lign-aloes, which the Lord hath planted, and as Cedar trees besides the waters.

Chaffinge, once he had opened this vein of Arcadian Protestantism in his sermon, went on to explore and exploit it. England was anxious. It was like "a darke, cold, stormy tempestuous night." Wouldn't anyone envy William the dead man his peace? He was like a man "a-bed and asleepe," while the rest of us were "vp and awake," suffering the storms and troubles of existence. There was a possibility that "the abomination of desolation, the idol of the Masse" would appear again in England. There was even the prospect of civil war again in England "of Ensigne borne against Ensigne, and Crosse against Crosse." But William, lucky man, would see none of it.

> We dreame of rest here, and contemplate vpon I know not what Elizian Fields, and Ayery Paradises vpon earth, whereas God knows, we haue here nought else but *desiderium quietis*, a desire to rest; onely in Heauen *quietum desideriorum*, rest to all our desires!

All worldly treasure is but mere beggary, all the pompe
and glory of this earth, but dung and darknesse, all pleasures whatsoeuer but nauseous and lothsome; in a word,
All flesh is grasse, and the glory of it as the flower of that
grasse, not *gramen* but *faenum*, withered grasse; withered
before it be plucked up.

The whole Herbert family would have been in the congregation
listening to Chaffinge's magnificent words. Surrounded by the pomp
and glory of Baynard's Castle, they could scarcely have believed what
he had to say. They would have loved and not despised the "Elizian
Fields and Ayery Paradises" at Wilton, and would not have considered
the dazzling collection of paintings that Philip Pembroke was then already gathering as "dung and darknesse." All flesh may have been
grass but was lovely for that; the sermon fell on deaf ears. Philip's
Wilton was to be a shrine to beauty, and a particular form of high-
minded, Italianate beauty for which Pembroke and the king shared an
appetite. Wilton's brand of Arcadianism was clearly descended from
the elevated world Philip Sidney had made there fifty years before. For
more than ten years, there is no sign whatsoever that the Pembokes
had any kind of quarrel with the king.

Philip's upbringing and his frame of mind had been formed in the
rumbustious atmosphere of James's court, and at least according to
Clarendon, he remained rough in that Jacobean way. Clarendon—his
enemy in the Civil War—saw him as a clumsy oaf, a man left over
from an earlier age, who got away with his rudeness and stupidity because he was rich and influential. He would make himself look more
significant than he was by

discoursing highly of justice and of the protestant religion,
inveighing bitterly against Popery, and telling what he used

to say to the King, and speaking frankly of the oversights of the court that he might not be thought a slave to it. He had been bred from his cradle in the Court, and had that perfection of a courtier, that, as he was not wary enough in offending men, so he was forward in acknowledging, even to his inferiors, and to impute it to his passion, and ask pardon for it; which made him to be thought a well-natured man. Besides, he had a choleric office, which entitled him to the exercise of some rudenesses, and the good order of the Court had some dependence on his incivilities.

This bitter and grudging description of one courtier by another was written many years afterward. Others wrote of Philip's kindness and grace. Even Clarendon, in a passage of his manuscript that he struck out of the published history, confessed that he felt "great kindness for him and was never without a desire to serve him, having been formerly beholding to him for many civilities when there was so great a distance between their conditions." He was in fact "a man to be relied on in point of honour and fidelity." Something of the complexity of Philip Herbert's real character emerges from that cancelled aside. He was both a civilized and an angry man.

As Lord Chamberlain he presided over a court that was far more refined and controlled than anything James I's courtiers would have known. Charles was an intensely pious person. He never went hunting in the morning before he had been at public prayers and would not tolerate even the lightest and wittiest of jokes about religion in his presence. A certain chillness had come about the court when he succeeded his father. "He was not in his nature very bountiful," even the hyperloyal Clarendon later admitted. "He paused too long in the giving, which made those to whom he gave, less sensible of the benefit." He insisted on precision and orderliness. He liked quiet. He didn't enjoy the company of strangers nor of very confident men. Presumptuousness was the ultimate source of failure at the Caroline court, largely perhaps because Charles himself was not intellectually confident. There was a sense of inner weakness about him, which showed itself as stiffness, rigidity. He was, in fact, a cultural puritan, disliking excess or even gaiety, and once saying that the victory in a drinking contest of a particular earl—not named in Clarendon's story—was nothing to be proud of, "that he deserved to be hanged." Soon afterward, when the earl came "into the room where his Majesty was, in some gayety, to shew how unhurt he was from the battle, the king sent one to bid him withdraw from his Majesty's presence; nor did he in some days after appear before him."

The ramshackle warren of the old palace at Whitehall, where some two thousand rooms, many of them not redecorated since the 1550s, were surrounded by a labyrinth of closets, garrets, and kitchens, would not have appealed to a king who required clarity, order, propriety, and calm. Nor would the unfailingly public nature of his own existence have satisfied him. One instruction issued by Charles reveals the habits of the Jacobean court he hoped to reform: "None of our bedchamber whatsoever are to follow us into our secret or privy room when we go to ease Ourself, but only our Groom of the Stool."

All of this means that the geometry of the relationship between Philip Pembroke and the king was complicated. At one level, Philip was a rough old Jacobean, more used to frankness than refinement, precisely not the sort of figure with whom the king felt at ease. Philip also had behind him the old Pembroke tradition of maintaining a critical distance from the luxuries of court, a distance Chaffinge and others were urging him to maintain. Against that, it was of course significant that Philip and the king had been brought up together. They had known each other all their lives. They also shared a deep love of

Italian art. When opening deliveries of paintings from his agents in Italy, Charles chose to have Philip alongside him (with Inigo Jones and others) to judge the paintings' quality, something the king had never done with William Pembroke.

It was a relationship in which intimacy and distance were sewn tightly together. The ambivalences within it can be seen as a reflection of something larger: of the Pembrokes' long relationship to the crown, and more than that of what had happened to the idea of Arcadia in the fifty years since Philip Sidney wrote his romance at Wilton. Arcadia had begun as a covert attack on courtliness and tyranny. But in the intervening years, the court itself had adopted Arcadia. By the 1630s, withdrawal from court to a life of (imagined) Arcadian purity, a return to the goodness of the old world, was something enthusiastically embraced by the king and court. The anti-courtly drive of Arcadianism was itself a courtly phenomenon, never more central to courtliness than in the prewar years of Charles's reign. Throughout the early seventeenth century, proclamations had been made "commanding the repaire of Noblemen, knights and gentlemen of qualitie, unto their mansion houses in the Country, there to attend their services, and keepe Hospitalitie." Just as the coherence of the kingdom depended on the largesse of the king, the workings of the country required the hospitality of the great lords in what was called their "countries." The urgency of these appeals heightened under Charles.

Whitehall 28 November 1627

The Kings most excellent Majestie, taking unto his royall con-
sideration the present state of the times, together with the great
decay of Hospitality & good house-keeping, which in former
ages was the honour of this nation, the too frequent resort, and

ordinary residence of Lord spirituall and temporall, Knights
and gentlemen of quality, unto cities and townes, especially
into, or neare about the Cities of London and Westminster, and
manifold inconveniences which ensue by the absence of so many
persons of quality and authority from their countreys, whereby
those parts are left destitute of both relief and government, hath
thought fit hereby to renew the course formerly begun by his dear
father of blessed memorie.

This was repeated in June 1632, and those lords who refused to obey it and remained in London for the summer were prosecuted and fined in 1634, 1635, and again in 1637. These are precisely the years when Wilton was transformed from a Tudor to a Palladian house. As Lord Chamberlain, Pembroke would have needed to be more responsive to this idea than any other. More than that, though, the courtly-Arcadian fusion, the creation of an Italianate pleasure house in the midst of the Elysian beauties of his chalkland estates, would have seemed by the early 1630s as an inevitability. To make a palace in the trees was almost the only possible response to his inheritance.

In a fascinating way, the emergence of the new Wilton under Philip Pembroke's hands is his articulation of his predicament. It is deeply Arcadian but it is deeply courtly, too. It is of and in his Wiltshire estates but is intended as a place where king and court can feel at ease. John Aubrey's description of the new Wilton's origins is full of clues. "King Charles the first did love Wilton above all places," Aubrey wrote, "and came thither every summer. It was he that did put Philip first [*sic*] Earle of Pembroke upon making this magnificent garden and grotto, and to new build that side of the house that fronts the garden, with two stately pavilions at each end, all 'al Italiano.'" Philip's remaking of Wilton, urged on by the king, was not as a classical building but an Italian, part of the same cultural world as Titian and Tintoretto, even as San-nazaro's original Italian *Arcadia*. The old Tudor palace, larded with Henry's elaborate armorial glass and escutcheons, was hopelessly out of date, a remnant of the faux-chivalric world to which they had all subscribed twenty years before but that now seemed flat-footed and unsophisticated. The king's suggestion was first of all a summer idea: the new Wilton was not to be a pompous prodigy house of the kind the earlier generation had built, but a light and elegant thing. And the first element was to be the garden and grotto.

The scheme devised and installed by the Fleming Isaac de Caus— "the fat Dutch keeper hereof, a rare Artist," according Lieutenant Hammond on his 1635 visit—was huge, stretching a thousand feet from the house, but for all its scale, the garden was playful. De Caus was an associate of Inigo Jones. He had already worked on the Banqueting House in Whitehall and had built a grotto in the undercroft there. His work on the Wilton garden began in 1632 and peaked in 1634. There were long gravel walks with pots of flowers, embroidered platts, marble fountains, marble statues standing within the fountains, and covered arbors and raised terraces from which the plan could be viewed. Female deities, a statue of Susanna, perhaps in memory of Philip's dead wife, and the pair of Bacchus and Flora, the deities of fullness and fruitiness, loomed over the beds. At the far end a huge bronze Roman gladiator stood surrounded by cherry trees. Beyond him was a vaulted grotto in which the passage of the water through pipes could be made to imi-tate the singing of nightingales; and "Monsieur de Caus" could some-how, by a secret he never shared, make rainbows appear to the visitors. Elaborate underground and underwater machinery could make stone swans swim and stone balls float. No expense was spared, but gaiety rather than grandeur was the effect, a realm of delight through which the Nadder flowed. In the 1690s, when Celia Fiennes visited, the sequence of gardens was still "very fine with many gravel walkes with grass squaires, set with fine brass and stone statues—fish ponds and basons with Figures in ye middle spouting out water—dwarfe trees of all sorts and a fine flower garden—much wall fruite."

If all of this seems like the background to a masque made real, such an effect was also apparent at the time. This family had appeared in one performance after another at Whitehall. In 1631 Pembroke had played the "Judicious Lover," and his son-in-law the Earl of Carnarvon, the "Valiant" in Ben Jonson's *Love's Triumph*; the earl's two eldest sons, Charles, Lord Herbert, and Philip Herbert, had come on in *Tempe Restored*, in February 1632, as two of the children portraying "the influences of the stars on divine beauty."

Right in the middle of the garden's construction period, in the early 1630s, one of the most expensive masques ever staged, *The Shepherd's Paradise*, was designed by Inigo Jones and performed by the queen and her ladies in Somerset House on Twelfth Night in 1633. The masque lasted an interminable seven or eight hours, was largely inaudible, and was celebrated as one of the most boring explorations of Platonic purity ever devised, but two of its backdrops, for which drawings survive at Chatsworth, seem to bear an extraordinary relationship to Wilton. The first is labelled by Jones "The Shepherds Paradise." Behind the dancing masquers, the courtly audience would have seen a colonnade of parklike trunks receding from them. The trees are loose and easily flowing. They provide a frame for the view of the great house in the way that a formal colonnade would have done—and did in other masques designed by Jones—but here the lines have become sinuous, and seductive. This is order so orderly that it can afford to let any stiffness go. The trees have about them that elegant, relaxed poise of sprezzatura, a form of disdain or carelessness, the grace that comes from inner nobility, the charm of effortlessness. This cultivated wildness approaches to within hailing distance of the great house. Beyond the trees, and within their embrace, one sees the palace itself as a model of classical restraint, of exactness and overt order, with an elegant and neatly laid out garden in front of it. Jones drew this as de Caus was building the great Renaissance garden but probably before any work had begun to transform the house. The house he has drawn is not as Wilton would emerge in a few years' time—although with its two terminal pavilions and central emphasis, it is not unconnected to it—but the relationship of house, garden, hill, and park is identical. It seems at least possible that in this sketch of paradise, the form to be taken by the new Wilton first emerged. Before anything had appeared in stone or mortar, the image of Wilton had already floated before the eyes of the court as part of a shepherd's paradise.

Inigo Jones was certainly involved from the start. As the royal architect, for a rebuilding which was the king's idea, he was the natural choice. He certainly knew the Herberts. There is a remote chance that he may have travelled to Italy with William Pembroke as a very young man, but in later life he certainly knew both brothers well. As successive Lords Chamberlain, they would have dealt with him regularly over his masques. He had also been to Wilton long before, when, in 1620, James I had been staying there and their conversation had turned to Stonehenge, ten miles north of Wilton, on the edge of Salisbury Plain. William Pembroke had sent for Jones to investigate the monument. He soon realized it was Roman. The Ancient Britons had been incapable of art. It was the Romans who "gave first rise to civility in this island" and so Stonehenge could not be druidical, nor an emanation of the soil, but was clearly the imposing on a wild ancient country of an imperial idea. It was not recognizably Roman in its decorations, but that was deliberate. The Romans chose a form of architecture, the Tuscan Order, "best agreeing with the rude, plain, simple nature of those they intended to instruct. [And] of this *Tuscan*

Order, a plain, grave, and humble manner of *Building*, very solid and strong, Stoneheng principally consists."

Jones's analysis of the Bronze Age monument reveals his cast of mind: civilization came from abroad, in fact from Italy. There was no point in looking for homegrown models for architecture, but the classical system could, nevertheless, happily adapt itself to local circumstances. The massively eaved barn of a church Jones built in Covent Garden was chunky and Tuscan in style, deliberately avoiding the kind of finesse that in the early 1630s might have smelled of Roman Catholicism. And the great south front of Wilton also chooses simplicity and a lack of show, an external sobriety that is more suitable to a palace in the trees than are enrichment and elaboration. A drawing does survive of a much grander elevation for Wilton—four hundred feet long, double its present length, and with a large central portico and pediment—but there is no evidence that it was ever seriously considered, although that greater length of façade would have aligned itself more easily with the scale of the de Caus garden.

Work on the house probably began in 1635, even as the garden was being finished. An entry in the Pembroke household accounts for 1634–1635 mentions a contractor, Antony Hinton, gentleman, who was paid £1,200 "for works building the new garden and the lord Earl's house at Wilton by order of the lord Earl." Inigo Jones himself was busy completing the Queen's House at Greenwich, and so de Caus was instructed to "take downe the side of Wilton House which is towards the garden & such other parts as shall be necessary & rebuild it anew with additions according to ye Plott which is agreed." A Mr. Brookes was told first "to remove all the stuffe in ye roomes & Lodgeings of that side of the house which is to bee pulled down and rebuilt."

Beyond that, the actual building history of Wilton remains obscure. A catastrophic fire in 1647, which began, according to Aubrey, after fires had been lit "for airing of the roomes," destroyed this part of the house. If you climb into the attics above the Single and Double Cubes, you will find alongside the massive adzed carpentry of the new 1640s roofs, signs of the disaster: burnt bricks, sooted plaster, and the stub ends of the oak joists still in the walls. The joists have turned to charcoal where they met the air, but you can dig them out and still find, where the brick protected them, the clean sawn 1630s estate oak. But there is no telling if the rooms as they were rebuilt in the late 1640s and 1650s resembled what had been here before the fire. On top of that, major alterations to Wilton were made in the eighteenth and nineteenth centuries, and it is no longer possible to be sure that Wilton's great rooms are real Stuart interiors or later pastiches.

Nevertheless, Inigo Jones was certainly involved in the 1640s rebuilding, which was done largely by his pupil and nephew John Webb, and there is no doubt that if not in detail then at least in atmosphere Wilton still reeks of the Jonesian moment in English taste and sensibility. It remains the central Arcadian statement in England, a palace in the trees, a masque made real.

Philip Pembroke enriched the house with every picture he could. There were many inherited from his father and perhaps his grandfather: ministers and heroes from Queen Elizabeth's time, some of King Henry VIII, the Earl of Essex. But to them he added a great Italianate upper storey: Charles I on horseback, by Van Dyck, and a life-size picture of Peacock, his favorite white racehorse, "to both of which Sir Anthony gave many master touches." Perhaps among the first collectors in England to do so, he also brought the great modern pictures down from London so that Wilton became a great treasury of Italianate taste: Correggios; both oil paintings and sketches by Titian, including a particularly prized "head of an old man"; four or five figures said to be "by Giorgione"; a painting of the Four Seasons by Bassano; a "ritratto of a Venetian looking sidewaise & showing a full body by Tintoretto il filio"; a portrait of "ye King of Spayne at length by Tizian as big as the life"; and many others. These, described in the 1640s when they had been taken back up to London for safety, were to create the Wilton atmosphere.

An inventory made of the house in November 1683, on the death of the seventh earl, and preserved among the Pembroke papers, gives some sense of the enormous riches gathered at Wilton. The inventory roams through 158 separate apartments laden with goods and tapestry hangings, pictures and furniture, which if nothing else marks the oceanic gulf between the life conditions of this family and those scratching their existence in the chalkland valleys they could see from their windows. If there is a certain boniness and paucity to the copyholders' possessions, here you can scarcely move for the material goods: "a Fustian quilt"; "a blew damask carpet"; pair after pair of silk tapestry hangings; chairs covered in black damask; a Purple Room with a purple damask bed; a silver table and looking glass; cloth of silver curtains and a headcloth to the bed embroidered with gold; a close stool and three pads for it; Turkish carpets and warming pans; an Indian quilt; a crimson velvet sideboard cloth; cloth-of-gold cushions with gold fringe; maps, folios, and volumes; "rich China bowls tippt and bottomed with silver"; one Book of Common Prayer and one Bible, both embossed with the family arms in silver; one Japan china teapot; and enormous quantities of wine in the barrel. Among it all, part of the "Goods belonging to the Dyning Room," alongside "1 set of Elbow chairs" and "4 stools of shaggy purple," was "The picture of the family & other pictures in ye Dining Roome," together thought to be worth £1,200, by far the most valuable things in the house. The family portrait was by Van Dyck, and many consider it the greatest painting of a family ever made in England. It represents the climax of this family's fortunes, of this book, and of the Arcadian story it has pursued. The great painting by Van Dyck is the ultimate embodiment of the Pembroke world, a painting carefully framed around the ideas of inheritance, Arcadianism, nobility, and time.

But if these large themes are in play, it is also fundamentally a painting of a family. There could be no meaning in riches if there were no heirs to enjoy them. His brother William had died childless but Philip had been careful to assemble a family. Three children had died young, with great sorrow for the parents, in the years before 1620. But many others had survived. His daughter Anna Sophia had married his ward, the enormously rich Robert Dormer, who in 1628 had become the Earl of Carnarvon. Charles, Lord Herbert, and his brothers Philip, William, James, and John were the boys Thomas Chaffinge had referred to so encouragingly in his sermon. After the Duke of Buckingham was assassinated, Buckingham's daughter Mary Villiers and her brothers had come to live with the Herberts, as her mother had married a wild Irish Roman Catholic lord and the king did not want the Villiers children brought up Catholic.

To this ensemble, after the death of his first wife Susan, Philip added one of the most intriguing figures of Stuart England: Lady Anne Clifford, the Dowager Countess of Dorset. By the time she married Philip, in June 1630, only two weeks after William had finally been buried in Salisbury Cathedral, she had suffered years of bullying and denial by her first husband, her relations, by the king, and by the court in general. She was a product of the greatest of English families, her mother a Russell, her cousin the Earl of Bedford, and her father the Elizabethan buccaneer George Clifford, Earl of Cumberland, tournament champion, captain of the *Bonadventure* against the Spanish Armada in 1588, conqueror of the Spanish at Puerto Rico, and winner of the golden prize Henry Pembroke had offered for his first horse race on the Wilton downs in the 1590s.

The Clifford earls of Cumberland had been the great medieval magnates of the northwest, with one generation after another dying in battle. They controlled vast estates in the Pennines and the Lake District. Those lands always descended to the "heir of the body" of the current earl, regardless of the heir's sex. Anne Clifford's father died "of a bloody flux" without a son in 1605, but he left his lands to his brother.

For decades, Anne and her mother waged a legal battle to recover them, gathering stupendous piles of ancient documents by which to prove Anne's rights to them, compiling biographies of those noble ancestors, becoming an authority on the ancient constitution by which the great magnates of medieval England had maintained their independence of the crown. In 1609, she married the spendthrift rake Richard Sackville, Earl of Dorset, who sided with her enemies in trying to coerce her into surrendering her claim on lands that were rightfully hers. Dorset tried every way he could to make her conform to his and her uncle's patriarchal dominance: threats of separation, refusal to sleep with her when she knew she was fertile, shaming her in public by flirting with his mistress, Lady Penniston, cancelling her jointure—the income from the lands to which she would have a right if he died before her—terrorizing her servants, and taking away from her the daughter on which she doted.

Anne was tiny, only four feet ten inches, but indomitable. James's queen Anne gave her "warning not to trust [her] matters absolutely to the King lest he should deceive me," and when confronted with the demands of the Cumberlands as voiced by the king himself in 1617, she stood up to him with a courage that is astonishing for a twenty-seven-year-old woman, even more so with the court largely ranged against her.

> I beseech'd his Majesty to pardon me for that I would never part from Westmorland while I lived upon any condition whatsoever.

Unsurprisingly, her spirits had often sunk under the relentless pressure and lack of respect. Retreating to the comfort of a diary, she was often "sad to see things go so ill with me." She bore Dorset five children, two girls who survived and three sons, all of whom "dyed young at Knowle, in Kent, where they were born." After Dorset himself died in 1624, she came into her jointure of £2,000 a year, but Dorset's own heir and brother continued to persecute her, and her troubles deepened when she suffered a violent attack of smallpox "which disease did so marter my face that it Confirmed more and more my mynd never to marrie againe."

This was the woman Philip Herbert married at the Bedford house of Chenies on the first of June 1630. There were many surprised that he married her at all: a forty-year-old ravaged by smallpox, with the reputation for independence of mind and pugnacity of spirit. And why should she, a woman perfectly well provided for, enter into a marriage with a man whose own reputation was not entirely sweet-smelling? Partly there were material considerations: her meager income from the Sackville lands, his enormous wealth (an income of perhaps £20,000 a year), and his position at court. Gossip was against them: "nor did there want divers malitious illwillers to Blow and foment the Coals of discontent betwixt us," she wrote much later. But there were also many aspects of their two backgrounds which would have brought them together. Both would have considered they came from the ancient not the modern court aristocracy. Both had been tutored by the poet Samuel Daniel in their youths. The works of Edmund Spenser, Sir Philip Sidney, and Michael Drayton—all of them part of the Pembroke circle of patronage, all of them Arcadianists—were in her library. She even erected and paid for a monument in Westminster Abbey to Spenser, who had been her mother's client. Both families had long-standing connections to John Donne, who enjoyed Anne's company. She could talk of anything, Donne once said, "from slea-silk to predestination," the whole range of existence from God's mind to the kind of fluffy silk which would ball up like cotton wool. It is not inconceivable that this marriage was more than a corporate alliance and that these two battle-scarred veterans of the court world saw in each other the possibilities of happiness.

This is the family portrayed in the great Van Dyck portrait. In 1634, the long-laid plans for the wedding of Mary Villiers and Charles Herbert had come into focus. The convoluted, debt-ridden Buckingham estate was finally to be granted probate in March 1635, and the prospect of that tangle being resolved may have prompted the earl into action. Equally, his fifteen-year-old-son Charles was approaching the age when he would be sent abroad with a tutor to visit Italy. In July 1634, Mary's mother, the Duchess of Buckingham, settled on the outline of an agreement with the earl. Swathes of Pembroke lands in Dorset, Glamorgan, Monmouth, and Wiltshire were to be transferred to the young couple in return for the £25,000 Mary would bring in her wake. The great alliance of new money and old status, conceived in the 1620s as a solution to the deep split then threatening the court, was at last to be achieved.

Then, very nearly, disaster struck. Mary began to fall in love not with the intended heir, Charles, but with his younger brother. "The young lady began to affect the younger brother Philip Herbert," George Garrard, a court gossip, wrote,

> and of herself warned the Chamberlain, that she might marry him, saying he did apply himself to her more than my lord Herbert did; but the dutchess chid her out of that humour, and now she is marrid that affection will vanish.

This particular twelve-year-old girl was not going to shipwreck the elaborate corporate deal. The ceremony was eventually conducted at the end of Christmas 1634 "by the Archbishop of Canterbury in the closet at Whitehall. It was done privately, and few invited, and sooner than was intended."

The financial details had not been settled and were not to be until the following May, when a huge vellum document with four sealed blobs of sealing wax, each the size of a squash ball and deeply impressed with the seals of the participating parties, was finally signed: Mary's mother and stepfather, the Earl of Antrim; the Earl of Northampton (a courtier); Pembroke himself, Sir Thomas Morgan of Wilton and Ruperra; and Sir John Thorowgood of London (a government official) all witnessed the transfer and commitment of lands and money "in consideration of a marriage heretofore had and solemnized."

The money flows were enormous. The earl was to assign all his lands in Wiltshire, Dorset, Somerset, Monmouth, and Glamorgan to his son, keeping for himself only an interest in them for the rest of his life. There could, in other words, be no going back on what he now agreed to give to the new couple. The duchess, for her part, agreed to give her daughter "twentie thousand pounds of lawfull money of England." She would pay it in instalments of £4,000 a year for five years, beginning at Michaelmas 1634. In addition, Lady Mary was to hand over £5,000 from another inheritance, her grandfather's, which she had already received. The earl agreed to spend this money, plus an additional £15,000 of his own, on lands that he was going to give to the children and that would provide Lady Mary with the £4,000 a year jointure after Charles died. If either of them died "after the said intended marriage and before cohabitation or before the said Lady Mary shall atteyne the age of sixteene yeares," then the whole deal was off. All money was to be repaid to the duchess, and the earl was free of his obligations to either his son or Lady Mary. The deal was to be concluded "by making of conveyances and assurances by Counsell learned on both sides before Xmas next, as convenientlie as may be done." There was no thought whatsoever that these two people, aged fifteen and twelve, would sleep together until they were substantially older, perhaps not for the next four years.

One other development had occurred in these busy months: Pembroke's marriage to Lady Anne Clifford had collapsed. She had resisted his claims over her lands in the north. He had refused the claim she would traditionally have made over a third of his lands after he died, and together they signed a document in which each stated their claim:

> *Wee are content to referre the consideration of the reasonablenss*
> *of theis propositions, & what may be fitt to be done thereupon,*
> *unto the Rt Honble the Lord Priuy seale [a judge, the Earl of*
> *Manchester], & the Earle of Bedford [Anne's cousin and long-*
> *standing ally] & what they shall advise wee will performe and*
> *obsirue*
>
> Pembroke Montgomery
> Anne Pembroke

But this was only a symptom of a deeper underlying malaise. Anne Clifford had been shaped by her sufferings. It is no coincidence that she became a diarist, because her life had turned into one of withdrawal and privacy. "I stay'd much in the Country," she had written when with Lord Dorset at Knole, "having many times a sorrowfull & heavy heart, and being condemn'd by most folks because I would not consent to the agreement [with her husband], so as I may truly say I am like an owl in the desert." It would turn out no better with Pembroke.

> The marble pillars of Knowle in Kentt and Wilton in
> Wiltshire were to me often times but the gay Harbours of
> Anguish. Insomuch as a Wiseman that knew the inside
> of my fortune would often say that I lived in both those
> my Lordes great familyes as the river Roan [Rhone]
> or Rodamus runs thorow the Lake of Geneva, without

> mingleinge anie part of its streames with that Lake; For I
> gave myselfe wholly to Retyredness, as much as I could,
> in both those great families, and made good Bookes and
> verteous thoughts my Companions.

She had retired not into widowhood but into diaryhood, an exceptionally rare condition in the early seventeenth century, a river running unmingled through the waters of a family. Two further levels
of unhappiness should be added to this picture. Sometime in December 1634, in the days before the wedding between his son Charles and
Mary Villiers, Pembroke ejected Anne Clifford from his lodgings in
Whitehall. From then on, at least for the next fifteen years, she was to
live in one of his houses in Wiltshire or London, but only rarely with
him. The immediate cause is unknown, but the context is more pitiable
still. Anne became pregnant twice with Philip Herbert, bearing "two
sons that were born both before their time while I lived at Whitehall."
Both premature sons died at birth.

It is sometimes assumed that the frequent death of children in premodern England caused no grief in their parents. This is untrue. No
explicit record remains of Anne's reaction to the death of these Herbert
sons, but there is a letter from her mother, the Countess of Cumberland, written on the death of a son and heir of her own, Robert Clifford. Half coherent with grief, it is addressed to the family chaplain
and translator of the King James Bible, Dr. John Layfield:

> Oh miserable woman wretched in the hope of my Life, to
> loose a Child of that hope, of that Love, to mee a Rose,
> that sweet Robin pulled before the tyme, the only sonne
> of his Mother, tormented with sicknesse, so many weeks
> before. Oh troubles come in by floods my deare Lord in

dangers unknown for number myself sonneless, my hon-
nour brought down, my poverty increased my misfortunes
to my enemy's laid open they gain, when I loose.

These are the circumstances in which the "mighty large piece of
the Ea of Pembrooke and all his family by Vandyke" was made. Everything in this long story can be seen to contribute to its meaning,
and its strange and enigmatic qualities become clearer in the light of
the family's story.

It is a drama of fertility, time, and death, much of its meaning carried by the subtle ballet of the hands sewn through the picture. The
Earl and Countess of Carnarvon, on the right, are already the parents of a young heir, Charles, born two years before. They glow with
sexuality and health: Anna Sophia's bosom is deeply revealed, and
between her fingers she holds a single pearl, standing for the precious
heir whom she and her husband have conceived. Their hands dabble
together in an unmistakably sexual way, the only sign of human contact in the painting. Theirs is the realm of fecundity and fullness. But
still their eyes do not meet. No member of the family, in fact, looks at
any other. Each is alone in his glorious world, and none is more glorious than Anna Sophia's husband, Robert Dormer, earl of Carnarvon,
at this stage in his life a traveller and gambler, a notorious womanizer
and rake, and a man filled with the vigor of an active life.

Next to that fertile and engaging pair is its opposite: the hands of
the countess are folded together in a way that is repeated nowhere else
in the entire body of Van Dyck's work: an explicit gesture of enclosure
and melancholy, shut off from those around her. The marriage of the
Earl and Countess of Pembroke, both of them shadowed and pushed
back within the picture, is barren. Her sons have died, and their relationship has failed. Her averted eyes and her folded hands are the
gestures of a woman who is no longer "mingleinge anie part of [her]

streames" with this family. She is central but absent, her gaze averted, her relationship with everyone around her cut away and inarticulate.

Beside her, but not touching her, the earl, Lord Chamberlain, the high official who is in charge of the Royal Household, holds his white staff of office easily in the relaxed and lengthened fingers of his left hand. With his other hand he reaches forward to the virginal promise of Mary Villiers, gesturing openly toward the heart of the young woman who is to marry his son. These are the signs of power. She, however, holds a closed hand to her virginal womb, a form of self-preservation even as she is to be married. In the picture space she is nearly but not quite connected to Charles, Lord Herbert, in red, who holds his left arm out as if in love, an openness to the world, but the hand itself is reflexed and withdrawn, perhaps also a sign of his virginity.

These three pairs make a diagrammatic set: fertility achieved, barrenness accepted, breeding promised. The younger brother, Philip, sharing with his brother the reddish brown hair that had come down through the generations, hangs back on the edge of this group of six, not part of it and not quite distinct. Is it too much to see in his portrayal the story recounted by George Garrard, of love disappointed, of his place in Mary Villiers's heart usurped by his older brother, not because love required it but simply because their father and her mother insisted? And is there an element, in Mary Villiers's own look of disdain, of a discontent with this marriage that was forced upon her for dynastic reasons?

The final elements are the two sets of three children on the left of the painting. The three young Herbert boys on the ground are gloriously alive with their hounds and their books. The three young Herberts who died as children are above them as angels, throwing roses into the wedding party. The painting as a whole flickers between content and discontent, between a celebration of the beauty of existence and recognition of its sorrows and travails. As a whole it is not unlike Thomas

Chaffinge's sermon on mutability, time, beauty, inheritance, and grief. Behind them all, Arcadia recedes into an inscrutable perfection.

The painter was a man of the world, ambitious, rich, and realistic, and this painting is part of that urban, entrepreneurial world. If a sitter could not pay for his portrait—Van Dyck usually charged £50 to £60 for a full-length (three years' stipend for a country vicar), £30 for a half-length, and £20 for a head-and-shoulders portrait; the Wilton group portrait cost more than £500—the artist would quite happily sell it to someone else. Those who required portraits from him had to book a series of appointments in advance. He would never paint a sitter for longer than an hour at a time and would usually have assistants complete the painting once the head and hands were done. Sitters sent their clothes to the studio, where hired models posed in them and Flemish specialists, employed by Van Dyck, painted the sumptuous cloths. There was something of the factory about the process, but during the precious hours in which the master's eye was engaged with his subject, Van Dyck's easy manners and self-possession encouraged in those who stood before him what was called at the time "an eloquence of the body," a poise, a form of bodily control that implied spiritual and social distinction.

As they stood within the lit circle, Van Dyck charmed them as a photographer might. The way these people appear in his paintings was the way he encouraged them to appear in that discriminating atmosphere. Preliminary sketches of the two Carnarvons have survived: between those sketches and the finished oil painting, Van Dyck simplified some details of clothing, loosening and romanticizing it, but he did not change substantially the way the people stood or looked. These are portraits not inventions, even if what they portray was as much an aspiration as a reality.

Here, then, consciously drawing on roots that dive many generations and many decades back into the English past, is the climax of this

Arcadian civilization. Its regal air intersects with a subtle, individualized psychology. Its subject is nobility, but its method questions the simplicity of that word. For all the charm of its presentation, its alluring surface, this is not a trivial or decorative object. It is about power and vulnerability, and its dressing of that power in these silks is itself an Arcadian act. Its governing paradox is that the man at the center, the ageing earl, the most weakly portrayed figure on the canvas, is the man who is making all the decisions. Time is conquering him. Van Dyck would paint him again, two or three years later, worn down, sitting heavily within the frame, the vitality of hope ebbed out of him.

Overall, the atmosphere of the painting is not quite secure. There is nothing cruel in it, nor even unkind, but it is full of uncertainty, hesitation, and even surprise, a tentativeness that makes complacency impossible. Where are they? Not in a comfortable interior, as they would have been in both the sixteenth and eighteenth centuries, but half inside and half out, half in a theater, half in the margins of a palace. Nor is there a settled middle to the painting. What seems to be central flickers from the earl and countess to the young Mary Villiers, who stands in front of them. The geometrical center in fact hovers in the awkward space between Mary's head and the body of Charles, the young lord in red, a charged absence at the heart of the painting.

Once you become alert to this sense of insecurity in the painting, it seems pervasive. Look at Philip, the younger of the two glamorous young Herberts, wearing the color called "carnation" in the seventeenth century. There is no ease in him. His pose is uncertain and his face unsure. A little less edgily, his elder brother stands beside him, performing it seems to nothing but the air. Only the three young boys at the left-hand side, framed by their dogs, a greyhound and a setter, are immune to this atmosphere, yet to enter the world of knowingness, sophistication, and uncertainty inhabited by their elders. (But even the dogs carry a signal: the ownership of setters and greyhounds was made illegal by a royal proclamation in 1638. Any greyhound found within ten miles of the court was to be hanged. Their presence here could also be taken as a statement of lordly independence from royal autocracy.)

In the painting, each of the subjects' hands in turn gives, blesses, meets, contains, promises, protects, challenges, and suggests. There is a play here to do with love, family, selfhood, engagement, and distance, between closedness and openness, intimacy and removal, spread across the whole width of the picture. These are the signals fitted to this particular moment, a marriage but not yet a sexual union, which will have to wait until both bride and groom are older.

Van Dyck had a famous and treasured ability to give a scene the sense that it was a caught moment, to imply from his nearly mobile figures that within a second their perfect arrangement would change and collapse. It is a stilled dance. Transience was at the center of his art, and here it is set against its opposite. Behind the figures, two enormous certainties preside: the landscape of perfection on the left, receding into deep-shadowed calm, and in the center-right, the vast coat of arms on the cloth that hangs behind them all, the inheritance of nobility, an assertion of the permanence from which they come. But do those certainties transmit themselves to the anxious figures in the foreground? Or do they serve to throw those figures into question? How do the two glorious young men really compare to the solidity and fixity of the two fluted columns behind them? They seem momentary beings by comparison, balanced on the balls of their feet, no more lasting or substantial than the clouds or the putti or the fading of the sun.

The beauty and allure of this picture is its central acknowledgment that complacency and fineness cannot coexist. The highest condition, it seems to say, is one of uncertainty and doubt. A questioning form of irony and intelligence is applied here to a conventional ideal. The sense of movement and of the contingent in Van Dyck's baroque masterpieces is the embodiment of that uncertainty. A body that hesitates between the steps of a platform, that makes a gesture that is at the same time withheld, that displays a sense of grace but does so in shadow: these are the ambivalent qualities to which one instinctively still responds. Look beneath the surface of this painting and you see in it a story not of worldly glory but of transience and fragility, of failure and disconnection, of the place of death and the erosion of time even in the most perfect circumstances. This is a painting that might be entitled *Et in Arcadia Ego*. But that poignancy of decline and infertility is not the only meaning here. Its light falls not on a tomb but on the beautiful, pale, glowing optimism of the young faces for whom the future holds out buoyant promise.

The portrait was probably finished by the end of May 1635. By then, Pembroke had arranged that

> Lord Charles Herbert of Cardiff and his brother Philip Herbert Esquire sons of the Earl of Pembroke and Montgomery are by His Majesty's Licence going into France to travel.

The commander of the fleet in the Channel was instructed by the Lords of the Admiralty "to cause some of the ships of the fleet to transport the Lord Chamberlain's sons to Dieppe," and on June 6, 1635, the ship *Swallow* carried them there. They were on their way to Italy, the heartland of the civilization with which their father was in love.

In the middle of March 1636, nine months after the two boys had left England for the continent, the news reached London. They had been staying in Venice. Philip wrote a thank-you letter to Lord Feilding, Buckingham's nephew and the English ambassador, for the "excessive courtesies and great civilitie" he had shown to his boys when they were there. They had moved on to Florence and in that city, just after Christmas, Charles, Lord Herbert, died of smallpox. The earl "took the news most grievously" and did not emerge from his rooms in the Cockpit at Whitehall for more than a week.

It has often been said that the death of Charles ruined the earl's financial prospects because the great £25,000 Villiers dowry was withdrawn on his death. But that misunderstands the nature of the marriage agreement, which was designed to be equal on both sides. Mary Villiers's mother would no longer have to produce the money, but Philip, Earl of Pembroke, would no longer have to give the jointure of £4,000 a year to his widowed daughter-in-law. The deal had been balanced, and works at Wilton did not stop at Charles's death. The earl's annual income, including the £6,000 a year from his deranged sister-in-law, was now about £30,000 (at a time when it was possible to build a perfectly good manor house for £150.) There is, in fact, a slight and poignant memorial at Wilton to Charles's disappearance from the scene. In the hunting room, decorated with painted panels derived from Tempesta's scenes of different forms of hunt around the world—the bludgeoning of crocodiles and the sticking of ostriches, men hiding from their prey dressed as cows, or underwater wearing rocklike hats to trick the wild duck—the painter Edward Pierce inserted here and there images of the fourth earl and his heir. The boy who is represented was not Charles but the younger brother, Philip, who had risen to take his place.

Mary Villiers was still at Wilton in 1636 when Van Dyck painted her as a fourteen-year-old widow, low in the picture space, black bows on her bosom and at her waist for her dead husband, a rose in her hand as a sign that she would marry again. The king wanted her back at court, but Mary was refusing, even as early as March 1636, to succumb. Within eighteen months, she had married the king's cousin, James Stuart, Duke of Lennox, a young and naive Scotsman, "of small experience in affairs," fiercely loyal to the crown. Mary brought him her £25,000 dowry, and in doing that, this high-spirited and strong-willed woman swam out of the Pembrokes' lives.

Van Dyck's painting of a wedding had become an epitaph. It was, of course, a chance event, but after the death of Charles Herbert, the tide starts to ebb. The integration of court and country on which Philip Pembroke had based his life for so long, and of which Wilton was the symbol as the Palace in the Trees, now began to fall apart. The Pembrokes' quarrel with the king would soon be resumed.

A SAD AND MISERABLE CONDITION WE ARE FALLEN INTO

THE CATASTROPHE OF CIVIL WAR
1640–1650

By the beginning of the 1640s, all over England, the old arrangements began to break up. In May of that year, Pembroke's son-in-law, Robert Dormer, the Earl of Carnarvon, was trying to raise a militia in Buckinghamshire for the war against the Scottish Presbyterians. He was meeting with little but reluctance from a gentry who had been subjected to forced loans and "new unheard-of taxes" and who were not now interested in paying for the king's desire to spread a richly Episcopal church to Scotland.

> Concerning our soldiers, I make no question they will be forewith very well clothed, but I do not see a possibility of procuring the draught horses, the country is so averse to paying ready money. I have sent out my warrants twice, and met the country twice, but they will part with no money.

In Wiltshire it was worse. Pembroke and his sons accompanied the king to the north, but other Wiltshire gentry only sent money, at best. Some refused to do that. In the summer of 1640, soldiers were pressed from all across the county. John Nicholas, successor to Sir Thomas Morgan as steward of the Pembroke estates, wrote to his son Edward, clerk to the Privy Council in Whitehall. John was in the family house at Winterbourne Earls, in the beautiful valley of the Bourne, just north of Salisbury. "It begins to be bad enough here," he wrote on June 1, 1640.

> Yesterday, being Sunday, a company of soldiers which were pressed [for the war against the Scots], about Martin and Damerham, in Wilts., [on the southern slope of the downs south of Broad Chalke] passing through our parish towards Marlborough, where the rendezvous is appointed, took all they could catch in their way, and being resisted by the owners of such poultry and other provisions as they took, they beat many very sorely and at Idminston [a couple of miles up the valley from Winterbourne Earls] cut off the hand of one Nott, and hurt another very dangerously. . . . There were but five soldiers, they came by my house as I was at dinner, and asked for victuals, and your mother sent them a piece of beef and beer enough, wherewith they were well pleased; yet after this they did the mischief. It is an ill beginning. . . . I wish you would take more time to stay with us than you have done heretofore.

That image of the hand of the poor chalkland farmer Robert Nott—he died in 1660—being sliced off by a small platoon of passing soldiers introduces the 1640s, as if the gentleness and expressiveness of the hands in the Pembroke family portrait, the linking gestures between them, had turned to this.

The world had darkened. The king's use of his prerogative powers in the 1630s had thrown the entire basis of the state into question. "We must not only sweep the house clean below," John Pym, the leader of the radical party in the House of Commons, told Edward Hyde, one of the old Pembroke adherents, that summer. "We must pull down all the cobwebs which hang in the top and corners, that they might not breed dust, and so make a foul house hereafter; we now have the opportunity to make our country happy, by removing all grievances, and pulling up the causes of them by the roots."

This was the deepest possible change. The cluttered ancient arrangements that were the essence of custom no longer seemed adequate. The great jurist Sir Edward Coke had repeatedly quoted an old saw: "out of the old fields, as men saith, cometh new corne fro yere to yere." To Pym and his allies, that frame a mind no longer seemed valid. It had been betrayed by a crown that had ruled without a parliament for a decade, had imposed illegal taxes, had imprisoned people wrongfully, had suborned the judiciary, and was steering the church away from the purity of its Protestant Reformation and toward the sinks of Roman Catholic iniquity.

If the lord had betrayed the copyholders of the manor, the copyholders no longer owed him any allegiance. The mutuality had gone. Instead, for Pym and his followers, a kind of brutal clarity was needed, a sweeping away of the unreliable superstructure of monopolies, forced loans, income from the sale of wards, and all the other baggage of inheritance. The ancient constitution had failed. The king and his ministers had failed England, and England needed to move on to a more enlightened and clarified future. The king saw all this clearly enough. The idea of Pym's party in Parliament, he said, was "to erect a universal over-swaying power to themselves."

The deep disenchantment of England soon focused on the most powerful and uncompromising minister of the crown, Sir Thomas

Wentworth, Earl of Strafford. He was not only guilty, Pym thought, "of vanity and amours," but as president of the Council both in Ireland and in the north of England, he had tried to "subvert the ancient fundamental laws of these realms of England and Ireland and to introduce an arbitrary and tyrannical government, against law."

That spring, as the bill for the condemnation of Strafford was being debated in Parliament and in the Council Chamber, mobs gathered at Westminster and even within the precincts of Whitehall Palace:

> As any lord passed by [they] called *Justice, justice*! And with great rudeness and insolence, pressing upon and thrusting those lords whom they suspected not to favour that bill; professing aloud "that they would be governed and disposed by the honourable House of Commons and would defend their privileges." This unheard of act of insolence and sedition continued so many days, till so many lords grew so really apprehensive of having their brains beaten out, that they absented themselves from the house.

Eighty or so lords had heard the arguments for Strafford and against, but in the end only forty-six dared attend on the crucial day. Thirty-five of them voted for his death. Pembroke was among them. Only eleven lords dared to defend Strafford. Pembroke was acting according to the tradition he had inherited: a support for the ancient constitution against the inroads of royal government and its arrogant officers. On May 3, 1641, he moved still further against the king, telling the angry anti-Strafford crowd jostling outside Westminster Hall that "His Majesty had promised they should have speedy execution of justice to their desires," a set of words that reached the ears of Charles and his queen and condemned Pembroke in their minds. It was a moment when the old amalgam was falling apart and choices had to be made. Pembroke was on the side of the country, a position that was in effect Arcadia turned political.

On May 12, 1641, after the king had reluctantly given his authority for the act, Strafford was executed on Tower Hill for treachery against the English nation; a crowd of two hundred thousand exulted in his death. The king would never recover from what he thought of as his betrayal of a loyal servant. He was clear in his mind: Pembroke, even if acting in defense of the ancient constitution, had himself betrayed his sovereign and his duty. It was the conflict of idealisms that would lead to war.

The tension at Westminster in that hot and close summer would finally burst and destroy Pembroke's career in July. The trigger for the crisis was trivial but symptomatic of this complex, involuted world. As part of his wife's dowry, Philip, Lord Herbert, now the earl's eldest surviving son and heir, had come into possession of some lands in Sutton Marsh, in the south Lincolnshire fens. It was one of the most contested pieces of land in England. The rights of commoners, who had been accustomed to living off the wildfowl and fuel from the marshes, had been extinguished by a set of aristocratic landlords who had drained, improved, and privatized their property. Along with other drained fens, it had become the scene of regular riot and destruction

On top of that, Herbert's title to these fenlands was in dispute with, among others, the king's cousin the Duke of Lennox, now the husband of the very Mary Villiers with whom Philip, Lord Herbert, had once been in love and on whom Pembroke had once been relying for her dowry. As yet another ingredient in this tangle, Lennox's sister, Elizabeth Stuart, was married to Henry Howard, Lord Mowbray and Maltravers, the heir to the Earl of Arundel, part of the Howard family that had been long-standing rivals and enemies of the Herberts. Maltravers, of enormous wealth himself and one of the major investors in fen drainage, had in 1626 married this girl against the king's wishes. William Pembroke and Philip Montgomery, as Privy Councillors, had both been part of the decision to commit him to the Tower.

Now in the fiercely heightened atmosphere of the summer of 1641, polarized by the trial and execution of the Earl of Strafford in May, amid whispers of an army plot to take over Parliament in the king's name, and in the presence of the bellowing crowds outside the Parliament House, this angry nest of aristocratic enmities and rivalries came to a head. Lennox, Pembroke, and Maltravers, as well as Lord Seymour, an old rival of Pembroke for local influence in Wiltshire, were all members of a small committee of the House of Lords whose task it was to consider the petitions of the people. The young Philip Herbert was also in attendance himself, acting as a messenger between the House of Lords and the House of Commons. Pembroke had voted for the execution of Strafford; Maltravers had made himself conveniently absent for the day; Lennox was one of the eleven who had voted to save Strafford. The summer was hot and overpowering. Smallpox and the plague were spreading in the City. One puritan MP had proposed a bill "for the gelding of Jesuits." According to a document in the papers of the House of Lords, taken down from witnesses the following day, the tension burst at a meeting of the committee on July 19, 1641.

It began with a pedantic discussion about an ancient statute from the time of Henry IV that had been dragged up by one of the lawyers in one of the Sutton Marsh cases. The Duke of Lennox arrived late to the committee, heard the phrase "Sutton Marsh," and asked what they had been discussing. Pembroke, looking across the table and pointing toward Maltravers, said, "No man named Sutton Marsh till you named it."

> To which my Lord Maltravers replyed I never named it
> till you named it first, and I appeale to the Committee. To
> which my Lord Chamberlayne sayd—But you did. The

other answered—I did not; and so twise or thrise to and fro. Then said my Lord Chamberlayne—My Yea is as good as your No, to which my Lord Matravers—And my No as your Yea, and further sayd that he would maintayne that he had named it 20 tymes this day. To which my Lord Chamberlayne sayd that he durst not maintayne it out of that place. Then my Lord Matravers sayd, That he would maintayne it in any place, for it was true; To which my Lord Chamberlayne replyed that it was false. My Lord Matravers sayd, You lye. Whereupon my Lord Chamberlayne reached out his white staff and over the table strok him on the head. Then my Lord Matravers took up the Standesh [a stand for pen and ink] that was on the table before him, and my lord Chamberlayne goinge farther from him, he threw it after him but misst him. Then my Lord Chamberlayne came towards him agayne and over the table gave him a second blow with his white staffe.

It was a catastrophe. Pembroke had lost his temper often enough before and had even hit people with the staff of office, which Van Dyck had shown resting so elegantly in his fingers. But he was not to get away with it this time. His hurried, draft apology, written the same day as the incident, survives among the papers of the House of Lords, scratchy and no more than half legible:

> at the committee for
> am fallen into the dishonour of
> this House
> ~~for my offence~~ I am greatly sorry for that offence
> of your Lopps
> ~~of that House~~

to be most iust. So I in all   humility
submit my selfe thereunto

Both he and Maltravers were sent to the Tower. On July 21, Pembroke made his apology to the House of Lords for his "miscarriage towards your lordships." The opportunity was too good for the king to miss. He had long been exasperated by Pembroke's rough and uncourtly behavior and took the chance to "send to him by a gentleman usher for his staff." The symbol of authority was removed from him and his career at court ended in humiliation. Efforts by Parliament to have him appointed Lord Steward of the Household were rebuffed by the king. Pembroke, as the inheritance from his grandfather the first earl, from Philip Sidney, and from his brother might all have suggested, was being pushed into the arms of those who were opposed to the king.

It was utterly humiliating. Pembroke could not "choose but think 44 years' service ill requited to be thus disgracefully dismissed." The atmosphere at Westminster was filled with anxiety and threat. At the end of October an anonymous gentleman on horseback gave a porter a letter for Pym, with twelvepence to deliver it. When Pym opened it in the chamber of the House of Commons, a filthy and bloody rag that had been drawn through a plague sore fell from his hands. The letter said: "Do not think a guard of men can protect you if you persist in your traitorous courses and wicked designs . . . If this do not touch your heart, a dagger shall."

Early in January 1642, after word had reached the king that Parliament would try to impeach his Catholic queen, Charles went with a party of one hundred troopers to the House of Commons to arrest the leaders of the anti-Stuart faction. They had escaped before he arrived, but the military intervention was an irrevocable and disastrous step. Charles had become a king who was prepared to threaten the nation gathered in Parliament with military force. On January 10, he left London and gradually made his way north, attempting to persuade the country that his task was to defend the liberties of England against the prospect of an increasingly tyrannical parliamentary government. The body of England was pulling apart into head and limbs, each claiming they were the true heirs of the integrated whole. After Parliament decided to raise its own army in March 1642, war was inevitable. By May the king was in York, and from there, on May 30, 1642, he wrote to Pembroke. That letter, a folded foolscap sheet, has survived. It is the fulcrum of this story, the point at which this family's long double commitment to king and country splits apart.

> To our rt trusty & right wellbeloved Cosin & Councillor
> Philip Earle of Pembroke & Montgomery
>
> Wee greet you well. Whereas Wee have some occasions of importance highly concerning our person, honor, & Service, wherein Wee are very desirous to recieve your advise and assistance, having had experience of your Affection, Wisdome and Integrity, Our express Pleasure therefore is, And Wee doe hereby will and command you all delayes and excuses sett apart, to make your immediate repaire hither to vs, When you shall understand the particular & urgent causes of this our sending for you: Of wch you may in no wise faile, as you value the good of Vs & our Service. And for so doing this our letter shall be your sufficient Warr[ant]. Given at Our Court at York the 30th day of May 1642.

"Charles R.": the king had signed this letter, with its ominous mixture of command and entreaty, by putting his large feathery signature, the pen scarcely touching the paper, at the head of the secretary's text.

But Pembroke ignored it, and the letter remains today in the House of Lords where it arrived that spring day. England was en route to civil war. The two sides were gathering their troops all over the country. In August, after the harvest had been taken in and men could turn their thoughts to war, Charles raised his standard at Nottingham and began to collect his army around him. Robert Dormer, Earl of Carnarvon, was with him. The Earl of Pembroke, Dormer's father-in-law, was not.

The discontent had surfaced, and in Clarendon's words, "every man [became] troubled and perplexed." Sir Benjamin Rudyerd, the long-standing Pembroke client, who with William Pembroke had written private Arcadian love poems thirty years before, had said to the House of Commons in July 1642 that "If blood once again begins to touch blood, we shall presently fall into a certain misery and must attain an uncertain success." The sense of the community of England, of a single organism connecting crown and people through the ancient constitution, had broken down, and for the next decade, as they repeatedly expressed it, the body of the country was at war with itself. It was "an intestinal war," "the troubles," the "unnaturall war," "the late unhappie difference." For Philip Skippon, the roundhead commander at Marlborough in December 1642, the royalists were "a race of vipers, that would eat the passage to their ambitions through the entrails of their mother, the Commonwealth." The favorite term used by parliamentarians for royalists was *malignant*, as if they were a disease of the body. If they had possessed anything like the frame of mind that could produce this expression, they would have recognized the Civil War as a form of autoimmune disease, the tissues of the body filled with its own hostile antibodies, a war in which not only liberty but the entire *constitution* of the body—a word that in its political and physical senses still preserves this ancient analogy—was endangered.

The war was brutal, not only in its battles, where the proportion of dead in infantry units could at times reach 75 percent, usually under the swords of the cavalry, or in the aftermath of sieges, whether of towns or fortified manor houses, where rage and revenge exacted a terrifying price from the defenders. A man emerged from one of these sieges with his mind so destroyed that he spent the rest of his life crawling around on all fours, hoping to be mistaken for a dog. Nor only in the dreadful weather, the cold and rain, which beat almost ceaselessly, winter and summer, in the early 1640s. Nor in the disastrous harvests, particularly in the middle of the decade, which left swathes of England hungry and weakened. Nor in the attacks of the plague that ravaged the hungry villages. Wilton, Bemerton, and Fugglestone were all devastated by the disease, which killed some of the people and kept others shut up so that they could not work but "during wch tyme they were inforced to waste and consume that small porcion of estate wch they formerly had gotten by their hard labour to ye utter impoverishinge of them and theire families," so that "as they have died in the plauge so now will they dye with famen also." Village after village made "a miserable cry to the magistrates," imploring the authorities for aid.

More than that, the Civil War was a brutal eruption of anarchy, rape, theft, and violence, of gang dominance and gang attack, of pervasive lawlessness, which spread across the country, terrified ordinary people, gave free rein to thugs and thieves, and turned the roads through the Arcadian valleys of Wiltshire into places no ordinary man or woman would dare travel. Everything that sixteenth- and seventeenth-century England had feared, against which the idea of Arcadia had been set, became a reality in the 1640s: a breakdown of order and even of meaning, a sense that no one knew anymore what mattered or what they believed in. The only constant, becoming ever more urgent as the years of war and turmoil rolled on, was a desire for a better time, a time in the past, an increasingly golden age of peace and happiness.

Wiltshire was turned over time and again. Already by March 1643 "the ways are now very dangerous to travel in by reason of the interruption of soldiers." Pembroke abandoned Wilton for his London houses and sent his estranged wife, Lady Anne Clifford, to live in Baynard's Castle, where she could look after his paintings and treasures. Detachments from both sides camped from time to time in the great rooms at Wilton and at Ramsbury, with the troopers quartered in the stables, the household servants providing meals for the officers. Pembroke's son-in-law, the Earl of Carnarvon, on the enemy side, spent a night in the house with other cavalier commanders in late May 1643. The king himself spent a few nights at Ramsbury, and at the very end of the war the king's daughter, Princess Elizabeth, held court with one or two of the Wiltshire cavaliers for a few days at Wilton. Around these passing wartime ironies, the county became a battle zone, controlled by Parliament to begin with, then taken by the royalists making raids from Oxford; its many country houses became armored hardpoints in the war, besieged and stormed, first by one side then the other, often sacked with astonishing and terrible ferocity, the women raped, the children abused, while armies marched across the ravaged lands between them.

The men and women of the county found themselves in a labyrinth of contradiction, not sure how or why the country had come to this, nor what their part in it all should be. Where before they had known what their rights and restrictions had been, now they were to answer to strange masters on strange grounds. Arguments they were only faintly familiar with had erupted into their lives. "Do you not think the condition of the poor Countryeman hath not suffered a sad alteration," one anonymous Wiltshireman asked at the end of 1642, "from a state wherein he knew what was his owne, and was not capable of any violence for which he was not sure of a remedy and reparation, to this, where he receives commands under the penalty of plundering and hanging from persons of whom he never heard, for horses, for money, for personall attendance, for which he can find no ground?"

Few sights are more pathetic than the marks of illiterate Wiltshiremen from these villages, perhaps related to the symbols with which they identified their sheep in the common flocks, put at the end of the hundreds of petitions and complaints to the justices that detail the damage and destruction done to their lives in these years:

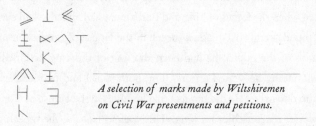

A selection of marks made by Wiltshiremen on Civil War presentments and petitions.

"'Tis indeed a sad and miserable condition we are fallen into," the anonymous Wiltshireman wrote. He was addressing his friend, an MP at Westminster. Why, he asked, had the war even begun? They were "weltering in one anothers bloud before we know why we are angry, and to see our houses and towns fired and our Neighbours and Friends taken prisoners, by men who do not onely speake the same language with us, but are of our owne families and of the same (or seeme to be of the same) Religion." Violence and viciousness had erupted in precisely the way the whole culture had been designed to prevent.

There was "a strange dejection in the spirits of the people," this Marlborough man continued, "& if I am not cozened, an inquisitive-nesse, by questions they did not use to aske. Who raised armies first? Why they did it? What the Commonwealth wanted? Whether the king hath denyed anything was not in his lawful power to deny?" And was the prize worth the grief that would inevitably come?

> That so many widowes must be made, so many children fatherlesse, and such a desolation brought upon the whole kingdome? With the like questions which in a little time

may raise such a storm as the cunning and power of both
houses cannot allay.

All certainty had gone, all trust and assurance. On Monday, December 19, 1642, when the country was deep into the first bloody phase of civil war, when the forces of king and Parliament had already shed each other's blood, Pembroke made a speech in the House of Lords. On the instigation of the queen, he had been shut out of the king's councils, and the anarchy he sensed around him, both social and political, had made him defensive. He did not feel that his allies in the House of Commons would remain allies for long. This was, as he said, the speech of an honest man, and all he was looking for was "an accommodation" between the warring sides. In its straightforwardness, its lack of guile, its deeply conservative conception of him as a grandee, and in its fearful, honest pleading with his peers, the speech might stand as his credo, his apology for himself and the decisions of his life. It was the statement of a man whose only intention was "to scape undoing."

The earl clearly liked what he said, as he had the speech printed and distributed. The words of his enemy and rival the fearsomely godly Lord Brooke were then also printed in response. In their two speeches, one can see, in fierce confrontation, the revolutionary opposed to the man for whom revolution is a greater disaster than the ills it aims to cure. It is the meeting of radicalism and gradualism, between the ferocity of first principles and the beliefs of someone such as the Earl of Pembroke, for whom continuity between past and future was more important than anything that might be put in its place.

THE EARL OF PEMBROKE'S SPEECH
FOR AN ACCOMMODATION
SUNDAY 19 DEC. 1642

My Lords,

I have not used to trouble you with long Speeches, I know I am an ill Speaker, but though I am no Scholler, I am an honest man, and have a good heart to my King and Country.

I have more to loose then many of those who so hotly oppose an Accommodation. I will not forfeit mine estate to satisfie their humour or ambitions. My Lords, 'tis time to look about us, and not suffer ourselves to be fooled out of our Lives, our Honours and our fortunes, to help those men, who when their turns are served, will dispise us; and begin to laugh at us already.

A fellow here of the Town, an ordinary scurvy fellow, told me the other day to my face, that he cared not if I left them to morrow; nay if all the Lords went to the King, they should do their businesse the better: yet my Lords, I think we have helped them. Now nothing will content them, but no Bishop, no Book of Common Prayer, and shortly it will be no Lords, no Gentlemen, and no Books at all.

My Lords, I wonder what we shall get by this war. We venture more then other men, I am sure I venture more then five hundred of them, and the most I can look for is, to scape undoing; we have but a narrow way to walk in: we hear every base fellow say in the street as we passe by in our Coaches, that they hope to see us a-foot shortly, and to be as good men as the Lords themselves; and I think they will be as good as their words.

My Lords, I am no Scholler, but I understand men. I have served the Kings Father, and Himself, and though I have been so unhappy to fall into His displeasure, no body shall perswade me to turn Traytor, I have too much to loose.

Lord Brooke then replied with a speech like a sword, a denial of every Arcadian principle of accommodation, gentleness, hierarchy, love, and custom:

> My Lords,
>
> His Lordship tells you much of what he has to lose, and into what great contempt the Nobility will grow, if there be not a speedy accommodation; and I fear some of these vile Considerations have hung Plummets [small lead weights] on some of our wings, which by this time would have mounted far higher; but these are the baits the enemy of godlinesse and true holinesse flings in the way, to discourage worldly mindes from fighting the good Fight of the Lord.
>
> They who are transported with naturall affection to their Fathers and Brothers, kindred, friends, will not keep us Companie; yet this troubles me the lesse, whilst I see those Noble Lords in my eye (upon whom I can never look enough) who, banishing those womanish and effeminate fancies, cheerfully undertook to serve against that Armie, wherein they knew their own fathers were; and on my conscience (I speak it to their honour) had they met alone, would piously have sacrificed them to the commands of both Houses.
>
> The Laws of the Land (being but mans invention) must not check Gods children in doing the work of their heavenlie Father. Let us proceed to shed the blood of the ungodlie.

All the ingredients were here of the destruction that unrolled across the United Kingdom for the next eleven years, founded on the idea that any damage—the killing of fathers by sons, the destruction of estates—was good and strong if done in the service of the word of God. Any doubts were effeminate fancies, any law a tissue of worldly invention. The custom of the manor had lost all authority.

The result of such sweeping certainty on both sides was that for the next few years a harrow would be dragged across the body of England. No part of the country suffered more than Wiltshire and its surrounding counties, the borderlands of royalist influence both around Oxford and to the west, with parliamentary control in the country around London.

There was a pervasive feeling that wickedness was loose in the land. And in its wake came an unprecedented level of hatred: Parliamentary prisoners taken in the first months of the war were forced by their royalists guards in Oxford to drink the water in which the guards had previously washed. Nothing was safe from the thieving of the armies. The wonderful Quarter Sessions Rolls, on which much of this book relies for its evidence, were preserved only because in January 1643 the Wiltshire justices, wondering how the "sessions records may be preserved in this time of danger," ordered "a strong chest with two locks and keys for that purpose be provided and kept in the vestry house of Warminster church."

Rough gangs of pressed soldiers roamed the valleys. "When service happens," one recruiting sergeant boasted, "we disburden the prisons of thieves, we rob the taverns and alehouses of tosspots and ruffians, we scour both town and country of rogues and vagabonds." War legitimized violence and theft. Soldiers staying in Salisbury in the spring of 1643 set fire to the beds they had slept on. Others raided a butcher's shop and threw the pig carcasses into the Avon. In the small chalkland village of West Lavington, about eighteen miles north of Wilton, on Sailsbury Plain, one of these savage gangs broke into the house where the young Henry Penruddock of Compton Chamberlayne, whose father was famous as a Catholic and royalist sympathizer, was staying, exhausted after days in the saddle. He was asleep in a chair in the house and woke to find the troopers in the parlor, armed, the women shrieking and fluttering around them. One of the men pulled him up by the hair, knocked him down, and "broke two pistols over his head, without so much as tendering him quarter." Another, said to have been "a collier," perhaps a charcoal maker, famously independent men of the woods, "swore that he should die for his father's sake, and putting a pistol to his belly shot him dead."

A steady stream of casual death, theft, and violence was done to ordinary people. Abraham Hale of the House of Correction at Devizes was forced "to entertayne the Prest souldiers & to make pvision for them wch came to Seven pounds fifteene shillings & Seaven pence," never paid. On March 25, 1644, in Warminster, a young mother at home alone with her child was surprised to hear a man called George Long knock on her door,

and two soldiers in Armes with him and the said Long and one of the souldiers required the peticoner to open her dore who answered she would not unless he was an officer. Then the said Long said he was as good as any officer whatsoever and ymediately by force broke downe a windowe leafe wch fell into the house upon a paile of water whereby both window leafe and paile of water fell on yor peticoner and her child wch dod so bruise the child that it fell sick and shortly after dyed. Yet not being contented they also brake up the dore and enterd the house by force and then the said Long fel to byting pinching and scratching of yor peticoner saying & swearing in most execrable and ignominious manner shee was a witch and therefore hee would have her blood wch he drawed from her in great abundance.

There is no explanation in the records of why Long and his armed friends attacked her and killed her child. At the same time, George Reynolds was asked to be high constable of the hundred but declared himself incapable "haveing byn by souldiers soe heavily abused & beaten yt he is not able to ride nor travel."

Carriers had "corne and malt taken from them by a turbulent multitude by reason whereof they cannot travel with the said comodities and therefore many poore people in those parts are in great distresse for want of the same." Widows were robbed, villages burned, and attacks made on hedges and other enclosures. The chance was taken to carry out revenge killings under the cover of ideological difference. After the war, the courts were full of cases trying to decide whether individual deaths were murders or were done in the cause of duty.

All over Wiltshire, parks were broken into and deer chased with greyhounds and shot. Incidents of sheep stealing peaked, and anyone who attempted to retrieve the stolen sheep ran the risk of gangs of men coming to find them. Thomas Astill of Peasemore recovered sixteen of his sheep and was driving them home when he "was overtook by a man on horse back with dogges & other men wth Clubbes who took the sheep away from him." The gang then threatened to take Astill and his neighbors to Devizes "& have them tyed neck to heels together & afterwards hanged for demanding and medling with the sheepe."

The people of Horningsham, Maiden Bradley, and Kingston Deverill, three villages at the far western end of the Wiltshire chalk, applied to the justices for permission to take the law into their own hands. The war had left them plagued by thieves:

> the number of Felons have greatly multiplied in and
> about our parishe by whom we are dayly robbed of our

cattell (especially our sheepe) wth much bouldnesse not
spareinge sometimes our very howses to our great dis-
couragement in the buildinge and keepinge of sheepe the
over throwe of tillage and soe to the generall damage of
the whole Comonwealth

They wanted a warrant from the court that would allow them to
attack and arrest their enemies. But the court, which had worked only
intermittently during the war, did not trust this vigilante law. The petition of the three villages is signed by the justices: "Noe order."

If that is a signal that some fragment of the system of law was still
operating, many other places suffered from the ebb and flow of armies
to which the whole county was subject, attacked in turn, plundered in
turn, taxed in turn, and then, for many, "barbarously burned." Gentry
like the Penruddocks would receive the familiar imploring-cum-
threatening letters demanding "£100 for our necessary support and
maintenance of our army"—this was from the king's camp—"And
of this service we cannot doubt since if you should refuse to give us
this testimony of your affection you will give us too great a cause to
suspect your duty and inclination both to our person and the peace."
Lesser folk were simply bullied into the provision of goods and services. Thomas White of Potterne, near Devizes, had taken from him

as much Beare, Stronge water and Sack as came to the Sume
of xii li or neare thereabouts and carried the same to a place
called Rundwayehill [Roundway hill] with promise to pay

which of course he never was. The armies took food and carriage
on tick, but by the time payment was due, had moved on. A mason
from Meere, for the want of building work, took to buying and selling cheeses. He was told to take two hundred Wiltshire cheeses to

Oxford "for his Majesty's provision there," half of the payment on credit. But he was never paid the sixteen shillings he was owed for the cheeses, nor the shilling a day for himself and his three horses for eight days.

Worse still was when an army detachment took up residence where you were living. There was no avoiding what was called "free quartering"; the landowners simply had to provide. In Easter week 1645, Thomas Randoll of Fisherton Anger, between Bemerton and Salisbury, had quartered on him

> of Sir William Walers Army six men for eleven dayes viz
> until the twentieth of April aforesaid whereof three were Ensigns, one Chirugion a quartermaster and a Marshall 3li 6s

In the previous November, the mayor and aldermen of Salisbury had been ordered to provide "upon sight" twenty bushels of wheat, twenty quarters of oats, twenty dozen candles, twenty bushels of salt, twenty flitches of bacon, and twenty quarters of meat "whereof we shall exact a punctuall account off yow as yow will answer to the Contrary." The Pembrokes' old steward John Nicholas, of Winterbourne Earls, was "never free from billeting of soldiers of both sides, some times thirty, forty or fifty men and as many horses three or four days and nights together." He took to hiding in his pigeon loft when army detachments were seen coming down the road.

No side was better than the other. When Lord Percy's soldiers were quartered in the village of Odstock, on the Ebble, in 1644, they defaced the parish register, drawing wild, looping, carefree scrawls all over one page and an irreverent rhyme, now partly blodged out, on another:

> God mad[e] man and man mad[e] [money]
> God mad[e] bees and bees mad[e] hone[y]

When Cromwell's troopers entered Winchester in 1645, they used the priceless medieval documents in the cathedral's muniment room to make kites.

The royalists who landed in Salisbury in December 1644 were particularly destructive. On a series of ninety-eight little torn notes and scraps of paper the citizens of Salisbury recorded their losses to the troopers of Sir Marmaduke Langdale's famously aggressive cavaliers: shops broken up and plundered; widows robbed; a man deprived of his doublet, hose, and shoes; blankets and a carpet taken; gloves, stockings, and hats stolen. One man, John Russell, a cobbler, had everything stolen and then found he had "a poore sick soldier lieth uppon my hands and I am not able to release him." William Philipps had a hat taken off his head, all his clothes stolen, both wool and linen, and "they kame a kene aftere word & had a plondeare a kene." Richard Durnford had his wife's petticoat taken; Bennet Eastman, four pounds "taken out of his pockets in money"; Hugh Smith, his Bible.

The other side was no better. An old man made a pitiable list of the goods in his house, all of which had been taken by parliamentarian soldiers:

> 7 pairs of sheets, 3 brass kettles, 2 brass pots, 5 pewter dishes, 4 shirts, 4 smocks, 2 coats, 1 cloak, 1 waistcoat, 7 dozen candles, 1 frying pan, 1 spit, 2 pairs of pot hooks, 1 peck of wheat, 4 bags, some oatmeal, some salt, a basketful of eggs, bowls, dishes, spoons, ladles, drinking pots, and whatsoever else they could lay their hands on.

The violence left the country littered with victims: men who had been pressed for service with one or other of the armies, who had deserted, been imprisoned, and driven into penury; men falling sick "with a disease called the Mesells" after being exposed to the unprecedented wartime movement of people; and many men claiming pensions for the injuries they had received in the war. Richard Rickette was "a poor lame mayned man a carpenter at worke at Ridge"—a Pembroke possession to the west of Chilmark—who had been "dangerously wounded crippled & disabled for all future service or labour whereby both himself and a small child is left wholly to the Charitie of his neighbours for their releefe & sustenance." The justices decided that the parish itself was "to releeve him according to the necessity of the party." There were men who had been shot in the back and were unable to work; a man blinded, "having lost the sight of both eyes by a cut across his face and left for dead" in Salisbury. Hundreds were left homeless and destitute in the towns that had been stormed and burned, filled with "heaps of rubbish [and] consumed houses, a multitude of which are raked in their own ashes. Here a poor forsaken chimney and there a little fragment of a wall that have escaped to tell what barbarous and monstrous wretches there have been."

Under the strain of such levels of violence and invasive theft, the social fabric stretched and broke. Men in the villages refused to play their part as tithingmen, the essential keepers of order. Those who had been chosen tithingman before the war found no one willing to take the duty on from them. Parishioners in Lacock were presented to the justices in July 1641 for failing to do their communal work, the essential mechanism for the workings of the village:

> John Pountney, Martin Gass, for not doing his six hours service
> Ambros Browne came not in with his plow to do his six
> days worke (same John Rumsey and Nicolas Barett)
> John Banks for doing but 3 dayes service (same Richard
> Ashly, William Frie)
> John Bush for not scowring his ditch along Nash way
> John Davis for not clensing his ditch along Nash way

Others would not or could not contribute their share of the taxes and rates levied by both sides. Village by village, Wiltshiremen complained that they were being forced to carry the burdens of war alone. Many individuals refused "to pay their rates with their neighbors towards the charge of the prest souldiers."

> Robert Locke the Tythingman at Wylye and Anthony Ballard the Constable, had
>
> > disbursed and layd out of their owne purses divers sums of money for the setting out of soldiers for his Majesties service this last summer out of the Tythinge of Wily aforesaid
> >
> > Whereupon a rate hath bin there made by the said Tything for the collecting of such summes of money as were to be paid out of the said Tythinge
> >
> > Roberte Greene, Henry Patient and John David doe refuse to pay the severall rates imposed upon them by the said Tything whereby your said peticioners are likely to pay the said monyes out of their owne purses beside all their great travaile and chardges already in the premises by them expended.

The rest of the village needed "to beare their burthen with their neighbours." It may be significant that both Locke and Ballard were members of long-standing Wylye families, who had maintained the workings of the village over several generations. (The Ballards had the inn the Green Dragon.) None of the three men named—Greene, Patient, and David—appear in the survey of the village made in June 1631. They were newcomers, perhaps parliamentarians, not prepared to contribute to the general fund or to the royalist cause.

Communal payment for communal goods was the customary expectation of the manor, but war meant that neighborliness itself was under threat. Villages became even less tolerant of difference than they had been before. Vicars such Thomas Lawrence at Bemerton had clearly drifted into unpuritan churchmanship and it was reported by his neighbors "That he do & did usually ducke and make obaysance to the communion table at the entering in to the church and at the goinge forthe and did always bowe at the name of Jesus." Anyone who stepped outside the norm, who was said "to have conveyed armour into Scotland, who had spoken treason or done felonie," was reported to the authorities. Edward Williams of Marborough was presented in 1641 for saying "there was base rogery in that book," when talking about the Book of Common Prayer. Increasingly confident puritan ministers campaigned against dancing, music, games, and drink. John Newman, minister of Upavon, on the north side of the plain, addressed the justices as though he were their moral physician, giving them a sermon on the good and healthy life:

> There is a greate complaint of bastardies, sheep-stealers, hedgbreakers, quarrellers and ye like. Would you be eased of these diseases? Believe it, they gather into Alehouses as humers doe into ye stomack. Doe you but drive them thence with som strong Physick, and you hele our towne and villages of infinite distempers.

People were beginning to pursue their private ends and neglect the needs of the community. The inhabitants of Tippett found their sheep dying of foot rot after "Henry White gent" neglected the water channels on his own land and allowed their common meadow to remain flooded. The royalist Lord Seymour was presented "for flotting his meadowe called long Meadowe for destrowing the Kings high way." Susan Long of Warminster "delivered to one Henry Garratt, blacksmith, a fire pan to have the same mended, but the said Garratt deteyneth it and telleth yor peticoner she shall come by her pan as she can for (saith hee) there is noe law." *There is noe law*: that might have been the motto inscribed over 1640s Wiltshire. War had dissolved the bonds of custom.

The ground was slipping under old meanings and structures. An intriguing petition came in to the justices in 1646 from the villagers of West Knoyle, on the very edge of the chalk, about sixteen miles west of Wilton. It was against "William Willoughby Esq, Lord of the said Mannour of Westknoyle concerning Rates and payments for the service of the king & Parliament." Willoughby was a royalist who would be implicated in a futile royalist Wiltshire rebellion in 1655 led by the Penruddocks against the Commonwealth, and this petition is a moment of revolution against him. In a small Wiltshire village, the ordinary copyholders make a requirement that the future should be fair, that the lord of manor should not ride in on the deference of his tenants but that he, too, should pay his way and should be no burden on the common man. Before the war, Willoughby had paid only a third of the parish rates or taxes, although his demesne lands represented far more than a third of the productive land in the parish. Previously, the parishioners had submitted to this unfairness, "hee being their landlord, and these payments then but small in respect of the tymes now." But times had changed; the amount that the villages had to contribute to war expenses on both sides, "daiely and weekly," was so great that the men and women of West Knoyle felt this was no longer fair.

> Therefore we most humbly do peticion you to soe order
> this busynes that hee may now beare and pay equall share
> with us according to his and our estates, which he refuseth
> to doe, although his demains be worth 300 li per annum
> besides the parsonage there, worth 60 li per annum which
> wee heare to fore never questioned in making our rates.

Willoughby refused to budge: "hee will pay but according to his former rate, which comes but to 26 shillings 7 pence a weeke and some of his said Tennaunts doe pay 9 shillings 10 pence halfpenny which is verie unreasonable and unconscionable that hee should soe free himself and lay the burthen upon his country who pay more payments as fines [on entering a copyhold], heriots [on the death of a copyholder] and yearly rents."

There is even a suggestion that, at the most internalized of levels, the power of authority had evaporated. In 1647, Grace Stokes, the wife of Henry Stokes, a glazier from Fisherton Anger, just on the edge of Salisbury, came to the justices to complain about a girl called Susanna Candby who was the daughter-in-law of William Locke, the husbandman from Wylye. Grace had taken Susanna on as her apprentice for three years. Susanna had, at least in the past, suffered from scrofula, a disease of the lymph nodes in the neck, which was severely debilitating and erupted in rough, raw pustules. Since the early Middle Ages, it had been known as the king's evil and was thought to be curable by the touch of the monarch. When Susanna first came into Grace's employment, she was

> extreamely troubled with a disease called the Evill Which
> when yor peticoner perceived asked her how long she had
> bin troubled with it, as also whither she was cured of it. she
> answered that she had bin with the King and was cured and
> did amend.

Grace took her on, but in the circumstances of the war the magic no longer worked. Grace found herself with a girl so sick she was useless as an apprentice and she wanted to be rid of her. Susanna, it turned out,

> hath bin and nowe is soe vehemently troubled with ye said
> disease that she is not able to helpe herselfe and is almost

redy to perish for want of Cure, to ye greate griefe and
damadge of yor poor petr.

As usual, the records have nothing to say about the outcome of
the case, nor whether it was thought reasonable that a sick girl could
be dispensed with in this way, nor any reason why the king's cure no
longer worked.

Alongside this erosion of old meanings was a longing for peace
and for a return to the conditions before the war. As early as October 1642, the leading Wiltshire gentry petitioned the king for peace,
as did the burgers of Salisbury. For the first time in the world of
seventeenth-century politics, women began to make their voices
heard in these petitions for peace, but as the damage, taxation, violence, and—increasingly—disease and hunger took its toll, a fiercer
and more directed reaction emerged from these villages. Each side was
taking more than £700 a week out of Wiltshire at the height of the
war. From the spring of 1645 onward, the men of Wiltshire, combin-
ing with their counterparts from Somerset and Gloucestershire, gathered themselves into the bands known as the Clubmen, opposed to all
armies, all incursions, and all taxations, whether for the king or for the
Parliament. The Clubmen were attempting, in fact, to restore locally
the peace that national politics had denied them.

In July 1645, the parliamentarian general Sir Thomas Fairfax told
his masters in London what he had heard about the Clubmen. "They
pretended only the Defence of themselves from Plunderers, but not to
side either with the king's Forces or the Parliament's, but to give Free
Quarter to both: They list themselves under several Officers daily,
and meet in great Bodies at their Rendezvous, and boast they can have
Twenty Thousand Men at Four and Twenty Hours Warning for assembling them together." It was Wiltshire gathering its own power.
The Clubmen were, at least apparently, well organized, sending mes-

sages throughout the valleys and summoning the men from the fields
by ringing the church bells.

> For Distinction of themselves from other Men, they wear
> White Ribbons, to shew, as they say, their Desires of
> Peace. They meet with Drums, flying Colours, and for
> Arms they have Muskets, Fowling-pieces, Pikes, Halberts,
> great Clubs, and such like. They take upon them to inter-
> pose betwixt the Garrisons of either Side.

Salisbury itself provided seven hundred clubmen, "some with
Pikes and Muskets, and others with Carbines and Pistols," and in
mid-July they and others from all over the Pembroke estates and
from farther afield—four thousand in all—gathered at a rendezvous
in the great Saxon forest of Grovely, on the ridge above Wilton where
Philip Sidney had loved to ride. There they heard "certain Articles
read and proposed to them, which they all assented to by giving
a Shout."

It must have been a moment of self-reassurance, the reassertion of
self-defense against the inroads of anarchy and alien ideas. The leaders
of the Wiltshire Clubmen included two Pembroke tenants: Thomas
Bennett of Broad Chalke and William Gould of Alvediston. Both of
them signed petitions sent by the Clubmen to both king and Parliament, "for procuring a Peace," telling both of their woes.

> More deeply than many other Parts of this Kingdom [they
> had] tasted the Miseries of this unnatural intestine War,
> which have been the more extremely embittered unto them
> by the Pressures of many Garrisons both here and in the
> neighbour Counties, and the opposite Armies continually
> drawn upon them by the reason thereof.

They had given up hope of a negotiated peace and had been forced to take the future into their own hands. All they wanted was "the true Reformed Protestant Religion; and next, as free-born *English*, not degenerating from the Virtues of their Fathers, by all possible and lawful Means to preserve and uphold the native Inheritance of their Laws, their Liberties, and Properties, which they equally hold in Esteem even with Life itself." They were asking for a restoration of the custom of the manor. The very instinct that had led Englishmen to war in 1642—a defense of the ancient—now led them in their desire for peace. "Immesurable Taxes, continual Free Quarter, and uncessant Plunderings," they told the king, "have scarcely left Your poor Suppliants sufficient for the Support of Life. Our purses have bin exhausted, corn eaten up, cattell plundered, persons frighted from our habitacons and by reason of the violence of the soldiers our lives are not safe."

The simple desire for certainty, for structures by which they could pay their rents, have their debts honored, make their living, and maintain their wives and families "from utter ruin and decay," was all that drove them. They wanted "peaceably [to] return to their wonted habitations and to the obedience of the established laws."

But it was a fantasy. The reality of the Clubmen's impotence and posturing was made apparent on August 4, 1645, when Cromwell, at the head of the New Model Army, brushed them aside. The brief engagement was at the Iron Age fort on Hambledon Hill, just over the county border in Dorset, where the Clubmen had gathered, shouting taunts at Cromwell's disciplined ironsides. "I believe we killed not twelve of them," Cromwell wrote to Fairfax that evening, "but cut very many and put them all to flight. We have taken about three hundred; many of which are poor silly creatures, whom if you please to let send home, they promise to be very dutiful for time to come, and will be hanged before they come out again."

It was a 1640s version of the long story this book has described: the meeting of a retrospective idealism with the overwhelming facts of power.

This is the background to Philip Pembroke's own involvement in the war. He behaved in a way that was little different from the thousands of Wiltshiremen who were first uncertain which way to turn, felt perplexed at the catastrophic outcome of events, wavered one way and then another, and felt deeply attached both to the ancient constitution and to the king who had betrayed it. But the 1640s was not a time for understanding, and Pembroke was ridiculed and despised for his flickering and uncertain behavior. Clarendon claimed that Pembroke became a parliamentarian because he wanted to protect Wilton and thought Parliament the stronger side. Others thought his rivalry with the Seymours, the great family from the north of the county with whom the Herberts had sparred since the 1540s and who had become ardent royalists, explained what Pembroke had done. Neither was right; the explanation is simpler. The tradition of which Pembroke was a part, and which this book has described, could only have led him toward Parliament. The "life of loyalty," which one satire attributed to him, was loyalty to what? Perhaps to himself, to Wilton, to his family's culture, to a true reformed church, to the Covenanting Scots, to the hunting he had loved since he was a boy, and to a world that was lost, destroyed from both ends, by an increasingly authoritarian crown and an increasingly radical Parliament and army.

He became something of a joke to his contemporaries. The royalist Earl of Dorset, in a letter to his son-in-law, a parliamentarian, wrote sarcastically that "You cannott suffer, while you have soe sure and constant a man amongst you as the earl of Pembroke . . . Paraselsus himselfe [the great sixteenth-century alchemist and pharmacologist] cowld never have fixed the mercuriall spirit thatt predominates in his breast: if hee weere alive to practise on him."

The brilliant satirist Samuel Butler published the definitive verdict:

> *Pembroke's a Covenanting Lord*
> *That ne'er with God or men kept word*
> *One day he swore he'd serve the King*
> *The next was quite another thing*
> *Still changing with the Wind or Tide*
> *That he might keep the Stronger Side*
> *His Hawks and Hounds were all his Gaze*
> *For them he made his daily Prayers*
> *And scarce would lose a hunting Season*
> *E'en for the sake of darling Treason.*

Parliament sent him out to gather the militia on their behalf. In 1642 he was appointed "Generall for the Western part of the Kingdom" and Lord Lieutenant in Wiltshire, Somerset, Hampshire, Dorset, Devon, Cornwall, and the Isle of Wight. If it looked for a moment as if his grandfather's Tudor fiefdom had somehow reappeared a century later, that was mere illusion. Pembroke had no military expertise and, at nearly sixty, was too old to be an active soldier. He soon withdrew to the comfort of his rooms in the Cockpit at Whitehall, taking part in the increasingly unreal debates in the House of Lords, where at times in the 1640s Pembroke and two or three other peers were the only figures on the empty benches under Inigo Jones's vaulted ceiling.

Repeatedly, Parliament sent him as one of their commissioners to negotiate with the king. But that, too, came with its humiliations, as Parliament would not allow the commissioners freedom to negotiate without reference back to Westminster. Late one night, in the very cold January of 1645, at the negotiations between the two sides at Uxbridge, Pembroke came to pour his heart out to his old friend and client Edward Hyde, later to be Lord Clarendon, who was one of the king's commissioners at the negotiations. Pembroke sat with Hyde for many hours, trying to persuade him that the king should consent to Parliament's demands. Hyde was adamant that the crown could not submit, as the only outcome of that submission would be tyranny in England. Pembroke then confessed that he, too, thought "there was never such a pack of knaves and villains as they who now governed in the parliament." Pembroke was "of the moderate party," and they needed this treaty to work. Otherwise there would be a coup and England would become a republic. Hyde "told him if he believed that, it was high time for the Lords to look about them, who would be then no less concerned than the King. [Pembroke] confessed it, and that they were now sensible that they had brought this mischieve upon themselves, and did heartily repent it, though too late, and when they were in no degree able to prevent the general destruction which they foresaw." Only if the king agreed to their demands would they be able "to recover all for him that he now parted with, and to drive those wicked men who would destroy monarchy out of the kingdom, and then his majesty would be greater than ever."

Hyde thought Pembroke and his fellow parliamentary commissioners both contemptible and ridiculous, "so broken were they in their spirits, and so corrupted in their understanding, even when they had their own ruin in view." Pembroke left him late in the evening, a pitiable sight, scarcely the same man who had posed for William Larkin with his ostrich fathers and his coral bracelet so long before.

The family had fallen apart. Pembroke's sons had stayed with him. Two of them, Philip and James, became members of Parliament. But his glamorous son-in-law, Robert, Earl of Carnarvon, had become a leading and courageous cavalry commander on the other side and had been killed, casually, in the evening of the first battle of Newbury in 1643, when a parliamentary trooper recognized him after the battle was over and ran him through with his sword. Carnarvon's wife, Anna Sophia, had very nearly died of smallpox the same year. Their son, Charles, the young boy born in 1632 and represented by the pearl between Anna Sophia's fingers in the great Van Dyck portrait, was painted by his successor the young Lely perhaps in that year. The young boy's pose looks as if it deliberately reflects his father's in the family portrait, one foot raised on a step, his head turned to look, the color and manner of his clothes also a form of inheritance from his father. In the background, the Arcadian trees were painted by Lely withered and broken under the blast of war. It is just possible that this painting was made for Pembroke, the boy's grandfather, a sign that his love for his daughter's son spread across any ideological divide. Among the executors' accounts preserved at Hatfield is an item: "Paid to Mr Lilly painter for severall pictures made for the late earle of Pembroke the sume of £85."

After the defeat of the king and the fall of his headquarters at Oxford, in July 1646, Pembroke was sent to Newcastle with Parliament's propositions. Charles had been given a copy privately sometime before. He asked Pembroke and the other commissioners

> whether they had powers to treat with him on the Proposi-
> tions or in any way discuss them. On their answering that
> they had no such powers, and had only to request his Maj-
> esty's *Ay* or *No* as they stood, "Then, but for the honour of
> the business," said the King testily, "an honest trumpeter
> might have done as much."

It was a good remark, symptomatic of the collapse of any authority Pembroke might have had. Pembroke stayed with the king as

Charles was moved under house arrest to the giant Elizabethan palace of Holdenby, in Northamptonshire, walking with him on "the Long Gravel-Walk" of the garden there, maintaining a fond and "mirthful" relationship with a man who had known him all his life, "and not without some difficulty held pace with him, his Majesty being quick and lively in his Motion." When on June 3, 1647, the king was kidnapped by the army officer George Joyce, on Cromwell's orders, arriving at Holdenby at dawn, with five hundred armed troopers behind him and "a cockt pistol in his hand," Pembroke went with the king in the coach to Cambridge, Newmarket, and eventually to Hampton Court.

In these years of disaster and dissolution, Pembroke's affection for the king grew and flowered. The king was not allowed his old Gentlemen of the Bedchamber to attend him, and Pembroke arranged for his cousin Thomas Herbert to play that role. Herbert watched the two of them carefully. "The earl of Pembroke (let others say what they will) loved the King in his Heart, and had certainly never separated from him, had he not (by the Procurement of some ill-willers) been committed to the Tower, and his White Staff taken from him, only by reason of a sudden and unhappy falling out."

Thomas Herbert also recorded the most poignant of all tales to do with Pembroke at the very end of Charles's life, a prisoner in the unhappy, Orwellian world of Westminster in 1648, with its whisperings and deceits, its sense of unbridled power lurking an inch or two beneath the surface of life, the air of mutual treachery. Thomas Herbert had at times been failing to wake up in the morning and the king had tried through the offices of the Earl of Pembroke to get him a repeating watch with an alarm. Herbert, in the third person, described a visit to Pembroke's rooms in the Cockpit at Whitehall. Pembroke

> then as at sundry other times enquired how his Majesty did,
> and gave him his humble Duty to him, and withal ask'd

[Herbert], if his majesty had the Gold Watch he sent for, and how he liked it. Mr Herbert assured his Lordship, the King had not yet received it. The earl fell presently into a Passion, marvelling thereat; being the more troubled, lest his Majesty should think him careless in observing his Command; and told Mr Herbert, at the King's coming to St James's, as he was sitting under the great Elm-Tree, near Sir Benjamin Ruddier's Lodge in the Park, seeing a considerable Military-Officer of the Army pass towards St James's, he went to meet him, and demanding of him if he knew his cousin Tom Herbert, that waited on the King? The Officer said, he did, and was going to St James's. The Earl then delivered to him the Gold Watch that had the Alarm, desiring him to give it Mr Herbert, to present it to the King. The Officer promised the earl he would immediately do it.

But neither king nor Herbert had seen anything of the watch.

My lord, (said Mr Herbert) I have sundry times seen and pass'd by that Officer since, and do assure your Lordship he hath not delivered it me according to you Order and his Promise, nor said anything to me concerning it, nor has the King it I am certain.

What were they to do? Could they accuse this military high-up of theft from the king? Not then.

But such was the Severity of the times, that it was then judged dangerous to reflect upon such a person, being a Favourite of the time so as no notice was taken of it.

Herbert did of course tell the king this story. "Ah," he said. "Had he not told the Officer it was for me, it would probably have been delivered; he will know how short a time I could enjoy it."

In January 1649 Pembroke was appointed by parliamentary ordinance to the court that was to try the king. But Pembroke could not bring himself to attend and remained in his beautiful rooms in the Cockpit, from where he "swore he loved not to meddle with businesses of life and death and (for his part) hee would neither speake against the ordinance nor consent to it." He had not signed the king's death warrant but he had done nothing to save him.

The king was executed on January 30, 1649. One of his last acts before he stepped out from the Banqueting House window and on to the wintery scaffold was to give Thomas Herbert his gold watch. Pembroke, with his old friend the Earl of Salisbury, watched the execution, quite dispassionately, from his lodgings in the Cockpit. On the scaffold, Charles I prayed to God: "Look upon my misery with Thine eye of mercy and let Thine infinite power vouchsafe to limit out some proportion of deliverance unto me." John Milton would reveal in *Eikonoklastes* that this prayer was not the king's own but was a quotation from *Arcadia*. By using it, Milton maintained, the king had polluted "prayer itself, by borrowing to a Christian use prayers offered to a heathen god, a prayer stolen word for word from the mouth of a heathen fiction praying to a heathen God; and that in no serious book, but the vain amatorious poem of Sir Philip Sidney's *Arcadia*." For Milton, it was symptom of everything that was wrong with royalism: no access to the divinely revealed truth, no belief in liberty, no pride in what a freeborn God-fearing Englishman should take pride in. And Milton had no trouble binding together the two Arcadias.

Anyone who still longed for this crown-dominated Arcadian world, Milton wrote, showed

themselves to be by nature slaves and arrant beasts—not fit
for that liberty which they cried out and bellowed for, but
fitter to be led back again into their old servitude like a sort
of clamoring and fighting brutes, broke loose from their
copyholds, that know not how to use or possess the liberty
which they fought for, but with the fair words and promises
of an old exasperated foe are ready to be stroked and tamed
again into the wonted and well-pleasing state of their true
Norman villeinage, to them best agreeable.

This was probably true. The English could not bear too much
liberty, nor the fear of tyranny, which came in liberty's wake. *Eikon
basilike*, the king's own (ghosted) justification of his life and kingship,
went through thirty-six editions in 1649 alone. Hunger for a Restoration had surged on the execution of the king.

Pembroke himself would be dead within a year, a year during
which the new regime would continue to humiliate him. The Council of State discussed whether they should demolish his castle in Cardiff; whether his art treasures should be sold along with the king's
for the good of the country; whether soldiers should or should not be
quartered in Durham House, the earl's London residence since 1640;
whether he should be allowed to keep the keys to the doors and gates
into St. James's Park, or if they would be better off in the hands of
Colonel Pride. On March 19, 1649, the House of Lords was abolished
by an act of Parliament that declared that "The Commons of England
[consider] by too long experience that the House of Lords is useless
and dangerous to the people of England." Although there had been
talk the year before of making Pembroke a duke, he now became
a member of the House of Commons, sitting alongside his sons, as
member for Berkshire, a move ridiculed in the London broadsheets as
"an ascent downwards."

Pembroke was not well. He was seriously ill in May, again in June, and again in July, running up apothecaries' bills for £122 over the summer. His digestion was failing him, and the painful affliction returned in the autumn. Mr. Metcalfe, the apothecary, was paid ten shillings a day for attendance, making large quantities of "alterative ale, issue powder and deobstructive electuary" to get the bowels working. The most expensive was sweet powders containing musk and amber, which were thought to aid the digestion and "intestinal elimination." Everything known to seventeenth-century medicine was thrown at Pembroke:

> Sweet fenall seeds, liquorice and coriander seeds, acqua cardiata, acqua cinnamon, syrup of roses, Syrup of citrons with Rhubarb, Syrupe of dryed roses, Syrupe of Limons, Syrupe of the Juice of Citrons, Syrupe of raspberries, Syrupe of Corrall, Two Ivory Clyster pipes prepared, Maiestry of pearle, Maiestry of Corrall, Crabbs eyes, Salt of Wormwood, Salt of scurvie grass, Confectio de Hyacinth, Conserve of Red Roses, Conserve of Rosemarie flowers, Chymicall oyle of wormwood, White sugar candy, Sweetes with musk and amber, purging potion with rhubarb and on Christmas day, a cordiall julipp with with syrupe of pomegrannutts

On Christmas day he had a "syrupe of marsh mallows with liquorice and maydenhaire" followed by conserve of bugloss and borage, a mysterious "Box of tabletts" along with "Syrupe of jujubes." On and on the treatments went until January 28, 1650, when he had a possett, a gargarisme with syrup, a cataplasm, and finally "a cooling Julipp," which would cost his estate 2s 8d and after which he died. The sum total for all of this was another £177 17 10, the price of good house. The executors were having none of that and reduced the bill by £65.

On Pembroke's death, bitter, spoof accounts by secret royalists of his last hours were quickly printed and published on the streets of London, the ranting visions of a man guilty of killing his king, of pursuing nothing but his own appetites. "Dam' me," Pembroke is meant to have muttered on his deathbed,

> there 'tis againe, a man without a Head, beckoning me with his Hand, and bending his fist at me; what a pox art thou? Speake, if thou art a man, speake; speake, speake; zblood, canst thou not speake without a Head?

Then, after his guilt, his desires:

> O mistress May. Come to bed Sweet-heart, come, my Duck, my Birds-nye; Zblood I must go to Salisbury to-morrow, bring me my Boots quickly; Zounds will not the Rogues bring me more Money; zblood that Cock's worth a Kings Ransome, a runs, a runs, a thousand pound to a Hobby Horse; Rub, Rub, Rub, a pox. Rub a whole hundred Tubs. Tell them I'll restore those *Pictures* and *Modells* I had from S. Iamses; the seiling of the banquety-House at White-Hall, tell them is as fit for my parlor in Ramesbury mannor as can be. I come, I come, good Devill lead the way. When Rebellls dye Hell makes a Holly-day.

The long arc the Pembrokes had traced from the 1520s had now returned to earth. Their status had gone, and the family was deep in debt; the fourth earl's horribly convoluted estate took five years to sort out. The executors' accounts survive at Hatfield. Friends, neighbors, and relations all came crawling out of the woodwork with promissory notes and obligations at dice or cards. The bills came in. Most of the earl's London pictures were sold to pay off the creditors. Connoisseurs toured the rooms to inspect them. Lands were mortgaged and jewels pawned. Valuers picked their way through the great rooms in Durham House, the Cockpit at Whitehall, Baynard's Castle, Wilton, and Ramsbury.

But this was more than a personal catastrophe. The world had changed, and the central place in the workings of England that the Pembrokes had occupied for so long was no longer available to them. The England they had known was now broken. Their conservative revolt against the crown had in turn released huge revolutionary energies in the country, which had swept away their old dreams of a renewed and potent nobility. England, infused with these dreams of radical and universal freedom, was now for ten years to be subjected to a brutal military dictatorship that the threat of freedom had summoned from the republican authorities.

In this fierce and polarized world, the balance and organic integrity of Arcadia could be little but a forgotten memory. Only the ex-royalists, savagely fined by the new regime and creeping back to their damaged and neglected estates in the depths of the country, could turn to the consolations of poetry and the beautiful, quiet life, a wan and defeated ghost of what the Arcadian dream of a good country had once been. The quarrel with the king was over because the king was dead. But as Clarendon had predicted, the status of the earls who had indulged in this quarrel for so long collapsed with the king they had finally and so catastrophically opposed. The old world had gone, and England would never be the same again.

HEAR THIS, O YE THAT SWALLOW UP THE NEEDY

THE DESTRUCTION OF DOWNLAND SOCIETY
1650–1830

The crown was restored in 1660, but not everything was restored with it. England could scarcely go back to the system or the mentality on which the prewar country had once relied. The war itself had been too deep and disturbing a rupture. There was no going back. The earls of Pembroke each in turn became the man of his moment: restoration rakes (one a multiple murderer), eighteenth-century connoisseurs, army officers, and conservative politicians. But around them, in the chalkland valleys they owned, as elsewhere, a disaster unfolded.

The Anglican divine Richard Baxter wrote a homily in 1691 on *The condition of poor farm tenants*. "The old custom was," Baxter wrote nostalgically, "to let lands by lease for lives or for a long term of years, and to take a fine at first and a small yearly rent afterward, and so when a man, with his marriage portion, had taken a lease he lived comfortably afterward and got somewhat for his children." That is the air of retrospective regret for a land of lost content. The pattern of human relationships had been folded into the habits of the land. The wife's dowry had paid the fine with which the couple entered into the copyhold, and the man's life's labor prepared for his children to do the same.

"But now in most countries," Baxter continued, meaning in most parts of England, "the custom is changed into yearly rack-rents," meaning not only that custom itself was over and done with, but also that the new annual rents were equal or nearly equal to the value of what the land could produce in the year. His subtext went far deeper into moral outrage. The new rents had been racked, bent, stretched, and strained to the point where they were no longer morally legitimate.

"The poor tenants are glad of a piece of hanged bacon once a week," Baxter told his gentlemanly audience, the grandsons of those who had read John Norden's treatise on mutuality as the essence of state management at the beginning of the century,

> and some few that can kill a bull eat now and then a bit of hanged beef, enough to try the stomach of an ostrich. He is a rich man that can afford to eat a joint of fresh meat (beef, mutton or veal) once in a month or fortnight. If their sow pig or their hens breed chickens, they cannot afford to eat them, but must sell them to make their rent. They cannot afford to eat the eggs that their hens lay, nor the apples or pears that grow on their trees (save some that are not vendible) but must make money of all. All the best of their butter and cheese they must sell and feed themselves, and children, and servants with skimmed cheese and skimmed milk and whey curds.

The change from copyhold to leasehold and rack rent, which began in earnest in the seventeenth century and would continue until deep into the nineteenth century, was the deepest possible transformation of the social fabric of England. Where people before had, as Baxter implies, eaten their own produce, now their produce amounted to a single thing: money. The yeomen copyholders became what Baxter was already calling in the 1690s "the poor enslaved husbandmen" of England.

Few landlords, he said, "scruple raising rents to as much as they can get, when poor men, rather than beg and have no dwelling, will promise more than they can pay; and then, with care and toil, make shift as long as they can." The idea of a balanced community, of mutuality in rights and obligations, of control of the government of the manor through the custom of the manor: all that had been collapsed into a simple cash deal. If you could pay the rent, you could stay on the land. If you couldn't, you couldn't. The natural drift of such a system was the replacement of an integrated copyhold community with a monopolistic landlord and a gang of rightless, dependent, impoverished tenants. Huge noncommunal farms would have on their margins scatterings of paupers' cottages, precisely the pattern that developed in these valleys in the nineteenth century.

In the period covered by most of this book Arcadianism was essentially a political idea, an idealism intended to embrace the whole of society. In the eighteenth century, that wholeness disappeared and Arcadianism lost its social dimension. In the making of the great eighteenth-century parks, and in the taste for the refined Meissen figures or Fragonard prettinesses, there was no political or social freight. The pink-cheeked shepherdess and her satin-suited swain, set in the smoothed contours of the English landscape school, was a slick of suavity, the most expensive wallpaper ever devised. Arcadia in the eighteenth century became décor, not a hope for society. Its money-cushioned languor became a commodity to be bought, an accessory to market success, not a criticism of individualism, market, or state. This eviscerated Arcadianism became effete, the symbol of everything against which the hunger of the Romantics for a vivid reality would react. Eighteenth-century Arcadia had lost its soul and become the country in a Savile Row suit, decorated with hermitages and tree clumps that were no more than pale, polite ghosts of their great Renaissance forebears.

Accompanying a smoothing out of the parks was a devastation of rural society. Jump to the end of August 1826, and William Cobbett is riding through the green and gold chalkstream valleys of the Wiltshire Downs. He cannot believe that he is seeing a place of such unparalleled and dreamlike beauty.

> This is certainly the most delightful farming in the world. No ditches, no water-furrows, no drains, hardly any hedges, no dirt and mire, even in the wettest seasons of the year: and though the downs are naked and cold, the valleys are snugness itself. They are, as to the downs, what *ah-ahs* are in parks or lawns. When you are going over the downs, you look *over* the valleys, as in the case of the *ah-ah*; and if you be not acquainted with the country, your surprise, when you come to the edge of the hill, is very great. The shelter in these valleys, and particularly where the downs are steep and lofty on the sides, is very complete. Then the trees are everywhere lofty. They are generally elms, with some ashes, which delight in the soil that they find here. There are, almost always, two or three large clumps of trees in every parish, and a rookery or two (not *rag*-rookery) to every parish. By the water's edge there are willows; and to almost every farm there is a fine orchard, the trees being, in general, very fine, and this year they are, in general, well loaded with fruit. So that, all taken together, it seems impossible to find a more beautiful and pleasant country than this, or to imagine any life more easy and happy than men might here lead.

It is difficult to think of two people in English history more different than Philip Sidney and William Cobbett, but here they are as one. "During the day I crossed the river about fifteen or sixteen times, and in such hot weather it was very pleasant to be so much amongst meadows and water." Cobbett's wonderfully expert eye ranged over the stack yards, the barley ricks, the wheat ricks, and hayricks, the enormous barns, some over 250 feet in length, the vast 400-acre fields, the flocks with 4,000 sheep and lambs in them, and the overwhelming abundance of straw:

> Cattle and horses are bedded up to their eyes. The yards
> are put close under the shelter of a hill, or are protected by
> lofty and thick-set trees. Every animal seems comfortably
> situated; and in the dreariest days of winter these are, per-
> haps, the happiest scenes in the world;

They might have been, but they weren't, because amid this astonishing fecundity and richness—it was a painting by Constable made flesh—were scenes of such devastating poverty that Cobbett came away sickened and ashamed. The predictions of Richard Baxter had come true. The men and women who lived and worked in these Arcadian valleys were "tormented by an accursed system that takes the food from those that raise it, and gives it to those that do nothing that is useful to man." These valleys would be the most delicious places on earth

> if those, whose labour makes it all, trees, corn, sheep and
> everything, had but *their fair share* of the produce of that
> labour. What share they really have of it one cannot exactly
> say; but I should suppose that every labouring *man* in this
> valley raises as much food as would suffice for fifty or a
> hundred persons, fed like himself!

In taking my leave of this beautiful vale, I have to express my deep shame, as an Englishman, at beholding the general *extreme poverty* of those who cause this vale to produce such quantities of food and raiment. This is, I verily believe it, the *worst used labouring people upon the face of the earth.* Dogs and hogs and horses are treated with more civility; and as to food and lodging, how gladly would the labourers change with them! This state of things never can continue many years! By *some means or other* there must be an end to it; and my firm belief is that that end will be dreadful. In the meanwhile I see, and I see it with pleasure, that the common people know that they are ill used; and that they cordially, most cordially, hate those who ill-treat them.

Cobbett turned to the Bible, using the voice of Amos the prophet to excoriate the landlords who had destroyed the communities that had once occupied these valleys:

Hear this, O ye that swallow up the needy, even to make the poor of the land to fail, that we may buy the poor for silver, and the needy for a pair of shoes. Shall not the land tremble for this; and every one mourn that dwelleth therein? I will turn your feasting into mourning, saith the Lord God, and your songs into lamentations.

Norden's idea that community should be based on love had simply disappeared. The parliamentary enclosure movement of the previous century had eroded and, in some places, removed the last rights of the copyholders to keep their animals on what had been the common grazings. The whole idea of communality evaporated. The great landowners, the Pembrokes included, reacquired the commons and gradually removed the customary rights on them. The families that had been copyholders became landless farmworkers, dependent on the cash wages paid for their labor. What looked like an equality and even liberty in the market was in fact a form of rightlessness.

The wars with France that persisted throughout the long eighteenth century, until 1815, created a falsely inflated market, delaying the recognition of what had happened. After Waterloo, at the end of the Napoleonic Wars, the catastrophe struck. Prices fell, rents shrank, poverty became usual, the old families of the chalkland valleys failed, and new men entered in their place. Banks called in their loans and landlords their rents. Bankruptcies, seizures, arrests, and imprisonment for debt colored the lives of these villages. Men came to be hired for as little as a week at a time. Many farmers lost everything and even applied for the handouts from a social welfare system that had been devised in the sixteenth century and could not cope with anything resembling this. Any suggestion of continuity, of the custom of the manor, of practices observed "time out of mind" would have been laughed into oblivion. This was the world for which Arcadia was nothing but a prettiness seen from a drawing room window, which made Cobbett feel ashamed.

The presence of the free market in labor and land was nothing new. Many deeds from the thirteenth and early fourteenth centuries have survived describing the deals conducted by small landowners in and around Wilton. But the growing sense that the market was king—whether in land or labor—became the crucial transformation in early modern England. In the first earl's survey made in 1567 there were twenty-one copyholders in Wilton itself and three free tenants, who could sell their land if they wished. By the time of the survey done for Philip Pembroke in 1631–1632, there were only five copyholders and twenty-two tenants "by indenture," holding what were effectively modern leases. By 1831 there were two hugely rich farmers in Wilton, both tenants of the earl. Neither did any farmwork himself—too grand—and both relied for their riches on employed laborers. Not a single man worked his own land. That tradition and that connection had gone. Instead, Wilton had a population of 113 adult male agricultural laborers, the men whom Richard Baxter had called "the poor enslaved husbandmen of England," and whom Cobbett saw as the "*worst used labouring people upon the face of the earth.*" Almost 500 of such men, rioting in the 1830s against the tithes paid to the church and the introduction of mechanical threshing machines, against the pauperization of their lives, were transported to Tasmania, with men from Wylye, Bishopstone, Bower Chalke, and Ramsbury among them. Fifteen others were hanged. In those figures, and in that conclusion, one can see the death of a communal idea.

Arcadia had been the dream of power. Only the powerful could indulge in its fantasy of wholeness, because it relied in the end on an imposition of authority. It was everything that the world of Adam Smith, and of the triumphant and beneficent market, would not approve. It was, in that sense, also the dream of illiberal beauty, of a calm and richness that emerged not because individuals had been allowed to pursue their individual ends but because they had submitted to a protective authority.

Our modern nostrils quiver and bristle at this idea. Can happiness and contentment really come from such radical limitations on individual freedoms? Can the system really be justified when so few seem to benefit in their silks and gilded rooms and so many are condemned to a life of poverty and drudgery in their small poor houses at the edges of their damp river meadows?

But look at what happened to these villages in the course of the eighteenth century, and the condition to which their inhabitants had sunk by the time Cobbett came to see them. Could one not see their fate as a justification for the earlier social system. It had of course denied rights to the individual. It had favored the coherence of the community over those rights. It had understood, in an extraordinarily modern way, the need for the ecological balance that Philip Sidney had seen in the grasses growing equally together in an Arcadian lawn.

Another question emerges from that: Was the vitality of the chalk-land valley communities dependent on a powerful overlord? Or could anything resembling the vivid communal life embodied in "the custom of the manor" have survived in a system that did not depend on hier-archy and dominance? Maybe not. Communities need to obey agreed laws, and those laws need to be imposed.

This, in the end, is surely the moral of the Pembrokes and their Wilt-shire valleys. They were defending their own against an encroaching state. As individuals, they were clearly fallible, corrupt, self-seeking, vacillating, irresolute, irascible, and at times less than articulate. But their story is not about individualism; it is about their joint belief in a version of the communal, in which principles both of hierarchy and of mutual-ity were deeply embedded. That is a strange pairing to modern minds. We think that hierarchy is bound to be domineering, and that mutuality cannot have hierarchy as one of its elements. The virtue of the Arcadian-ism this book has described was that, in an evolved and balanced way, it understood how to accommodate these contradictory principles.

It is important, of course, to recognize that those who were most en-ergetic in promoting this system were those who benefited most from it. Did the poor really like the stasis and exclusion of the copyhold manor? Probably not. The eruption of popular anger and violence in the Civil War might well be seen as the expression of a rage whose origins were in generations of oppression and denial that the old system had imposed.

Nor is it likely that the elite rural idyll was something the Pem-brokes' tenants wholly subscribed to. George Herbert's description of his parishioners as a dumb and sullen lot, scarcely dancing their way to the fields or church, must have some truth in it. Arcadianism didn't always feel Arcadian if you were a member of the caste. Nor, importantly, were the people of these valleys unreconstructed rustics, as Herbert and others were tempted to describe them. The streets of Salisbury, until controlled and cleared by the city authorities, were as chaotic and frightening and as full of importuning and sometimes aggressive beggars as the streets of Calcutta. Much of the valley of the Nadder, to the west of the city, was busy with traffic and distinctly suburban in character by the early part of the seventeenth century.

So, for all the communal ideology, there is a divergence between the wish-fulfillment ideals of the Pembrokes and the reality of ordinary lives. The examples toward the end of this book of all the stresses and strains in the run-up to the Civil War—the seeking for market solutions to chronic poverty, the disobedience of communal laws, and the ever-present sense of violence and abuse—all that may well have occurred earlier, but the evidence has not survived. Documents from the Tudor decades are much thinner on the ground than those from the early seventeenth century, particularly the quarter sessions records, which survive in quantity only from the beginning of the reign of James I. The dream of perfection undoubtedly sheltered in its heart both a systematic limit placed on the individual and his liberties and a natural human effort to escape and resist that limitation.

It was an exploitative world: How, except by exploitation, could the earls have paid for their luxuries from the rents and fines of their copyhold tenants? But it was also a world that in its ideals and practice was alive with a sense of jointness, of a joint enterprise between the different connected parts of the social organism. It lived above all in its gatherings: at the village courts, at the masques and tournaments, at the hay harvest and the wheat harvest, at the plays in the candlelit halls, at the great funerals, and eventually at the desperate hilltop meetings during the Civil War. It is a world that has entirely disappeared, but one whose virtues disappeared with its faults.

BIBLIOGRAPHY

Manuscript Sources

SWINDON AND WILTSHIRE RECORD OFFICE

A1/110 Great Rolls of Wiltshire Quarter Sessions (1631E/151 for the libel sung by Jane Norrice of Stoke Verdon; 1642H/158 and 1646T/179 for marks of the illiterate villagers)

G23/1/40 A list of losses by the citizens of Salisbury, December 1644

P2/L/268 William Locke's Inventory, 1660

P5/1626/11 Probate inventory reused to record costs of parliamentarian soldiers quartered in Fisherton Anger, 1645

212B/7181 Final agreement on marriage of Charles, Lord Herbert, and Lady Mary Villiers, 1635

784/1 Parish Register of Odstock, Wiltshire, 1541–1745

1553/25 1563 Survey of "Terrae Pembrochianae"

2057/A1/2 Pembroke estate surveys and Wilton domestic accounts, 1630s

2057/F1/2 George Owen, *A Catalogue of all the Earls of Pembroke*, c.1625

2057/F1/14 Sermon delivered at the funeral of William, 3rd Earl of Pembroke, 1630

2057/F2/1 *Catalogue of the nobilitie of England*, 1628

2057/F2/36 Garter Statutes drawn up for 3rd Earl of Pembroke

2057/H1/1a Inigo Jones/John Webb drawings

2057/H5/1 Wilton House inventory and valuation 1683

2057/P1/49 Plan to accompany sale particulars of Pembroke estates at Bower Chalke, Broad Chalke, Stoke Farthing, and Bishopstone, 1919

2292/2 A transcript of a letter about the capture of Marlborough during the Civil War, mid-nineteenth century

SHEFFIELD ARCHIVES

EM1351–1362

Elmhirst Muniments: Executorship and Financial Papers of Sir Robert Pye

Articles of Agreement between the La. Dutchess of Buckingham and the Earl of Pembroke and Montgomery, 1635

HOUSE OF LORDS JOURNAL OFFICE

Main papers

10/14/7/3527 Pembroke dispute with Mowbray, July 1641

10/1/23 Summons to York from King Charles to E of Pembroke, May 1642

Note x.B.B. 108 Pembroke's draft apology, July 1641

10/14/9/3616 Assessment of estates, Feb 1643

10/1/130 Appointment as Ld Lieutenant Monmouth, July 1642

10/1/139 Letter re demands for money, Dec 1642

10/1/142 Servants to Oxford, Jan 1643

10/1/156 Cutting down trees and killing deer in Hyde Park, August 1643

PUBLIC RECORD OFFICE, KEW

SP 14 State papers domestic, James I

SP 16 State papers domestic, Charles I

SP 18 State papers domestic, interregnum

SP 25 Council of State papers

HATFIELD HOUSE

Accounts, general, 12/19

Bills, 247, 670

BRITISH LIBRARY

Sloane MS 4014 Thomas Moffet (or Muffet) illustrated manuscript volume of spiders and insects

Add MSS 40630 f 234 Wiltshire Committee for Sequestrations

Add MSS 30305 f 76 Letter to Sir Thomas Fairfax re Clubmen

Add MSS 34195 Pembroke's row with Maltravers

Printed Sources

Adamson, John. "The Baronial Context of the English Civil War." *Transactions of the Royal Historical Society*, 5th series, 40 (1990), 93–120.

———. "Parliamentary Management, Men of Business, and the House of Lords, 1640–49." In Clive Jones, ed., *A Pillar of the Constitution* (London, 1989), 21–50.

———. "Politics and the Nobility in Civil-War England," *Historical Journal* 34 (1991): 231–55.

———. *The Noble Revolt: The Overthrow of Charles I*. London: Weidenfeld & Nicolson, 2007.

Alpers, Paul. *What Is Pastoral?* Chicago: University of Chicago Press, 1996.

Aubrey, John. *The Natural History of Wiltshire*. Wiltshire Topographical Society, 1847.

Aylmer, G. E. *The Struggle for the Constitution*. Blandford Press, 1975

Barnes, Susan J., Nora de Poorter, Oliver Millar, and Horst Vey. *Van Dyck: A Complete Catalogue of the Paintings*. New Haven, Conn.: Yale University Press, 2004.

Batey, Matey. *Alexander Pope: The Poet and the Landscape*. Barn Elms Publishing, 1999.

Beal, Mary. *A Study of Richard Symonds: His Italian Notebooks*. Garland, 1984.

Berry, Edward. *Shakespeare and the Hunt*. Cambridge University Press, 2001.

Bettey, Joseph. *Wiltshire Farming in the Seventeenth Century*. Wiltshire Record Society, 2005.

Bold, John, with John Reeves. *Wilton House & English Palladianism*. London: HMSO, 1988.

Buchanan-Brown, John, ed. *John Aubrey: Brief Lives*. New York: Penguin, 2000.

Bremmer, Jan, and Herman Roodenburg. *A Cultural History of Gesture*. Polity Press, 1991.

Brigden, Susan. *New Worlds, Lost Worlds: The Rule of the Tudors 1485–1603*. New York: Penguin, 2000.

Brown, Christopher. *Van Dyck*. Phaidon, 1982.

Burgess, Glenn. *The Politics of the Ancient Constitution: An Introduction to English Political Thought, 1603–1642*. New York: Macmillan, 1992.

———. *Absolute Monarchy and the Stuart Constitution*. New Haven, Conn.: Yale University Press, 1996.

Campbell, Mildred. *The English Yeoman*. New Haven, Conn.: Yale University Press, 1942.

Carlton, Charles. *Going to the Wars: The Experience of the British Civil Wars, 1638–1651*. Routledge, 1992.

Chaffinge, Thomas. *The Iust Mans Memoriall*. Nathaniel Baxter, 1630.

Chandler, John. "The Country Parson's Flock: Bemerton in 1632," *Sarum Chronicle* 6 (2006).

Clarendon, Edward, Earl of. *The History of the Rebellion and Civil Wars in England*. 6 volumes. Ed. by W. Dunn Macray. Clarendon Press, 1888.

———. *His maiesties answer to the propositions presented to him at Hampton Court . . . by the Earle of Pembroke and others*, 1647 (WSRO 2057/F6/4).

Clifford, D. J. H. *The Diaries of Lady Anne Clifford*. Alan Sutton, 1990.

Colvin, M.M. "The South Front of Wilton House." *Architectural Journal* cxi (1954).

Cook, Hadrian, and Tom Williamson, eds. *Water Meadows: History, Ecology and Conservation*. Windgather Press, 2007.

Cornwall, Julian. *Revolt of the Peasantry, 1549*. Routledge Kegan Paul, 1977.

Cressy, David. *England on Edge: Crisis and Revolution, 1640–1642*. Oxford University Press, 2006.

Cunnington, B. H., ed. *Records of the County of Wiltshire, Being Extracts from the Quarter Sessions Great Rolls of the Seventeenth Century*. George Simpson, 1932.

Cust, Richard. *Charles I: A Political Life*. Pearson Longman, 2005.

Davidson, H. E. *The Sword in Anglo-Saxon England*. Boydell Press, 1994.

de Caus, Isaac. *Wilton Garden*. London: Peter Stent, 1654.

Duncan-Jones, Katherine. *Sir Philip Sidney: Courtier Poet*. Hamish Hamilton, 1991.

————, ed. *Shakespeare's Sonnets*. Arden Shakespeare, 1997.

————, ed. *The Countess of Pembroke's Arcadia (The Old Arcadia)*. Oxford World's Classics, 1999.

Ekwall, Eilert. *Concise Oxford Dictionary of English Place-Names*. Clarendon Press, 1960.

Erickson, Amy Louise. *Women & Property in Early Modern England*. Routledge, 1993.

Firth, C. H. *The House of Lords During the Civil War*. Methuen, 1974.

Fletcher, Anthony. *The Outbreak of the English Civil War*. Edward Arnold, 1981.

Foister, Susan. *Holbein in England*. Tate Publishing, 2006.

Girouard, Mark. *Robert Smythson & the Elizabethan Country House*. New Haven, Conn.: Yale University Press, 1983.

————. *The Return to Camelot: Chivalry and the English Gentleman*. New Haven, Conn.: Yale University Press, 1981.

Gordenker, Emilie E. S. *Anthony Van Dyck and the Representation of Dress in Seventeenth-Century Portraiture*. Brepols, 2001.

Hammond, Lieutenant. "Relation of a short survey of the Western Counties." In *Camden Miscellany*, xvi, Camden 3rd Series, lii, London: Royal Historical Society, 1936.

Hannay, Margaret P. *Philip's Phoenix: Mary Sidney, Countess of Pembroke*. Oxford University Press, 1990.

Hannay, Margaret P., Noel J. Kinnamon, and Michael Brennan. *Domestic Politics and Family Absence*. Ashgate, 2005.

Harris, John. "Variable Geometry." *Country Life*, September 15, 1988.

Harris, John, Stephen Orgel, and Roy Strong. *The King's Arcadia: Inigo Jones and the Stuart Court*. Arts Council, 1973.

Henderson, Paula. *The Tudor House and Garden*. New Haven, Conn.: Yale University Press, 2005.

Herbert, George. *George Herbert: The Complete English Works*. Ann Pasternak Slater, ed. Everyman, 1995.

Herbert, William, and Sir Benjamin Rudyerd. *Poems* (1660), 2nd ed. London 1817.

B. Herrup, Cynthia. *A House in Gross Disorder: Sex, Law and the 2nd Earl of Castlehaven*. Oxford University Press, 1999.

Hill, Christopher. *The Century of Revolution, 1603–1714*. Thomas Nelson, 1961.

Historical Manuscripts Commission. *Reports and Calendars*, several dates.

Houses of Parliament. *Petition of parliament to the King, delivered by Lord Pembroke and others; with the King's answer*, 1642 (WSRO 2057/F6/2).

Howard, Maurice. *The Early Tudor Country House: Architecture and Politics, 1490–1550*. George Philip, 1987.

Hunter, Michael. *John Aubrey and the Realm of Learning*. Science History Publications, 1975.

Hutton, Ronald. *Debates in Stuart History*. Palgrave Macmillan, 2004.

James, Susan E. *Kateryn Parr: The Making of a Queen*. Ashgate, 1999.

Jordan, W. K. *Edward VI: The Young King*. Allen and Unwin, 1968.

Kerridge, Eric, ed. *Surveys of the Manors of Philip, Earl of Pembroke and Montgomery, 1631–2*. Wiltshire Archaeological and Natural History Society, 1953.

―――. "The Movement of Rent 1540–1640." *Economic History Review*, 2nd ser., VI (1953).

Klein, Lisa M. "Lady Anne Clifford as Mother and Matriarch." *Journal of Family History* 26, no. 1 (Jan. 2001): 18–38.

Larkin, James F. *Stuart Royal Proclamations, Vol II: Royal Proclamations of King Charles I, 1625–1646*. Clarendon Press, 1983.

Larkin James F., and Paul L. Hughes. *Stuart Royal Proclamations. Vol. I: Royal Proclamations of King James I, 1603–1625*. Clarendon Press, 1973.

Latham, Agnes, ed. *William Shakespeare: As You Like It*. Methuen, 1975.

Laurence, Anne. *Women in England, 1500–1760: A Social History*. Weidenfeld and Nicolson, 1994.

Lees-Milne, James. *The Age of Inigo Jones*. Batsford, 1953.

Lever, Tresham. *The Herberts of Wilton*. John Murray, 1967.

Lewin, C. G. "Housekeeping in Salisbury, 1640." *Sarum Chronicle* 5 (2005): 14–25.

Lockyer, Roger. *Buckingham*. Longman, 1981.

———. *James VI & I*. Longman, 1998.

Long, C. E., ed. *Richard Symonds's Diary of the Marches of the Royal Army*. Cambridge University Press, 1997.

Maclachlan, Tony. *The Civil War in Wiltshire*. Rowan Books, 1997.

Mazzola, Elizabeth. *Favorite Sons: The Politics and Poetics of the Sidney Family*. Palgrave Macmillan, 2003.

Millar, Oliver. *The Age of Charles I: Painting in England, 1620–1649*. Tate Gallery, 1972.

———. *Van Dyck in England*. National Portrait Gallery, 1982.

Montagu, Walter. *The Shepherds' Paradise*. The Malone Society, 1997.

Morrill, John. *Tudor and Stuart Britain*. Oxford University Press, 1996.

Morris, Christopher, ed. *The Journeys of Celia Fiennes*. Cresset Press, 1947.

Nichols, John. *The Progresses of Queen Elizabeth I*. John Nichols, 1823.

Nightingale, J. E. *Memorials of Wilton*. George Simpson, 1906.

Norbrook, David. *Writing the English Republic: Poetry, Rhetoric and Politics, 1627–1660*. Cambridge University Press, 1999.

———, ed. *The Penguin Book of Renaissance Verse*. Penguin, 1992.

———. *Poetry and Politics in the English Renaissance*. Oxford University Press, 2002.

Norden, John. *The Surveiors Dialogue*, 1610.

O'Callaghan, Michelle. *The "Shepheards Nation": Jacobean Spenserians and Early Stuart Political Culture, 1612–1625*. Oxford University Press, 2000.

Ollard, Richard. *Clarendon and His Friends*. Hamish Hamilton, 1987.

Orgel, Stephen, and Roy Strong. *Inigo Jones: The Theatre of the Stuart Court*. 2 vols. University of California Press, 1973.

Panofsky, Erwin. "Et in Arcadia ego: Poussin and the Elegaic Tradition." In *Meaning in the Visual Arts*. Doubleday 1955.

Parfitt, George. *Ben Jonson: The Complete Poems*. Penguin, 1996.

Pembroke, Sidney, earl of. *A Catalogue of the Paintings & Drawings in the Collection at Wilton House*. Phaidon, 1968

Powell, Anthony. *John Aubrey and His Friends*. Hogarth Press, 1988

Powell, J. M. *Mirrors of the New World: Images and Image-Makers in the Settlement Process*. Dawson, 1977.

Powis, Michael, et al., eds. *Broad Chalke: A History of a South Wiltshire Village, Its Land and People*. Broad Chalke Millennium Books, 1999.

Pritchard, R. E. *Mary and Philip Sidney: The Sidney Psalms*. Carcanet, 1992.

Pugh, R. B., and Elizabeth Crittall, eds. *Victoria County History, Wiltshire*. Oxford University Press, 1956–1965.

Rackham, Oliver. *The History of the Countryside*. Dent, 1986.

——————. *Trees and Woodland in the British Landscape*. Dent, 1993.

——————. *Woodlands*. New York: HarperCollins, 2006.

Ravelhofer, Barbara. *The Early Stuart Masque: Dance, Costume, and Music*. Oxford University Press, 2006.

Rowe, Violet A. "The Influence of the Earls of Pembroke on Parliamentary Elections, 1625–1641." *English Historical Review* 50, no. 198 (April 1935): 242–56.

Russell, Conrad. *The Causes of the English Civil War*. Oxford University Press, 1990.

——————. *Parliaments and English Politics, 1621–1629*. Oxford University Press, 1979.

Sharpe, Kevin. *The Personal Rule of Charles I*. New Haven, Conn.: Yale University Press, 1992.

——————. *Remapping Early Modern England: The Culture of Seventeenth-Century Politics*. Cambridge University Press, 2000.

Sharpe, Kevin, and Peter Lake, eds. *Culture and Politics in Early Stuart England*. Macmillan, 1994.

Shepherd Geoffrey, ed. *Sir Philip Sidney: An Apology for Poetry*. Manchester University Press, 1973.

Sil, Narasingha P. *William Lord Herbert of Pembroke, 1507–1570: Politique and Patriot*. Edwin Mellen Press, 1992.

Skinner, Quentin. *Liberty Before Liberalism*. Cambridge University Press, 1998.

Slack, Paul, ed. *Poverty in Early-Stuart Salisbury*. Wiltshire Record Society, 1975.

Sloan, Kim. *A New World: England's First View of America*. British Museum Press, 2007.

Smith, David L. *Constitutional Royalism and the Search for Settlement, c.1640–1649*. Cambridge University Press, 1994.

Smith, James. *Wilton and Its Associations*. Salisbury, 1851.

Smuts, R. Malcolm. *Culture and Power in England, 1585–1685*. Macmillan, 1999.

Starkey, David, ed. *The English Court from the Wars of the Roses to the Civil War*. Longman, 1987.

Stone, Lawrence. *The Crisis of the Aristocracy, 1558–1641*. Oxford University Press, 1967.

—————. *The Family, Sex, and Marriage in England, 1500–1800*. Weidenfeld and Nicolson, 1977.

Strong, Roy. *The Elizabethan Image: Painting in England, 1540–1620*. Tate Publications, 1970.

—————. *The Renaissance Garden in England*. Thames and Hudson, 1998.

—————. *Henry, Prince of Wales and England's Lost Renaissance*. Thames and Hudson, 1986.

Straton, Charles R., ed. *Survey of the Lands of William First Earl of Pembroke*. 2 vols. Roxburghe Club, 1909.

Thirsk, Joan. *Alternative Agriculture: A History from the Black Death to the Present Day*. Oxford University Press, 1997.

Thirsk, Joan, and J. P. Cooper. *17th-century Economic Documents*. Oxford University Press, 1972.

Thomas, Keith. *Man and the Natural World: Changing Attitudes in England, 1500–1800*. Allen Lane, 1983.

Thompson, Elizabeth McClure. *The Chamberlain Letters*. John Murray, 1966.

Tomlinson, Sophie. *Women on Stage in Stuart Drama*. Cambridge University Press, 2005.

Tuck, Richard. *Philosophy and Government, 1572–1651*. Cambridge University Press, 1993.

Underdown, David. *Revel, Riot, and Rebellion: Popular Politics and Culture in England, 1603–1660.* Oxford University Press, 1985.

Webb, John. *The Most Notable Antiquity of Great Britain Vulgarly Called Stonehenge,* 1655.

Williams, N. J. ed. *Tradesmen in Early-Stuart Wiltshire: A Miscellany.* Wiltshire Archaeological and Natural History Society, 1960.

Williams, Raymond. *The Country and the City.* Chatto and Windus, 1973.

Williamson, George C. *Lady Anne Clifford, Countess of Dorset, Pembroke and Montgomery, 1590–1676: Her Life Letters and Work* (1922). S. R. Publishers, 1967.

Williamson, Tom. *Shaping Medieval Landscapes: Settlement, Society and Environment.* Windgather Press, 2003.

Woolf, Virginia. "The Countess of Pembroke's Arcadia." In *The Second Common Reader.* Hogarth Press, 1932.

Worden, Blair. *The Sound of Virtue: Philip Sidney's* Arcadia *and Elizabethan Politics.* New Haven, Conn.: Yale University Press, 1996.

Worsley, Giles. *Classical Architecture in Britain: The Heroic Age.* New Haven, Conn.: Yale University Press, 1995.

——————. *Inigo Jones and the European Classicist Tradition.* New Haven, Conn.: Yale University Press, 2007.

Wotton, Henry. *Elements of Architecture.* London, 1624.

Wroughton, John. *An Unhappy Civil War: The Experiences of Ordinary People in Gloucestershire, Somerset, and Wiltshire, 1642–1646.* Lansdown Press, 1999.

INDEX

ILLUSTRATION CREDITS

View of Downland above Broad Chalke. David Reed/Alamy.

Bluebells and Oak Trees in Grovely Wood Wiltshire. Paul Glendell Photography/ Photographer's Direct.

The Ebble at Alvediston. © Warren A. Stallard/Photographer's Direct.

Wilton Estate map of the 17th Century, showing Grovely Wood. Reproduced by permission of the 18th Earl of Pembroke and Montgomery and the Trustees of the Wilton House Trust, Wilton House/Photo: (WSRO 2057/S/3) Steve Hobbs, Wiltshire Record Office.

A Wiltshire sheepfold, c. 1950s. Eagle Photos (Cheltenham) Ltd., 1951.

Haymaking. The Museum of English Rural Life, University of Reading.

Map of Wylye Village, 1742. (WSRO 628/7/1) Wiltshire and Swindon Archives/ Wiltshire and Swindon Record Office.

William Herbert, 1st Earl of Pembroke. Netherlandish, 16th century, oil on panel. National Museum of Wales.

Portrait of a Lady, unknown, thought to be Anne Parr, by Hans Holbein the Younger, c. 1540, chalk on paper. The Royal Collection © 2007 Her Majesty Queen Elizabeth II.

Silver medal of William Herbert, 1st Earl of Pembroke, by Stephen Van Hanwyck, c. 1562. © The Trustees of the British Museum.

"The Front of Wilton House," detail from the *Survey of Lands for the 1st Earl of Pembroke,* 1566, pen and ink on vellum. Reproduced by permission of the 18th Earl of Pembroke and Montgomery and the Trustees of the Wilton House

Trust, Wilton House/Photo: (WLN 275900) Steve Hobbs, Wiltshire Record Office.

Henry Herbert, 2nd Earl of Pembroke, c. 1590, oil on canvas. © National Museum and Gallery of Wales, Cardiff/The Bridgeman Art Library.

Mary Sidney, Countess of Pembroke by Nicholas Hilliard, c. 1590, watercolor on vellum. © National Portrait Gallery, London.

The Funeral Cortege of Sir Philip Sidney on Its Way to St Paul's Cathedral, 1587, engraved by Theodor de Bry. The Stapleton Collection/The Bridgeman Art Library.

William Herbert, 3rd Earl of Pembroke by Daniel Mytens, c. 1615, oil on canvas. Courtesy of The Weiss Gallery.

Philip Herbert, 4th Earl of Pembroke, attributed to William Larkin, c. 1608, oil on canvas. Audley End, Essex, UK/The Bridgeman Art Library.

Portrait of Lady Anne Clifford, 3rd Countess of Dorset by William Larkin, c. 1620. The National Trust Photo Library/Private Collection.

Shepherd's Paradise: Proscenium and Standing Scene, pen and black ink, Inigo Jones. © Devonshire Collection, Chatsworth. Reproduced by permission of Chatsworth Settlement Trustees.

Garden design from *The Gardens of Wilton* by Isaac de Caus, c. 1645, engraving. The Stapleton Collection/The Bridgeman Art Library.

Philip, 4th Earl of Pembroke, and His Family by Anthony van Dyck, c. 1634, oil on canvas. Reproduced by permission of the 18th Earl of Pembroke and Montgomery and the Trustees of the Wilton House Trust, Wilton House.

"Philip, 4th Earl of Pembroke, and his wife, Lady Anne Clifford," detail of *Philip, 4th Earl of Pembroke, and His Family* by Anthony van Dyck.

"Philip and Charles Herbert," detail of *Philip, 4th Earl of Pembroke, and His Family* by Anthony van Dyck.

"Lady Mary Villiers," detail of *Philip, 4th Earl of Pembroke, and His Family* by Anthony van Dyck.

"Anna Sophia Herbert and her husband, Robert Dormer, Earl of Carnarvon," detail of *Philip, 4th Earl of Pembroke, and His Family* by Anthony van Dyck.

Portrait of Charles Dormer, 2nd Earl of Carnarvon by Sir Peter Lely, c. 1644. Sotheby's Images, London.